Managing Software Deliverables

Managing Software Deliverables
A Software Development Management Methodology

John W. Rittinghouse, Ph.D., CISM

ELSEVIER
DIGITAL
PRESS

Amsterdam • Boston • Heidelberg • London • New York • Oxford
Paris • San Diego • San Francisco • Singapore • Sydney • Tokyo

Digital Press is an imprint of Elsevier.
200 Wheeler Road, Burlington, MA 01803, USA
Linacre House, Jordan Hill, Oxford OX2 8DP, UK

Copyright © 2004, John W. Rittinghouse. All rights reserved.

No part of this publication may be reproduced, stored in a retrieval system, or transmitted in any form or by any means, electronic, mechanical, photocopying, recording, or otherwise, without the prior written permission of the publisher.

Permissions may be sought directly from Elsevier's Science & Technology Rights Department in Oxford, UK: phone: (+44) 1865 843830, fax: (+44) 1865 853333, e-mail: permissions@elsevier.com.uk. You may also complete your request on-line via the Elsevier homepage (http://elsevier.com), by selecting "Customer Support" and then "Obtaining Permissions."

All trademarks found herein are property of their respective owners.

∞ Recognizing the importance of preserving what has been written, Elsevier prints its books on acid-free paper whenever possible.

Library of Congress Cataloging-in-Publication Data
Application submitted.

British Library Cataloguing-in-Publication Data
A catalogue record for this book is available from the British Library.

ISBN: 1-55558-313-X

For information on all Digital Press publications visit our website at www.digitalpress.com and www.bh.com/digitalpress

03 04 05 06 07 08 10 9 8 7 6 5 4 3 2 1

Printed in the United States of America

Contents

List of Figures xv

Foreword xvii

Acknowledgments xxi

Introduction xxiii
- i.1 Reasons for Using Software Program Management — xxiv
- i.2 Preparing an Organization for Software Program Management — xxiv
  - i.2.1 Project Initiation — xxv
  - i.2.2 Project Sponsorship — xxv
  - i.2.3 Tools Needed to Create an SPMO — xxv
  - i.2.4 Project Roadmaps — xxvi
  - i.2.5 Project Tracks — xxvii
  - i.2.6 Project Binders — xxvii
- i.3 Project Life Cycle in Software Program Management — xxvii
  - i.3.1 Systems Engineering Process — xxviii
  - i.3.2 Overview of the SEI Process Maturity Model — xxix
- i.4 Overview of This Book — xxxii

1 Understanding the SPMO 1
- 1.1 SPMO Mission Statement — 1
- 1.2 Roles and Responsibilities — 1
  - 1.2.1 Executive Stakeholder — 2
  - 1.2.2 Project Sponsor — 2
  - 1.2.3 Program Manager — 2
  - 1.2.4 Project Manager (PM) — 3
  - 1.2.5 Project Coordinator — 3
  - 1.2.6 Business Systems Analyst (BSA) — 3
- 1.3 Project Resources — 4

Contents

1.4	SPMO Organizational Structure	4
1.5	Software Program Management Service Areas	5
1.6	Performance Reporting	5
	1.6.1 Financial Management	8
	1.6.2 Vendor Management	9
	1.6.3 Vendor Planning	11
	1.6.4 Vendor Selection	11
	1.6.5 Establishing Contract Terms and Conditions	12
	1.6.6 Monitoring the Vendor	12
	1.6.7 Contract Closure	13
1.7	Issue Management	13
	1.7.1 Issue Escalation	14
	1.7.2 Issue Reporting	14
1.8	Quality Management	14
	1.8.1 Benefits of Quality Management	15
	1.8.2 Components of Quality Management	15
	1.8.3 Determine Performance Measurements	18
	1.8.4 Continuous Process Improvement (CPI)	20
	1.8.5 Software Process Improvement Organizations	21
1.9	Change Management	23
1.10	Change Management Plans	24
1.11	Business Requirements Oversight Committee (BROC)	25
1.12	BROC Roles and Responsibilities	27
	1.12.1 BROC Sponsor Role	27
	1.12.2 BROC Member Role	27
	1.12.3 SPMO Role in the BROC	28
1.13	The COHEN Bill of 1996	29
1.14	Chapter 1 Review	30

2 SEP Phase I: Initiation — 31

2.1	Forming a Core Team	34
2.2	Security Access	34
	2.2.1 Project Kickoff Meeting	35
	2.2.2 Risk Officer Appointment	35
	2.2.3 Core Team Roster Revision	36
	2.2.4 Project Customization Matrix	36
2.3	Project Framework Rules Document	37
	2.3.1 Planning Decisions to Be Made and Documented	37
	2.3.2 Tracking Decisions to Be Made and Documented	39
	2.3.3 Best Practices Decisions to Be Tracked and Documented	40
	2.3.4 Relationship Decisions to Be Tracked and Documented	41

	2.3.5	Target Completion Notice (TCN)		43
2.4		The Requirements Gathering Process		43
	2.4.1	Evaluate the Work Process		44
	2.4.2	Define the IT Requirements		44
2.5		User Requirements Document (URD)		45
2.6		Project Planning and Documentation Guide (PPDG)		47
2.7		Chapter 2 Review		52

3 SEP Phase II: Analysis and Detailed Planning Phase — 53

	3.0.1	Project Objective Statement (POS)	55
	3.0.2	Project Definition Document (PDD)	55
	3.0.3	Flexibility Matrix (FM)	56
	3.0.4	Project Definition Document Notebook (PDDN)	56
	3.0.5	Data Analysis Document (DAD)	56
	3.0.6	In-House Analysis	57
	3.0.7	Commercial Off-the-Shelf (COTS) Sources	57
	3.0.8	Near-Term Deliverables (NTD)	57
	3.0.9	Data Risk Analysis (DRA)	58
	3.0.10	Technical Analysis Document (TAD)	58
	3.0.11	In-House/Contractor Analysis (IHCA)	61
	3.0.12	High-Level Solution (HLS)	62
	3.0.13	Project Deliverables	64
	3.0.14	Bids/Proposals (BP)	64
	3.0.15	Develop a Request for Proposal (RFP)	64
	3.0.16	Funding Documentation (FD)	65
	3.0.17	Project Budget (PB)	66
3.1		Project Schedule (PS)	68
3.2		Critical Path (CP)	68
	3.2.1	Task Duration Estimates (TDE)	69
	3.2.2	Dependency Diagrams (DD)	69
	3.2.3	Optimization Tradeoff Plan (OTP)	69
	3.2.4	Resource Histogram (RH)	69
	3.2.5	Work Breakdown Structure Dictionary (WBSD)	69
	3.2.6	Risk Analysis (RA)	70
	3.2.7	Status Reports (SR)	71
	3.2.8	Variance Reports (VR)	72
	3.2.9	Adaptive Action Plan (AAP)	72
	3.2.10	Review Package (RP)	72
	3.2.11	Meeting Agenda (MA)	73
	3.2.12	Documents from Review Meeting (DRM)	73
	3.2.13	Waiver/Exception to Required Standards (WERS)	73

		3.2.14 Project Team Review Minutes (PTRM)	73
		3.2.15 Approval Letters (AL)	74
	3.3	Chapter 3 Review	75

4 SEP Phase III: Detailed Design Phase — 77

	4.0.1	SEP Deliverables Checklist	78
4.1	Quality Assurance Plan (QAP)		78
4.2	Human Factors Plan (HFP)		78
4.3	Human Factors Report (HFR)		80
4.4	Product Requirements and Specifications (PRSpec)		80
4.5	System Infrastructure Requirements (SIR)		82
4.6	Software Requirements Specification (SRS)		84
4.7	Interface Requirements Specification (IRS)		85
4.8	Performance Requirements Specification (PRS)		86
4.9	Data Development Plan (DDP)		86
4.10	Contracts/Agreements (CA)		87
4.11	Software Development Plan (SDP)		87
4.12	Database Conversion Plan (DCP)		88
4.13	Marketing Communications Plan (MCP)		91
4.14	Marketing Rollout Schedule (MRS)		91
4.15	Marketing Rollout Signoff (MRS)		92
4.16	Project Transition Letter (PTL)		92
4.17	Chapter 4 Review		93

5 SEP Phase IV: Construction Phase — 95

5.1	Software User Manual (SUM)		96
5.2	Software Installation Manual (SIM)		96
5.3	Training Manual (TM)		97
5.4	Operations and Maintenance Guide (OMG)		97
5.5	Development Process for Test Plans (TP)		98
5.6	SPMO Recommended Test and Certification Plans		102
5.7	Stress Test Plan (SsTP)		103
5.8	Integration Test Plan (ITP)		103
	5.8.1 Software Test Plan (STP)		104
5.9	Product Assurance Test (PAT)		104
5.10	User Acceptance Test (UAT)		105
5.11	MIS/Outside Certification Plan (MISCP)		106
5.12	Product Deliverables		106
5.13	Product Signoff and Certification Letters		106
5.14	Product Assurance Signoff Letter (PASL)		107

	5.15	Functional Certification Letter (FCL)	107
	5.16	MIS Certification Letter (MISCL)	107
	5.17	Data Certification Letter (DCL)	107
	5.18	Chapter 5 Review	108

6 SEP Phase V: Testing — 111

- 6.1 Review the Test Plan Checklist (TPC) — 113
- 6.2 Test Plan Checklist — 113
- 6.3 Test Logs and Incident Reports — 115
- 6.4 Test Domains — 116
- 6.5 User-Interface Errors — 118
  - 6.5.1 Functionality — 118
  - 6.5.2 Communication — 119
  - 6.5.3 Command Structure and Entry — 122
  - 6.5.4 Missing Commands — 123
  - 6.5.5 Program Rigidity — 124
  - 6.5.6 Performance — 125
  - 6.5.7 Output — 126
- 6.6 Error Handling — 127
- 6.7 Boundary-Related Errors — 128
- 6.8 Calculation Errors — 128
  - 6.8.1 Initial- and Later-State Errors — 128
- 6.9 Control Flow Errors — 129
- 6.10 Errors in Handling or Interpreting Data — 129
- 6.11 Race and Load Conditions — 130
- 6.12 Hardware Errors — 131
- 6.13 Source, Version, and ID Control Errors — 131
- 6.14 Testing Errors — 132
- 6.15 Test Plan Reviews — 132
- 6.16 Chapter 6 Review — 133

7 SEP Phase VI: Implementation — 135

- 7.1 Review SEP Deliverables Checklist — 136
- 7.2 Develop the User Training Plan — 136
  - 7.2.1 Scope and Objectives — 137
  - 7.2.2 Training Methods — 138
  - 7.2.3 Training Delivery — 138
  - 7.2.4 Training Facilities — 139
  - 7.2.5 Training Materials Development — 139
  - 7.2.6 Timing, Duration, Sequencing, and Dependencies — 139

	7.2.7	Training Estimates	140
	7.2.8	Hardware/Software Requirements for Training	140
	7.2.9	Training Roster (TR)	141
	7.2.10	Training Schedule (TS)	141
	7.2.11	Training Signoff (TSO)	141
7.3	Equipment Installation Plan (EIP)	142
7.4	Develop Installation Rollout Plan	143
7.5	Rollout Plan (ROP)	143
7.6	Rollout Schedule (RS)	144
7.7	Training and Implementation	144
7.8	Rollout Signoff (RSO)	145
7.9	Chapter 7 Review	145

8 SEP Phase VII: Support Phase   147

8.1	Software Transition Plan (SWTP)	148
8.2	MIS Hardware and Software Handoff Letter	148
8.3	Hardware Life Cycle Management Plan	148
8.4	Develop Support Plan	149
8.5	Software Configuration Management Plan (SCMP)	149
8.6	Service Level Agreement(s) (SLA)	151
8.7	Components of an SLA	152
	8.7.1 Help Desk Checklist	155
8.8	Phase Completion Approval Signoff Completed	155
8.9	Chapter 8 Review	156

9 SEP Phase VIII: Project Closeout   157

9.1	Disposition Phase	158
9.2	Disposition Plan	158
9.3	Closeout Actions	159
9.4	Postmortem Meeting Report	160
9.5	Close-out Paperwork (COP)	160
9.6	Archiving the Project	160
9.7	Closeout Ritual	161
9.8	Chapter 9 Review	161

10 Project Wizardry 101   163

10.1	External Factors That Dictate Success	163
10.2	Business Reasons for the Project	163
	10.2.1 Where Is the Business Fit?	164

	10.2.2 How Business Fit Influences Project Success	165
10.3	Project Customers	165
10.4	Project Objectives	165
10.5	End-State Visions	166
10.6	Making Success a Team Effort	166
10.7	Building Customer Confidence	167
10.8	Choosing a Development Strategy	168
10.9	Software Development Life Cycle (SDLC) Models	168
	10.9.1 How to Identify the Right Model	168
10.10	Setting Expectations: Staged Deliveries	169
10.11	Rapid Application Development (RAD)	169
10.12	Alternative SDLC Work Patterns	170
10.13	Other Alternative Work Patterns	170
10.14	Alternative Work Pattern Selection	172
10.15	Alternative Work Pattern Descriptions	173
10.16	Matching Resources to Business Need	177
10.17	Developing an Effective Approach to Software Projects	178
10.18	Having "Just Enough" Process	178
10.19	Optimizing Time, Cost, Function, and Quality	178
10.20	Building Realistic Project Plans	179
10.21	A Step-by-Step Process Using SEP	180
10.22	Identifying Tasks, Milestones, and Phases	180
	10.22.1 Using MS Project with SEP	180
10.23	Building a Project Plan Using the Template	182
	10.23.1 Adding Start and Finish Dates	182
	10.23.2 Inserting Additional Tasks and Subtasks	182
	10.23.3 Inserting Predecessor Tasks into the Project Plan	183
	10.23.4 Inserting Task Notes into the Project	183
	10.23.5 Inserting Resources into the Project Plan	183
	10.23.6 Tracking Task Completion	184
	10.23.7 Saving the Project Plan from the Project Template	185
	10.23.8 Updating the New Project Plan	185
10.24	Project Work Breakdown Structure	185
	10.24.1 Summary Work Breakdown Structure	186
	10.24.2 Project Work Breakdown Structure	186
	10.24.3 Contract Work Breakdown Structure	186
	10.24.4 Work Breakdown Structure Dictionary	187
10.25	Pert Charts	187
10.26	Gantt Charts	187
10.27	Performing Reality Checks and "Fit for Purpose"	188
10.28	Assessing Project Risk Factors	188

10.29 Risk Identification List ... 190
    10.29.1 Risk Assessment ... 191
    10.29.2 Risk Action Plan ... 192
10.30 Building Confidence in the Plan and Selling It Internally ... 192
10.31 Managing for Success: Day-to-Day Project Management Insights ... 193
    10.31.1 Focus on Process ... 193
    10.31.2 Put Theory into Practice ... 193
    10.31.3 Detect Early Warning Signs ... 194
    10.31.4 Set Communications Ground Rules ... 194
10.32 Daily Tracking and Management ... 195
10.33 Measuring Progress with Milestones ... 196
    10.33.1 Defect Detection and Prevention ... 196
10.34 Pressures to Expect at Each Stage ... 196
10.35 Managing Conflict Effectively ... 197
10.36 Estimating for Reality ... 198
    10.36.1 Size ... 198
    10.36.2 Complexity ... 198
    10.36.3 Capability ... 199
    10.36.4 Process ... 199
10.37 Creating an Initial Estimate and Revising Estimates ... 201
10.38 Handling Deadlines ... 201
10.39 Knowing When and How to "Give and Take" ... 202

11 Some Software Best Practices to Consider — 205

11.1 Project Integrity ... 206
    11.1.1 Practice 1. Adopt Continuous Program Risk Management ... 206
    11.1.2 Practice 2. Estimate Cost and Schedule Empirically ... 208
    11.1.3 Practice 3. Use Metrics to Manage ... 209
    11.1.4 Practice 4. Track Earned Value ... 210
    11.1.5 Practice 5. Track Defects against Quality Targets ... 212
    11.1.6 Practice 6. Treat People As the Most Important Resource ... 213
11.2 Construction Integrity ... 214
    11.2.1 Practice 7. Adopt Life Cycle Configuration Management ... 214
    11.2.2 Practice 8. Manage and Trace Requirements ... 217
    11.2.3 Practice 9. Use System-based Software Design ... 218
    11.2.4 Practice 10. Ensure Data and Database Interoperability ... 219
    11.2.5 Practice 11. Define and Control Interfaces ... 220
    11.2.6 Practice 12. Design Twice, Code Once ... 221
    11.2.7 Practice 13. Assess Reuse Risks and Costs ... 222
11.3 Product Stability and Integrity ... 223
    11.3.1 Practice 14. Inspect Requirements and Design ... 223

	11.3.2	Practice 15. Manage Testing As a Continuous Process	224
	11.3.3	Practice 16. Compile and Smoke Test Frequently	227

12 Putting It All Together — 229

- 12.1 Beyond SEP Methodology: Making It All Work — 230
- 12.2 SPMO Implementation Thoughts — 230
- 12.3 People Issues Revisited — 232
- 12.4 Project Management Tools — 233
- 12.5 Study Design and Background Facts — 235
- 12.6 Next Steps — 237
- 12.7 Additional Resources for Managing Software Projects — 237

Glossary — 239

Common SPMO Acronyms and Abbreviations — 261

A Roadmaps — 265

B Answers — 285

- B.1 Chapter 1 Review — 285
- B.2 Chapter 2 Review — 287
- B.3 Chapter 3 Review — 289
- B.4 Chapter 4 Review — 290
- B.5 Chapter 5 Review — 292
- B.6 Chapter 6 Review — 294
- B.7 Chapter 7 Review — 295
- B.8 Chapter 8 Review — 297
- B.9 Chapter 9 Review — 299

C Software Notes — 301

- C.1 Installing the Intranet-Based Software — 301

References — 303

Index — 305

List of Figures

Figure i.1 Default Intranet SPMO Start Page.	xxvi
Figure i.2 The Process Roller-coaster.	xxviii
Figure i.3 Five Levels of the SEI/CMU Process Maturity Model.	xxx
Figure 1.1 The SPMO Organization.	4
Figure 1.2 Focus of Software Process Improvement Organizational Components.	22
Figure 2.1 SEP Phase I: Initiation Roadmap.	31
Figure 2.2 Project Initiation Form.	33
Figure 2.3 Security Access Sheet (SAS).	35
Figure 2.4 Customization Matrix.	37
Figure 3.1 SEP Phase II Roadmap.	53
Figure 3.2 Flexibility Matrix.	56
Figure 3.3 Cost Estimate Worksheet.	67
Figure 3.4 Project Budget Template.	67
Figure 3.5 Project Gantt Template.	68
Figure 3.6 Risk Analysis Matrix.	70
Figure 4.1 SEP Phase III Roadmap.	77
Figure 4.2 SEP Deliverables Checklist.	79
Figure 4.3 Requirements Traceability Matrix (RTM).	85
Figure 5.1 SEP Phase IV Roadmap.	95
Figure 5.2 SEP Phase IV Deliverables Checklist.	96
Figure 6.1 SEP Phase V Roadmap.	111
Figure 6.2 SEP Phase V Deliverables Checklist.	112
Figure 6.3 Incident Report.	116
Figure 7.1 SEP Phase VI Roadmap.	135
Figure 7.2 SEP Phase VI Deliverables Checklist.	136

Figure 8.1 SEP Phase VII Roadmap. 147
Figure 8.2 SEP Phase VII Deliverables Checklist. 148
Figure 9.1 SEP Phase VIII Roadmap. 157
Figure 10.1 Project Plan Using SEP. 181
Figure 10.2 The Radio Dial Analogy. 197
Figure 12.1 SPMO Scope and Methodology Domain. 231

Foreword

Some books are written by folks who are good writers, but have never actually done the work. Some books are by smart theoretical types who describe how the work *should* be done. Other books are regurgitations of yet other books. Pick a way to write one, and there is a title out there somewhere on the subject in one style or another. Few books, however, are written by people who have "been there and done that, have the T-shirt, starred in the video, and wrote the book." Well, this is one of those types of books.

Corporate IT software program management has always smelled like unneeded bureaucracy to me. Lots of people, paperwork, meetings, templates, forms for all, project critical reviews, more forms, financial spreadsheets, and so on. Bleah! Who needs it? Being a technical person by nature and training, my immediate reaction to such efforts has always been distrust and disdain. Then, I saw what I call "John's way."

I have known John for several years and have worked with him extensively both as a consultant and later as a coworker at the world's largest Web hosting company, where he ran the Information Technology (IT) department. When John arrived, IT was a real mess. If you wanted an internal network connection and an Internet connection, someone had actually set up an IT policy where you would be issued two laptops to access both connections (no kidding). Getting access to e-mail was like being dragged over carpet tacks and then dipped in alcohol—very painful, but not life threatening. Forget asking for help with an application-related problem on your system: You got the "ticket of death" from the ticketing system and you might get called back—someday. Along came John—or JR, as those of us who know him best tend to call him.

John is an interesting guy. When you start learning more about John over time, you find that he ran a software development shop for the War Plans Division in the Air Force at the Strategic Air Command for several years, has a Ph.D. in psychology, and is fluent in Chinese and Thai (if you ever get a chance to go to lunch with John, go to a Chinese restaurant, get him to order lunch, and watch the reactions). He has run very large multinational IT organizations, done the mainframe thing, done the Web translation thing, and run large, distributed IT organizations in many countries. Experience is something he doesn't lack when it comes to project management and deployment of ugly technologies to folks that have no clue how to use them. John is also a gadget junkie and always has the proper array of the latest technologies at his beck and call.

As a coworker, I coerced him to come to work for our company to assist us with several large projects that needed help in focus, execution, and cost overruns. John came in, got the troops organized, and initiated John's way—Corporate IT Software Program Management—for all the projects underway. These included a complete change of financial systems, sales systems, customer ticketing systems, IT organization, help desk systems, and a dizzying myriad of other smaller systems too numerous to remember. In less than 60 days, the projects—all of them—went from totally unmanaged disasters to well-tuned, humming machines of management excellence. The troops were happy, goals and milestones were actually being achieved, deliverables were happening, management was happy—you name the benefit, it was there. Oh, and we saved more than $60 million as well.

I can't say I was a bystander. In fact, I was right in the middle of much of it because my department, information security, was in the middle of a lot of the projects underway. John spent some time educating me on the processes, and then I saw paperwork and went screaming down the street, hair on fire (well, what little I have left). I did come back eventually and found that process, not paperwork, was the key, and that process and discipline of execution are keys to success.

With time, I have come around to John's way. It really works—in theory and in practice. I have seen it work in at least three major corporations first hand. The results are well worth the efforts. Projects actually get done in a predictable fashion. Anomalies are accounted for and accommodated. Financial details are managed, leadership and execution of tasks are measurable and quantified, and the bureaucracy is not all that bad. When you walk out of a project meeting, you don't feel like your time has been wasted and that you have not accomplished anything. I spent many years having that feeling. John's way is better. I don't feel that way when working with his project teams.

If you are reading this book, you are on your way to committing to a better way to get projects and tasks out the door. It will take some effort to internalize John's way, and it will not be easy at first. But, like a duck on the water, you will soon be swimming smoothly along and making progress with every stroke. I follow John's way for small and large projects, and I use his ideas for keeping track of the multitude of tasks I have to deal with every day in my job. Yes, I work for a very large company with very large projects and very large problems. I have also done four startups and recommend the techniques and ideas in this book strongly for that environment as well. The system works equally well for an entire range of businesses and efforts. Take the next step and read this book. Follow the examples and internalize John's way. It will change your outlook on actually getting projects out the door and make you successful. And, your weekends will become free, your job will be fun to go to because you are making scheduled deliverables, and you will have time to do real work again.

Dr. Bill Hancock, Ph.D., CISSP, CISM

Vice President, Security and Chief Security Officer

Cable and Wireless

October 2003

Acknowledgments

I would like to dedicate this book to my dear wife, Naree. I would like to thank her for her infinite patience, for putting up with all of those occasions when I was buried in the construction of this book, for all of the hours she tolerated me sitting at the computer writing, for all of her words of encouragement, and most of all, for her love and understanding, without which this book would never have been written.

I would also like to thank my old friend Al Braaten from Microsoft for having the patience to read and reread my manuscripts, providing thoughts, comments, and the occasional correction. My brother, Jim Rittinghouse, who worked many hours providing constructive comments on the book, has made it a better product, and I thank him for that. Dr. Tony (Vern) Dubendorf deserves thanks for all of the effort he put into editing and providing sanity checks on my material. Thomas Beltz of American Systems Corporation deserves a special thanks for his contributions on software best practices. Finally, Dr. Bill Hancock, who was actually the inspiration for my forward progress on this book, deserves many thanks. Having known Bill for more than a few years now, I learned from him that a book can be written at 35,000 feet at night just as easily as at the computer at home (not really, but I would not tell Bill otherwise). Most of all, I would like to thank all of those folks who have worked with me to see so much done in so little time.

Introduction

The material in this book describes a set of processes that comprise an effective Software Program Management Office (SPMO) function for use in a corporate IT setting. Every business that has people performing project management activities has a need for these processes. In some instances, an organization may already have an SPMO chartered with overall responsibility for each project managed in an enterprise. In those cases, this book will either provide validation of their efforts, or it will provide some new techniques and useful approaches that can be utilized to further improve on their overall implementation of the SPMO. In most cases in business, however, an SPMO is unheard of. Each project managed in the enterprise is unfortunately managed separately from all others (at great cost in both time and money to the enterprise).

From the perspective of a Chief Information Officer (CIO) or Chief Technology Officer (CTO), this lack of an SPMO function leads to serious shortfalls in the overall management, administration, execution, standardization, and reporting of projects. To effectively administer all of the activities involved in just one project is difficult enough, but for the average CIO, it is normal to have 10 to 20 projects running concurrently under the supervision of a few program managers. Is it any wonder that most projects implemented in corporate America fail to meet their established initial goals?

In order to successfully achieve the desired goals for each of these projects, an effective leader must rely heavily on well-defined, industry-proven, standardized processes to manage these projects. This book will show you, the business leader, how to quickly and effectively implement the basic building blocks for an SPMO function within an enterprise and utilize the corresponding processes that will enable an organization to begin managing its resources in an effective, standardized manner. Along the way, the methods defined herein will also enable you to begin to help your organization lay the foundation work needed for beginning an ISO 900X certification.

i.1 Reasons for Using Software Program Management

There are several very good reasons for starting corporate implementation of an SPMO. Foremost among these reasons is effective cost management. Using a proven framework of well-defined, industry-proven processes enables a business leader to leverage knowledge gained from other business leaders who have been in similar situations. The processes and procedures used in software program management are, by design, risk mitigators and cost savers. They are viewed as best practices that have been implemented and refined over time and tested in many organizations. Standardization of such processes will allow a project team to plan and execute a project in a manner that avoids any major surprises to upper management in an organizational status review meeting. Processes that are designed with such built-in procedures as audit and status reporting will also allow cross-functional teams to communicate issues more effectively.

i.2 Preparing an Organization for Software Program Management

Once you, as the business leader, have made the decision to try to establish formal software program management in your organization, there are some preparations to be made. You will need to write some internal communications that begin to talk about the new Software Program Management Office (SPMO). You will need to explain to your user community how the SPMO will assist all of the program managers in executing internal projects using the new procedures. Part of this communication should introduce the concepts of a corporate Systems Engineering Process (SEP), formalized project initiation, and project sponsorship.

Another important point you will need to communicate in your message to the organization is process standardization. You can explain the advantages of having well-defined, best-practice processes as they relate to cost savings in implementation of your internal projects. You can also describe the added benefits, such as a lower cost of training, faster ramp-up time for projects, better communication across the organization, better budget controls, and so on.

Finally, you may want to prepare the organization for an ISO certification. In your communications, you can explain how ISO requires an organization to begin to "*say, do, prove, and improve*" on its internal processes. Software program management helps enable an organization for ISO pre-certification by implementing a set of standardized processes. While software program management may not provide everything needed in your organization to become fully ISO 9002 certified, it will certainly go a long way toward achieving that goal.

i.2.1 Project Initiation

Projects usually begin when a user, most often someone in the Project Sponsor's organization, submits a written request for something to be done. This is accomplished using a Project Initiation Form (PIF). The user will complete the PIF and submit it to the SPMO. The SPMO will process the request, performing such tasks as logging the request, reviewing it against outstanding corporate goals, and so on, and contact the Project Sponsor to set up a meeting to review the request.

i.2.2 Project Sponsorship

Basically, a sponsor is someone with the authority and budget to authorize funds against the costs of doing project work. Let's face the facts: If no one is willing to pay for doing a project, it just doesn't get done! Project Sponsors take on such responsibility by formally signing a letter of sponsorship, known as the Sponsor Formalization Letter (SFL). The SPMO will prepare the SFL and obtain both written commitment of funding (at this point, funding only to investigate, not for the entire project) and approval to proceed on the project from the sponsor.

i.2.3 Tools Needed to Create an SPMO

The software that is available with this book has all of the documents, files, templates, databases, spreadsheets, presentations, and HTML files needed for you to quickly implement a minimal working, entirely functional intranet-driven SPMO in your enterprise. Everything described in this book is available in the download file. Instructions for obtaining the download and for installing the example intranet-driven SPMO are found in Appendix C of this book. All of the necessary files and documents on the intranet are linked and cross-referenced to the corresponding documents needed for

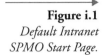

Figure i.1
Default Intranet SPMO Start Page.

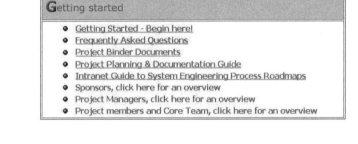

each phase of the SEP. A screenshot that depicts the SPMO intranet start page is shown as Figure i.1.

i.2.4 Project Roadmaps

In an effective SPMO, each phase of the SEP has a well-defined set of activities that should be accomplished in order to complete that phase. These processes have been illustrated on charts we refer to as phase roadmaps. As we begin to cover the details of each phase of SEP in the following chapters, we will start each chapter with a look at the phase roadmap for that particular phase. Each step of each track in the roadmap will be covered in detail.

As you will see, these roadmaps are an indispensable tool for the SPMO. They allow all involved parties to communicate in a standardized manner and clearly delineate the various roles and responsibilities. They also set expectations in an organization regarding people's understanding of what is next in the SEP. Adherence to these processes becomes internally enforced over time as the members of the organization gradually develop such expectations while working on projects managed in the SPMO environment.

i.2.5 Project Tracks

For every project, the following four key roles are needed:
1. SPMO
2. Project Sponsor (representing user needs)
3. Project Manager
4. Core Team

These roles are known as tracks in the SEP phase roadmaps. When executing each phase of the SEP, the SPMO follows a different track than the Sponsor or the Core Team would follow. In the Phase I roadmap (shown at the beginning of Chapter 1), you will see an additional track, called Project Requestor. Because the Project Requestor is usually a member of the Sponsor's organization, it is assumed that the Sponsor operates on behalf of the Requestor in all subsequent activities. For this reason, the Project Requestor will not appear as a separate track beyond the first phase.

i.2.6 Project Binders

For every project started in an organization, a set of documents is necessary to complete each step in each track of each phase of the SEP process. Collectively, these documents are referred to as a project binder. The project binder is maintained by the SPMO as work on a particular project is completed. It is very important that a complete record of all project-related activities, decisions, and so on be maintained by the SPMO during the entire life cycle of a project. Such records can help an organization handle the capitalization of costs, document the changes to and maintenance of a system, assist with project continuity, transfer responsibility, and so on. Do not take the value of these binders lightly.

i.3 Project Life Cycle in Software Program Management

The basic life cycle for a project within the SPMO is shown in Figure i.2. The process is really quite easy to understand, and it follows a logical process of identifying a need, planning for the project, designing the product, making it, testing it, getting it out to the users, and supporting it. The diagram also indicates a final step of project life cycle: closure. We use an

Figure i.2
The Process Roller-coaster.

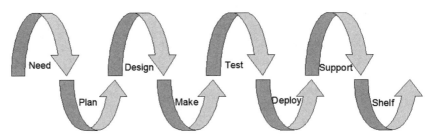

established framework of processes known as a Systems Engineering Process (SEP).

i.3.1 Systems Engineering Process

The SEP is a well-defined, detailed, phase-managed set of processes and procedures that make up an entire software project methodology. SEP is a hybrid of the waterfall methodology that started in the 1960s and, according to Edward Yourdon in his book *The Decline and Fall of the American Programmer*[1], it is still the most widely used methodology in practice today. All eight of the following phases of SEP are managed within the scope of the SPMO:

   I. Initiation
  II. Planning
 III. Design
  IV. Construction
   V. Testing
  VI. Implementation
 VII. Support
VIII. Closure

Each phase of the SEP will be described in greater detail in Chapters 2 through 9 of this book. It is important at this point to understand that an SPMO must embrace a methodology or framework within which work will be done. For our purposes, that framework is called SEP. The project documents and templates referenced herein are used to support SEP execution in an environment where multiple concurrent projects are common. Throughout this book, the management of software projects is based on an assumption of the establishment and standardization of processes and methodology within an IT environment. This book is also a starting point for helping your organization define and achieve the goals of the Capability Maturity Model[2], which was evolved from the Process Maturity Model at the Software Engineering Institute (SEI) at Carnegie-Mellon University.

i.3.2 Overview of the SEI Process Maturity Model

The SEI Process Maturity Model[3] consists of five distinct levels. In the first, or Initial Level, the organizational programmers operate in an ad-hoc fashion. There are no real organizational standards, and, if any exist at all, they are applied in an inconsistent, informal manner by the software development team. The recommended solution at this stage is, of course, implementation of stringent project management procedures. Management must commit to overseeing completion of the process, and both process and quality assurance implementation and training must begin. It is at this level, overcoming the Initial Level roadblock, that we will concentrate our efforts. The commitment required here is to create a standardized, flexible approach to ensuring the success of each project. The focus becomes one of preparing ourselves to achieve consistent, repeatable results by defining processes that prevent common errors. From the Initial Level, we can build a solid foundation that implements industry-standard best practices to assist us and ensure success.

At the second level in the SEI Process Maturity Model, the Repeatable Level, an initial definition of the software development processes has taken place. An organization has achieved a stable level of operation for software development. The organization has developed repeatable processes and has produced statistically acceptable variance tolerances over these development processes. Process groups have been established to ensure compliance with standards; an architecture for software development has been defined and is being adhered to at all levels of development. Finally, software engineering development methodologies are being introduced to the organization.

The next level, the Defined Level, has been achieved by very few organizations. At this level, a strong foundation has been established for the development process. Basic elements of process management have been set up to identify quality and cost factors. A process database has been established, and data-gathering and processing techniques are in place to allow the organization to make informed decisions about the product and management of its development.

The fourth level, the Managed Level, continues to focus the organizational efforts by automation of the data-gathering techniques. The data, which consists of more than cost and schedule data (such as basic software metrics), is used to refine procedures and techniques that support the software development process. Modification of processes based on the use of this data is the major task to accomplish at this level.

The last level described by the SEI Process Maturity Model is the Optimizing Level. You should view this level as a continuation of the previous level because the modifications take place at the Managed Level. The end result of the modifications made at the fourth level is reasonably argued to be the Optimized Level of the organization. This level is an end product of the maturity process and not really a step along the path to software development process maturity.

Baselining Your Organization

As an SEP manager, when you attempt to move your organization from its current state to an optimized level, it is recommended that you start at the beginning and move up the various levels as soon as you can. To that end, this book will provide you with some key recommendations in the next few paragraphs.

Assume Level One from the Beginning

As stated in the previous paragraph, assume you are operating at level one from the outset. If your organization is at level two, it is a simple matter to verify that the criteria for moving to the second level are met. On the other

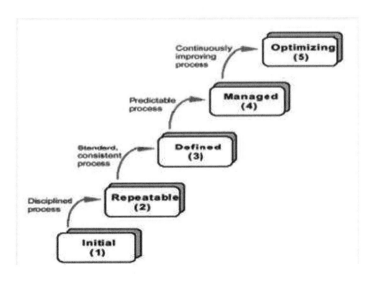

Figure i.3
Five Levels of the SEI/CMU Process Maturity Model.

hand, if your organization is really at level one, you need to establish the criteria for moving to the next level.

Establish Criteria to Move to the Next Level

A solid review of the basic criteria for attaining the Repeatable Level should be undertaken by your organization. At this point, you need to balance the needs of your organization with the absolute necessity of moving up to the Repeatable Level. In the end, much time and money will be saved by making this move, so you, as a manager, must not delay this effort. To establish these criteria, we recommend that you obtain a copy of the SEI Capability Maturity Model document. This document is an update of the initial SEI Process Maturity Model document. We further recommend that your organ-ization establish a working group to research what are perceived to be the most important first steps and implement those steps as soon as possible.

After the dust settles from this first strike to the "wild ones" in your organization, the creation of initial training programs is necessary to educate your personnel in what the organizational goals are. Quickly weed out or reeducate any dissenters who may become roadblocks to success, but remain open to fair and objective criticism from your personnel. Reward compliance with new standards by setting up shopwide recognition programs to provide an incentive to your people for doing it better than before. You should also strive to encourage the "wild ones" to develop and establish their own standards as a model for the organization's working group to use. By putting the monkey on their back, you task them with helping meet goals that adhere to SEP guidelines that your working group establishes. Once these newly developed policies and standards have been reviewed and approved by the working group, a higher degree of compliance is almost always assured.

Aspire to Move Onward and Upward

Encourage the people in your organization to help the process mature. As they achieve the goals set forth by the working group, their job becomes much easier. They become more productive and can satisfy requirements much better than before. Instill a new level of professionalism in your people. Do not allow them to maintain or acquire the attitude of the old-timer who "has been doing it this way for 20 years without problems, so there should be no reason to change now."

i.4 Overview of This Book

In the first chapter, we provide a high-level overview of the SPMO. We discuss what the mission of an SPMO should be and describe the roles and responsibilities of members of an SPMO. We discuss the software program management service areas the SPMO should address, such as performance reporting, financial management, issue management, vendor management, quality management, and so on. Finally, we describe a governing body for projects, the Business Requirements Oversight Committee (BROC), and explain the roles and responsibilities of the BROC membership.

Chapter 2 discusses the process of initiation of a new project within the SPMO. It covers the roles and responsibilities of the people working with the SPMO: the Sponsor, the Project Manager, and the Core Team. This chapter, as with all subsequent chapters through Chapter 9, describes each step in the corresponding SEP phase roadmaps and the prescribed actions taken by the project Core Team to complete the project. We discuss how the Core Team uses a Project Framework Rules Document to make key decisions and document those decisions. Finally, we close the chapter with a discussion of the Target Completion Notice, User Requirements Document, and the Project Planning and Documentation Guide.

Chapter 3 provides an overview of the project analysis and planning process. A High-Level Solutions Document is covered, and various evaluation techniques for risk mitigation are discussed. We cover project tailorability issues, defining the work necessary for successful completion of the project, performing data analysis, technical analysis, requests for proposals, budgets, schedules, estimations, change management processes, approval requirements, and so on. Each of the documents required in this phase is covered in detail.

Chapter 4 is an overview of the detailed design process. A presentation of quality and human factors issues surrounding quality management is provided. Detailed discussion of the development of specifications for system, infrastructure, software requirements, interface requirements, and performance requirements is covered. The latter part of this chapter covers creation of the various development plans needed for successful completion of the design process.

Chapter 5 discusses the construction phase of the development process. Herein, the user manuals, test plans, and software are created by various teams under the overall direction of the project core team. Coverage of the development processes, test planning and test case development, product assurance, deliverables, and certification requirements are included in this chapter.

Chapter 6 covers the actual testing of the project deliverables. Various techniques for managing a test process are explained. There is also an overview in this chapter of some key test issues that should be accounted for by the Project Manager and the Test Manager before and during the test cycle.

Chapter 7 discusses implementation of the system once the testing process has been completed. Issues regarding development and execution of training are covered in this chapter, and there is some discussion on how to properly prepare for a product rollout in an enterprise.

Chapter 8 explains the issues of product and user support. During the life cycle of the product, most of the cost incurred for the project will be in this phase of the process, and some discussion of techniques on how to mitigate such costs is included.

Chapter 9 explains how to properly bring a project life cycle to an end. It discusses what should be saved, why it should be saved, how to archive such material, and what can be learned from the past history of the product.

Chapter 10 provides some real-world insight into the day-to-day issues that Project Managers face. It provides some guidance on when and how to give and take, how to select the proper methodology for the project, and other things deemed project wizardly in nature.

Chapter 11 is devoted to best practices. In this chapter, material from a leading contractor/vendor is presented to explain the various "best-practices" consideration that will make your project stand out from others.

Chapter 12 brings together some thoughts on how this book can help you be a more effective manager of people. Some of the most important issues any project manager will have to cope with revolve around honing people skills and effectively interacting with and motivating them to achieve desired results.

Appendix A of this book provides illustrations of all the SEP phase roadmaps in a single place for ease of future reference, as well as some additional processes that are needed to fully implement the SPMO function. Appendix B provides detailed answers to the chapter review questions. Appendix C explains how to install the software that accompanies this book and how to tailor it to suit your organizational needs. For now, let's focus on the actions within the SPMO and what the SPMO staff's responsibilities are in helping the project requestor get a project started.

Understanding the SPMO

This chapter defines at a high level the mission of a corporate IT Software Program Management Office (SPMO). It outlines the major roles and corresponding responsibilities for each member of the SPMO and project team. It explains the functions of the various positions people working in the SPMO occupy and, more importantly, it covers a wide variety of issues that are often overlooked when projects start.

1.1 SPMO Mission Statement

"To ensure the successful implementation of Enterprise programs and projects developed within an environment of continuous process improvement."

To achieve success in this process, an SPMO will provide a standard set of tools and processes for program and project delivery. The SPMO will be tasked to provide planning, reporting, and administrative support for enterprise projects, and it will be responsible for facilitating project communications from the Core Team out to the organization.

1.2 Roles and Responsibilities

The following sections describe the roles of participants in projects that are run by the SPMO. These descriptions may also be used as a guideline for projects that are run by functional groups outside the SPMO.

NOTE: Roles may differ from the titles belonging to individuals who are functioning in an organization with specific responsibilities. For example, a Technical Lead in the development group may play the role of a Project Manager for a new initiative in that group. For our purposes, it is important to remember this book references roles and not titles.

1.2.1 Executive Stakeholder

This is the person to whom the Sponsor usually reports. He or she is responsible for reviewing the weekly status reports and schedules that are provided by the SPMO. The Executive Stakeholder is the owner of the entire program and represents it to the senior executive staff as needed. In many instances, the Executive Stakeholder and the Project Sponsor are one and the same person. He or she may also be asked to provide strategic direction and make decisions on highly critical issues and project prioritization. Most importantly, this person will approve the overall funding for the program (otherwise, it never gets off the ground).

1.2.2 Project Sponsor

This person is the functional owner of the project (typically the vice president of the business unit driving the project or a director of an area within that business unit). The Sponsor is also responsible for providing strategic direction to the project. The Sponsor is the person with financial accountability, and he or she agrees, via the Sponsor Formalization Letter, to apply resources to a project, including the formal appointment of a Project Manager. The Sponsor is the focal point for project decisions that are beyond the Project Manager's scope, as well as acting as the project representative to upper management. Sponsors agree to review and approve all deliverables (as appropriate), in addition to approving all project phase transitions.

1.2.3 Program Manager

This function is responsible for soliciting standard reporting and Systems Engineering Process (SEP) methodology information from various Project Managers and Coordinators regarding subprojects of a major project (defined as a project that spans more than one business unit in an organization.) The Program Manager is responsible for sharing information with other business units and communicating relevant major project information to and from other business units to individual Project Managers. The Program Manager may sometimes be mistaken for the Project Sponsor because his or her role is much more involved at the day-to-day level. The Program Manager is much more of a decision maker, but project staff often do not distinguish between the manager and the role of the Sponsor. Project Managers often report directly to the Program Manager when they are assigned to the SPMO by the Project Sponsor in an Appointment Letter.

1.2 Roles and Responsibilities

1.2.4 Project Manager (PM)

The Project Manager works within a functional group that usually belongs to the Sponsor. The Project Manager is the primary point of contact for a project. He or she is responsible for day-to-day management of project tasks, including schedule management, project definition, architecture and implementation plans, resource needs identification, vendor selection, and many other specific items required for a successful delivery. The Project Manager is also responsible for providing the Project Coordinator in the SPMO with all appropriate and completed SEP methodology documentation, reports, and any other additional project-specific information requested.

1.2.5 Project Coordinator

The Project Coordinator works directly with the Project Sponsor and provides various services offered by the SPMO (the service areas of the SPMO are further detailed in this chapter).

The Project Coordinator ensures that all project management processes are consistent with SEP methodology. He or she provides reports, status updates, and pertinent project information to the SPMO manager and the Sponsor for continuous tracking and cross-functional monitoring of a given project. The Project Coordinator collaborates with other Project Coordinators within the SPMO to facilitate communications about different projects in progress across the organization. The Project Coordinator is tasked to identify, track, and synchronize project interdependencies. This person resolves issues that arise when such interdependencies exist.

1.2.6 Business Systems Analyst (BSA)

The BSA is responsible for analysis of business and user requirements. He or she also monitors projects that affect business units. The BSA would typically oversee requirements for delivery of a specific business system (e.g., customer relationship management, sales automation tools, or financial package etc.). The BSA works closely with user representatives and the Project Manager to identify, classify, and mitigate project risks, perform cost-benefit analyses, and provide input regarding product and tool selection. This person serves as a liaison between the development team and the user. It is the BSA's responsibility to ensure that user needs are properly communicated to and implemented by the developers. The BSA is generally an expert in the business processes and knows all of the details of business process execution inside and out. This person is a resident expert in the area of the business you are working to support.

1.3 Project Resources

Project Resources are responsible for completing specific tasks on a project. They are usually managed by a team lead or by the Project Manager. They may be external or internal to the organization and may include architects, planners, end-user representatives, developers, engineers, analysts, database administrators (DBAs), system administrators, technicians, testers, trainers, coordinators, and so on.

1.4 SPMO Organizational Structure

The following diagram (Figure 1.1) depicts the line structure of a typical SPMO-driven project. The Executive Stakeholder has one or more Project Sponsors in his or her organization. Each Project Sponsor works in the SPMO shop with a Program Manager, who is assigned by the SPMO to drive the project to completion. The Project Sponsor is responsible for the appointment of a Project Manager in his or her organization. This Project Manager will have a project coordinator who works in the SPMO assigned

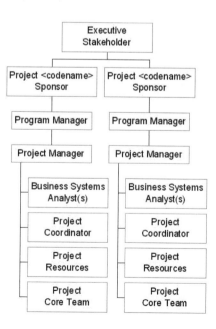

Figure 1.1 *The SPMO Organization.*

to the Project Manager's project team. The Project Manager will also have BSAs and other project resources (e.g., data analysts) assigned on an as-needed basis. It is the Project Manager's responsibility to form a project Core Team and start moving the project forward through the SEP life cycle process. The Project Manager will work under the Program Manager's supervision. This ensures adherence to all SPMO standards, policies, and procedures and helps in the standardization process.

1.5 Software Program Management Service Areas

The SPMO is set up to run as a service organization. It provides project-related services to all business units across the company. These services include the following:

- Performance Reporting (including schedule and status reporting)
- Financial Management
- Vendor Management
- Issue Management
- Quality Management
- Change Management
- Risk Management

1.6 Performance Reporting

Project performance reporting involves documenting the project's performance against the plan. This reporting addresses a variety of audiences (and levels of responsibility), both internal and external to the project. The objective of performance reporting is to provide consistent and regular reports that recognize progress made or lost in the project. Another objective is to provide the project team with early warnings of potential problems. This type of reporting will also provide senior management with information that can be used to keep the project operating smoothly and enable adequate communication among key parties.

Benefits of performance reporting include providing a means to ensure that the project makes orderly progress toward key milestones by charting progress metrics. The reports tie performance reports and project financials together for a consolidated picture of the overall status of a project. These reports are designed to capture all project information regarding scope, schedule, cost, and quality. These reports will recognize and target multiple audiences and tailor the information to each audience. The SPMO implements and executes performance reporting.

The five components of performance reporting are:

I. Establish program standards
II. Request and collect data
III. Consolidate information
IV. Reporting development and continuous improvement
V. Reporting Communications

Performance reporting is a means used to formally establish project standards. Project standards should define the reporting and communications process and team organization, the personnel roles, including participation in project management, and the project reporting frequency. Performance reporting effectively communicates the information produced in the course of project execution to the entire organization.

In order for a report to be meaningful, it must contain relevant, timely data. The SPMO uses various reports to collect and disseminate this data from multiple sources in an organization. The SPMO is likely to collect data from Project Progress Reports (which are weekly recurring reports) and from the Project Plan (usually maintained in a software product used for project management). The SPMO can determine and track overall project scope and cost using project status reporting. Any new or significant issues and problems can be gleaned from Project Status Reports and the Project Issues Database. The SPMO can track vendor costs and performance by reviewing vendor invoices and Status Reports.

Reports should consolidate information and summarize project data, targeting it to the appropriate audience in the organization. Reports that are sent to members of the Core Team often become attached as status updates to the Core Team members' report to their business leaders. Performance reports should focus only on the project level, and they should be quite specific in nature. It should always be assumed that a report leaving the SPMO will be used publicly within the company. This assumption may seem overly cautious, but it is better to be safe than sorry. There have been instances where reports have circulated back to a company CEO before a business leader could meet and brief the CEO on the project. Imagine the embarrassment the Sponsor must have felt in this particular circumstance! Projects have even been canceled in such circumstances.

Report development and Continuous Process Improvement (CPI) require that the Core Team members take some time in planning the reports, devising a method where they can continuously monitor project progress and periodically improve on the report structure, format, and content. At the same time, the Core Team should always ensure that any report meets the following criteria:

- Targets a specific audience
- Is accurate in all regards
- Is consistent with other project data
- Is understandable and not filled with jargon
- Is usable—it must serve a purpose to the recipient
- Is analyzable and timely in nature
- Enables prediction of project performance
- Identifies potential problems (and propose solutions if possible)
- Is approved by and useful to all project stakeholders
- Is published and distributed to all interested parties

An example format of the required elements of a project performance report includes the following:

- *Scope of deliverables:* Planned, actual, and projected
- *Cost:* Planned, actual, earned, and estimated at completion
- *Schedule:* Planned, actual, and estimated
- *Quality:* Planned, actual, and projected achievement
- *Risk:* Planned, actual, and projected reduction
- *Benefits:* Planned and achieved
- *Issues:* Defined, corrective actions taken, status, management actions required

Communications reporting involves effective communication to the organization. The objective is to ensure the delivery of the right message, sent by the appropriate party, to the necessary audience(s), through appropriate channels. Successful implementation of communications reporting positively affects the work environment and relationships with sponsoring organizations, employees, and other stakeholders.

1.6.1 Financial Management

Financial management involves control and management of the program's budget and other finance, as well as providing financial reporting for the project. Objectives of sound financial management should ensure that all costs relating to the progress of the project are planned and tracked, including operating expenses, capital expenditures, and man-days. Financial management involves reporting on the status of projects related to, but not under, Core Team control, such as those activities that affect the overall project (e.g., infrastructure development). Financial management should allow a team to quantify, support, and maintain all financial aspects of the business case for the project. The SPMO generally performs performs or assists the Project Manager in performing the financial management functions needed for any given project.

NOTE: This section documents only the critical components of project-related financial management and reporting. It does not address financial reporting typically required for companies (i.e., general and subsidiary ledgers, balance sheet, income and expense statements).

Financial management establishes financial guidelines for projects underway in the SPMO. It enables the SPMO to compile budgets using Cost Estimate Worksheets. The SPMO can then periodically quantify and maintain the financial aspect of the business case and conduct periodic financial analysis. The SPMO can maintain financial control of the project and oversee the results. With sound financial management, the SPMO can assist in estimating realistic project budgets and establish and maintain a project chart of accounts, which logically categorizes the financial activities of a project. To properly perform project-related financial management, the SPMO must collect data from the various affected units of the organization, prime and subcontractors, and suppliers, to name but a few.

In order to create and maintain the costing and budgeting elements for a project, the SPMO must determine if the cost is in line with the business and project requirements and decide on an approach for handling project costs. This includes determining the most likely types and sources of project costs. Types of costs include direct labor and materials (i.e., direct charges to project accounts) and indirect costs (i.e., allocations of costs to project accounts) incurred during the course of project execution. The SPMO must determine all sources of cost, including those of the sponsoring organizational unit, the prime contractor (if one is involved), subcontractors, and suppliers. The SPMO must also determine an estimating approach and decide which factors will force inclusion or exclusion of various cost elements into the overall project scope.

Project initiation requires the SPMO to work closely with the Project Manager and Core Team members to define detailed estimates and obtain budget authorization. The SPMO will set up a cost-control mechanism to initiate the project and begin tracking actual expenditures. Once the project has been initiated, the SPMO will establish a project baseline and begin to solicit estimates from the project management team on project-related payroll and other expenses (usually by headcount or hours tracked). Project Sponsors are tasked to ensure proper assignment of budget by having the finance representative on the Core Team work with the finance organization to set up a cost center and allocate funds for the project to the new project cost center.

The SPMO is chartered to monitor and control project costs. To accomplish this task, the SPMO must receive all invoices requested for payment, implement an invoice approval process, collect all invoices in a repository, and track the invoices against projected budgets. The SPMO is responsible for tracking payment authorizations and verifying that payments have been made in a timely manner. Finally, the SPMO will report the results of all projects' financial status.

In order for the SPMO to report financial results properly, it must prepare financial reports on a monthly recurring basis. It must gather data from project accounting reports and input actuals into the reports. A summary of the financials by project is sent to the various Project Managers for review. The Project Managers are expected to determine variances and provide explanations for significant deviations from the plan. It may require the SPMO to reforecast financials based on new data obtained from the Project Manager. Finally, the SPMO will consolidate the data into a "roll-up report" to senior management.

1.6.2 Vendor Management

Vendor management involves assisting Project Managers with the selection and management of resources obtained from outside the organization. This may include consultants, suppliers, or contractors. It can also include products and services that are part of the business capability (such as software or physical assets) or tangibles used to create a business capability (such as office space or temporary workers). The goal of vendor management is to achieve the project's objectives by assisting in the selection of vendors and establishing a business relationship with them in order to purchase appropriate technologies, products, and services. Vendor management should establish contracts and manage any changes to the contract, assist in the management of vendor personnel, and efficiently use internal resources and skills by identifying opportunities to supplement internal capabilities with qualified vendors.

The benefits of effective vendor management are cost savings obtained by working closely to obtain quality products and services, development of relationships and partnering alliances with vendors, and development of standards for vendor quality, metrics, reporting, pricing, and billing. These standards ensure that all vendors in compliance, and, as software program management matures, all units in the company will expect such standards to be enforced. Vendor management staff in the SPMO should work with the legal department to create standard wording (boilerplates) for common contract clauses. They should identify and establish priorities for vendor selection criteria.

It is very important for the vendor management team to fully understand the business arrangements between the sponsoring organization and the vendor (and any business partners). There may be larger issues at stake outside the scope of a single project. The SPMO vendor management staff must gain efficiency in internal resources and skills by identifying opportunities to supplement internal capabilities with qualified vendors. This can only be done when standards to measure performance are in place.

The SPMO facilitates vendor management with the Project Manager, the Core Team, and all other stakeholders. Generally, it is best if only the SPMO representatives deal directly with vendors because SPMO staff nearly always have special training to help them deal with vendors in situations that create ethical problems, conflicts, or otherwise can lead to legal complications. There are five key components of vendor management:

I. Planning
II. Selection Assistance
III. Establishment of Contract Terms and Conditions

IV.   Monitoring

V.   Contract Closure

1.6.3   Vendor Planning

In vendor planning, the SPMO needs to identify all products and services required for the project. Sometimes this takes quite a long time and requires many meetings with business units and various members of the Core Team. This is especially true for very large projects ($20 million or more in scope). Next, the SPMO must identify the available budget and involve all groups affected by the use of each product or service. The vendor team is responsible for each product or service area (e.g., facilities, network, package) that must be identified. This must be communicated to the interested parties through the Core Team and through various reporting vehicles used by the SPMO.

During the selection process, the vendor team will work with the Project Manager to identify vendor candidates by developing a Request for Information (RFI) document that is to be sent to the candidate vendors. The vendors selected at this point are usually the best known or best referenced you can find. The vendor team will also define the selection criteria to be used to determine which candidates are chosen for the project. An important consideration is to ensure that before the RFI is sent out to vendors, all input to the process is included. It is not fair to the vendors to have multiple revisions of an RFI out to various competitors and to have each vendor responding to differing or altered requirements. Any changes subsequent to initial release should be change-managed and communicated through a formal RFI update process. If vendors feel you are wasting their time with frivolous changes, your credibility is likely to take a hit and responses will generally be hard to obtain in the future. It is also important for the vendor selection team to understand when they send RFIs out to vendors that their request is generally only one of many those vendors often receive.

1.6.4   Vendor Selection

The selection process for a vendor generally requires that the SPMO prepare and issue a Request for Proposal (RFP). The SPMO must also identify a vendor team member as the single point of contact to clarify issues. The final selection will be based on how well the vendor has met defined selection criteria, cost, and so on. One criteria that selection teams often overlook is how the vendor product strategy will play out with your specific enterprise needs 12 to 18 months down the road. It is important to know if you are buying a product that will likely be discontinued in three months, for example. The process of evaluating vendor proposals can be time-consuming and tedious, but it should not be taken lightly. As soon as possible, the SPMO should notify and remove candidates do not satisfy the criteria stated in the RFP. The final selection should be made by the consensus of the Core Team. Once the Core Team has made a selection, it should formally notify the legal department about the upcoming contract review.

1.6.5 Establishing Contract Terms and Conditions

At a minimum, the contract should define the commitment between the company and the vendor. The SPMO should work with the selected vendor and the organization's legal department to reach an agreement regarding the precise content and wording of the contract. The contract should stipulate a price and define how billing will be accomplished (include frequency of billing and to whom the bills should be sent). After the legal department has completed work on the contract, the SPMO should schedule a contract review meeting with the selected vendor to evaluate any new vendor alternatives and assess their impacts on the organization. Any changes to the contract must be taken back to the legal department and another review should be scheduled when legal has finished making the new changes. During the course of this sometimes protracted process, it is common for the Project Manager to concurrently seek and obtain funding approval from the Executive Sponsor.

1.6.6 Monitoring the Vendor

Once contracts are signed and everyone has agreed to what will be done by whom, it is the SPMO's responsibility to monitor the vendor to ensure that everything proceeds as planned. The SPMO should be ready to identify variances, report and track issues, process changes, resolve contract disputes, and ensure that timely and proper billing occurs with the vendor. When bills are received from the vendor, the SPMO should prepare and clear such billings with the Project Manager. If there are changes to the original contract—and there almost always are—the SPMO coordinates those contract changes in accordance with the project change-control process. SPMOs ensure that project teams assess the vendor performance and validate whether on not the vendor has satisfied the contractual requirements of the project. Any instances of noncompliance should be documented and raised as an issue with the Project Manager. If the Project Manager cannot get the issue addressed with the vendor, the SPMO will facilitate handing the matter over to the corporate legal department for resolution.

1.6.7 Contract Closure

The SPMO is tasked to ensure that the vendor has met all contract obligations and the project has met its commitments to the company. The SPMO must verify that project users perform an acceptance review to validate whether the product or service delivered has met all expectations and commitments. Finally, the SPMO should verify that the Project Manager has notified the purchasing department after a successful completion of the acceptance review in order to release final payments to the vendor.

1.7 Issue Management

Issue management facilitates identification, analysis, escalation, reporting, and resolution of the project's issues. Any decisions to be made regarding the development of the business capability or the management of the project are classified as an issue. Issue management will enable the project Core Team to create strategies that effectively address potential barriers to project success. Issue management should be carried out at all levels within the project. The issue management process should ensure that issues are resolved at the appropriate level and are communicated as appropriate. Sometimes, organizations set up a Change Control Board (CCB) to process and prioritize issues as they arise.

Issues are resolved with action items, which can span a single project or multiple projects. Issues can escalate, and they should be proactively raised during the course of project execution. Having a formal issue management process achieves several important objectives, such as providing informed, proactive, and timely management of issues; allowing a team to analyze project concerns and issues, including those that span multiple areas; and ensuring that all stakeholders are informed of and participate in issue resolution. The benefits of formal issue management are also easily identified. It facilitates appropriate escalations for project issues that remain unresolved. Issue management can enable timely issue resolution through prioritization of service, schedule, costs, performance, or quality. Formalized issue management can improve quality; enable root-cause analysis; provide future project teams with key lessons learned, project history, and project metrics; and allow for future risk analysis through documentation of the issue and its resolution.

1.7.1 Issue Escalation

Sometimes a project team must escalate issues that impede the progress of a project and are beyond the authority of the Project Manager to resolve. These issues generally cannot be resolved by anyone within the Core Team. The escalation path is from the Core Team to the Project Manager to the Program Manager to the Project Sponsor. These issues may even need to be further escalated to the Executive Stakeholder or the company CEO, depending on the nature and severity of the issue. They are resolvable with action items and affect project scope, cost, schedule, projected business performance, or business capability. Multiple projects or releases can also be affected by an issue. Such issues do not have a clearly defined owner. The project team should focus on issues that are mission critical and those that are past due.

1.7.2 Issue Reporting

The Project Manager is responsible for regularly assessing the overall issue status (e.g., new issues per period, critical issues). He or she should monitor issue resolution progress and identify potential bottlenecks and/or increases in the number of open issues. These discoveries should be integrated into the issue status section found in the weekly project reports. Some examples of issue metrics include tracking the number of new issues and the number of issues resolved since the last reporting period, the timeliness of issue resolution by issue importance, mission-critical issues and their due dates, and the total number of open and closed issues.

1.8 Quality Management

Quality management involves ensuring that the expectations and quality requirements of the project are understood and actively managed. Effective quality management contains six components:

I. Expectation management
II. Quality verification
III. Process management
IV. Metrics
V. Continuous improvement
VI. Rewards and recognition

The objectives of quality management are to ensure the delivery of a quality product that successfully realizes the intended benefits[4]. The product must meet all of the expectations of the project stakeholders, and it should uniformly apply the approved principles, measures, standards, and methods of software program management. The quality program should create an environment fostering continuous improvement and actively manage and continue to leverage the knowledge capital of the organization.

1.8.1 Benefits of Quality Management

The benefits of quality management are obtained from implementing a philosophy of "build in quality" versus "inspect for quality." This really means one cannot rely on back-end inspections to achieve quality. The Project Manager is responsible for setting project expectations that ensure the project will deliver quality work. The expectation of "get it right the first time" should be shared among all members of the Core Team. To achieve all of these benefits and meet all user expectations, the quality management team should establish Continuous Process Improvement (CPI) as a team mantra. The team should be ready and willing to enable customer-driven measurement. Quality is achieved when your customers state that a quality product has been delivered. A truly effective quality program must empower people across the organization. Everyone is responsible for the quality of the project (e.g., there are no "other" people responsible for quality in this project). The quality program should maximize solutions by involving project members, the people closest to the problems, and it should provide ample opportunities for improvement within the project development environment.

Quality management is defined using two basic premises: (1) develop an explicit understanding of what quality means to the Sponsor and stakeholders, and (2) ensure that those requirements are deliberately and consciously built into the project at the start, rather than simply looked for at the end of the project. If you are dealing with vendors, make sure you come to a common understanding of quality measurements before starting work with them. In order for your expectations to be met, the vendor must know what is expected and what to deliver in terms of quality components.

1.8.2 Components of Quality Management

Having a solid understanding of the following key components of quality management can help to ensure these quality goals are always met:

- Managing expectations
- Quality verification
- Internal quality audit
- Process management
- Definition of metrics
- Reporting of quality metrics
- Continuous process improvement
- Establishing rewards and recognition
- Quality training and orientation

Managing Expectations. Managing expectations focuses on two key components: understanding stakeholder expectations and managing stakeholder expectations. In order to understand stakeholder expectations, you must understand who the project's key stakeholders are and be able to identify the best way to gather specific, relevant information about their expectations, including data collection, categorization, and prioritization of their expectations. It is a common mistake to assume that all stakeholders have the same expectations of a project.

A good-quality program will ensure that expectations remain realistic throughout the duration of the project effort. A good-quality program will periodically analyze progress on expectations and share expectations with the project team and stakeholders. It is important to address expectations that are not met and continuously monitor stakeholder perceptions regarding the project. The Project Manager must work with the quality team to keep expectations up to date and relevant. The Project Manager should strive to implement improvements that address expectations falling short of the desired level. Finally, the Project Manager must communicate expectation status and evaluate team progress on meeting those expectations.

Quality Verification. The most effective means of ensuring quality in a program is to verify it periodically as the project progresses from start to finish. This is done by identifying critical targets for quality verification and defining the criteria and processes for each of those targets. This will help you ensure that the desired quality levels are achieved. Some targets you should consider for your assessment are the deliverables, the processes, and the people.

For deliverables, you should include verification, validation, and testing. This would include the use of quality testing techniques such as stage containment and entry and exit criteria. Stage containment refers to a process of defining boundaries around which testing will occur. Entry and exit criteria are used to stipulate when testing begins and ends. When you are identifying such processes, consider evaluating your project compliance with such quality verification processes. You may also desire to benchmark against other known standards, such as the Project Realization Process (PRP), Capability Maturity Model (CMM), or ISO 900X audits. When assessing people, it is important to measure team satisfaction periodically. If all of the folks on your team are melancholy about their daily work, there is something wrong, you can be sure! You need to dig into this problem and work to resolve this matter quickly. Never underestimate the power of good team morale on a project. You should strive to address gaps in satisfaction by assigning responsibility, designating completion dates, and communicating the remediation plan to everyone.

Internal Quality Audit (IQAs). IQAs are performed to ensure that your business activities meet stated requirements and demonstrate the effectiveness of your quality systems. IQAs are basically plans with procedures for conducting internal assessments of your system. In conducting an audit, you should ensure that the audit is scheduled according to the importance of the activity and use objective independent auditors to carry out the assessment. They should document everything and follow up to ensure that any needed corrections are made. Communicate the results of the audit across the organization as needed, and document any and all corrective actions taken. Finally, verify the effectiveness of the corrections made and communicate that to the organization as well.

Process Management. The first step in process management is to clearly define and obtain agreement from all affected parties on what constitutes process boundaries. To accomplish this goal you must identify users and providers of the process, ensure the process is described at the appropriate level of detail, and identify how metrics and goals are tracked and collected for the process. You must provide for continuous evaluation and improvement of the process. You can use the following techniques to do this:

- Perform desk checks—look for gaps and redundant steps that add no value.
- Assess compliance with the process.
- Perform root-cause analysis on performance gaps.

- Discuss changes or improvements following the execution of a process.

Defining Metrics. For metrics to be of any value, they need to be measured against some criteria. It is the Core Team's responsibility to define the criteria for determining the appropriate metrics used in a project. The team should define the required measurement and reporting processes and identify the resources tasked to gather, analyze, and report metrics. They should next define a process for piloting the selected metrics, identify implementation requirements, and identify the requirements and the methods used to communicate these metrics and the corresponding results to the larger audience of the company. This process is sometimes referred to as determining performance measurements, which is our next topic.

1.8.3 Determine Performance Measurements

The requirements should be developed on the assumption that the system will provide a more efficient and/or more effective work process that supports the organization's mission. Performance measures for the work process should be developed to measure its progress toward accomplishing the mission. This is also a requirement of the Government Performance and Results Act of 1993 (GPRA)[5]. Ideally, some indicators that measure the impact of the project on the mission performance measures should be developed to measure the performance of a proposed system.

Performance measures must be developed for each proposed system, and a method for collecting that information must be established. Most of the performance measures should be indicators of how well the system is meeting the requirements defined for the system. Project team personnel who develop performance measures will likely require training. Performance measurement is sometimes defined as a group endeavor that seeks to improve the performance and accountability of an organization, process, program, product, or service. Some key steps to include in a performance measurement process are as follows:

- Agree on basic principles for mission, goals, and objectives.
- Brainstorm many ideas for measures.
- Select the best measures.
- Take action (i.e., develop a plan and monitor progress).
- Evaluate and calibrate the measures.

Performance measures that are sometimes used by private-sector firms to account for the value and impact of information technology are as follows:

- Process/product/service improvement
- Cycle-time reduction
- Customer satisfaction
- Cost-effectiveness

Some Information Management performance measures include the following:

- Percent change in life cycle costs
- Percent change in work process cycle time
- Percent change in acquisition time to deliver a product or service
- Percent change in product/service quality (e.g., fewer error rates in transactions)
- Percent change in customer satisfaction
- Percent change in information systems projects on schedule/within budget
- Percent change in systems that comply with architectures and standards
- Percentage of systems project management staff who meet acquisition and information management education and training requirements

Finally, over time, some valuable lessons have been learned through painful experience. These lessons include the following:

- Involve key stakeholders from the beginning.
- Place primary focus first on the most costly or troubled programs.
- Develop measures in the context of management plans and budgets.
- Choose measures that are results oriented and quantifiable and demonstrate value.
- Select a vital few projects to undertake at any time.
- Do not promise more than you can deliver.
- Educate and train stakeholders in performance measurements.

Report Quality Metrics. Provide reports that are easy to interpret and use. In order to understand and improve the quality of the development process, you should attempt to incorporate quality metrics for scheduled versus completed deliverables, the number of issues tracked per work group, and the average quality review turnaround time and duration. Compare the estimate at completion with the original baseline, and record the number of errors incurred during the test phase. All of these metrics provide benchmarks for future projects.

In addition to these metrics, it is often beneficial to conduct postmortem meetings. These are formal reviews at project completion that are used to identify any CPI opportunities. Solicit team-member feedback. This process is important to obtain and track feedback on all aspects of the project environment. To do this effectively, you should create Quality Action Teams (QATs). These teams are empowered to act as a virtual project team and are tasked to identify possible solutions to any CPI opportunity. Establish a CPI recognition program that provides incentives and rewards to encourage wider participation in CPI activities. Engage experts to provide accurate and objective assessments. This will help ensure quality services and delivery. Conduct stakeholder, team member, and user satisfaction surveys. These surveys will help the SPMO quantify the overall project satisfaction in combination with the postmortem documentation.

1.8.4 Continuous Process Improvement (CPI)

In order to implement CPI effectively, the SPMO must define an organizationwide CPI policy to ensure that improvement efforts are integrated into daily activities. One technique often used to increase project member involvement in CPI activities is to use corporatewide broadcast communications. This can be done with newsletters, project update sheets, e-mail, and so on. This type of communication helps build the level of participation by keeping a broader corporate audience informed. It also reminds the team that a larger audience than those in the conference room where they have been working has been following up on the progress of its efforts. It helps keep team members focused on the objectives and, in many instances, provides a form of positive recognition by association. If the project bombs for some reason, the reverse effect would likely hold true. Who would want his or her name associated with failure? It is another form of motivation that can be relied on to provide results. Many times in my career, I have heard people make the statement that a project would not fail on their account. People take pride in their work and want to do better. CPI simply enables this to occur.

1.8.5 Software Process Improvement Organizations

In a NASA Software Engineering Laboratory report[6], software process improvement researchers reported that software organizations historically exhibited significant shortcomings in their ability to capitalize on the experiences gained from completed projects. These researchers found that most of the insight gained through previous efforts had been passively obtained instead of having been aggressively pursued through specific planning and use of organizational infrastructures. Software developers and managers, although well-meaning and interested, generally do not have the time or resources to focus on building corporate knowledge or organizational process improvements. They have projects to run and software to deliver. Thus, collective learning and experience must become a corporate concern and be treated as a company asset.

Reuse of experience and collective learning should be supported by an organizational infrastructure dedicated to developing, updating, and supplying upon request synthesized experiences and competencies. This infrastructure should emphasize achieving continual sustained improvement. Software process improvement organizations are devoted to using lessons, data, and general experience from software projects to ensure that ongoing and future efforts use the experiences gained from previous activities to continually improve the associated organization's software products and processes. Most software process improvement organizations consist of the following elements:

- *Developers*—who design, implement, and maintain software. They also provide project documentation and data gathered during development and operations.
- *Process analysts*—who transform the data and information provided by the developers into reusable forms (e.g., standards, models, training) and supply them back to the developers. They provide specific support to the projects on the use of the analyzed and synthesized information, tailoring it to a format that is usable by and useful to a current software effort.
- *Support staff*—who provide services to the developers by supporting data collection and retrieval and to the analysts by managing the repository of information.

Although each element is separate and distinct from the others, these three components are intimately related to each other. Each component has its own goals, process, and plans, but when combined, all three components have the mission of providing software that is continually improving in quality and cost effectiveness. Figure 1.2 outlines the differences in focus among the three components constituting the software process improvement organization. It also provides you with a high-level picture of the software process improvement organization. It highlights the activities and information flows among its three components—namely developers, analysts, and support staff.

The developers produce and maintain software, but are not directly responsible for capturing the reusable experience. They provide the analysts with project and environment characteristics, development data, resource-usage information, quality records, and process information. The developers also provide feedback on the actual performance of the models produced by the analysts and used by the project. Therefore, with respect to software process improvement, the developers have global responsibility for using, in the most effective way, the packaged experiences to deliver high-quality software.

The analysts, by processing the information received from the developers, produce models of products and processes and return direct feedback to each project. They also produce and provide baselines, tools, lessons learned, and data, which are given parameters in some form in order to be adapted to the characteristics of a project.

Area	Developers	Analysts	Support Staff
Focus and Scope	Specific project	Multiple projects (specific domain)	Multiple projects (specific domain)
Goals	Produce, maintain software Satisfy user requirements	Analyze and package experience Support developers	Archive, maintain, and distribute development and maintenance experience
Approach	Use the most effective software engineering techniques	Assess the impact of specific technologies Package experience into models, standards, etc.	Maintain a repository of experiences, models, standards, etc.
Measure of Success	Delivery of quality software products on time and within budget	Reuse of empirical software experience by developers Improved products	Efficient collection, storage, and retrieval of information (data, models, reports, etc.)

Figure 1.2 *Focus of Software Process Improvement Organizational Components.*

The support staff sustain and facilitate the interaction between developers and analysts by saving and maintaining the information, making it efficiently retrievable, and controlling and monitoring access to it. They use tools that assist in collecting, validating, and redistributing data and reusable experience.

Remember, the ultimate goal of a software process improvement organization is to understand and repeat successes and to avoid failures. Therefore, the software process improvement organization's processes and operations must be based on solid and objective development experience. A measurement-based approach is needed for project management, evaluation, and decision making. Software measures are applied to process, product, and resources. Measurement is one of the basic tools available to the software process improvement organization for performing its tasks and to management for controlling and improving the efficiency of the whole infrastructure.

Establishing Rewards and Recognition. Establish a governing body for the rewards-and-recognition process within the project environment. The responsibilities of this team include identifying the types of behaviors to reward and providing initiatives that support the project's goals. Define all eligible participants by determining which groups or individuals are affected by the project deliverables. Establish award criteria, reward availability, frequency of award presentations, and responsibility for providing and bestowing the awards. Develop a communications plan for initial and ongoing initiatives that people will participate in and outline the process for how an individual or team participates in the rewards program.

1.9 Change Management

Change management is the process of managing proposed changes to project scope as defined during the requirements phase. This process will ensure consistent handling and escalation of all change requests. The primary objective of change management is to provide a defined process for managing changes to requirements and to set guidelines for approving and escalating change requests. This process will provide corporate executives and project members with timely information regarding changes to requirements. An obvious benefit of a successful implementation of change management will be a positive effect on the work environment and relationships with sponsoring organizations, employees, and other stakeholders by minimizing scope creep and requirements churn.

When establishing a change management program, ensuring consistent handling and escalation of change requests is critical. You should obtain Project Sponsor support for the change management process. The Sponsor must be assured that his or her project is following a well-defined process and is not going outside the boundaries of this process to include new scope (and cost). All requirements should be baselined before a change management process is implemented.

1.10 Change Management Plans

Change management has been defined as an integrated communications, training, workforce planning, and evaluation approach to assisting managers, supervisors, and employees with transitioning effectively into a new way of accomplishing work. These key elements are further detailed in the following paragraphs.

Communications. In order to be effective, the team must be able to assess the effectiveness of current and proposed business practices, to convey the capabilities of the chosen software solution, to engage groups affected by automation or business practice change (stakeholders) in a meaningful exchange of information, to provide accurate information regarding design and implementation timing and progress, and to foster acceptance of new methods of work. These abilities are enhanced by stakeholder involvement through good two-way communications. Because the importance of the communications effort is high, in addition to this change management plan, a communications plan detailing the specific efforts that will be made to engage stakeholders should be developed.

Training. The success of any implementation depends on having well-trained end users who are comfortable with their knowledge and skill in using both the SEP approach and the deliverable being managed. Good training fosters acceptance of new work processes, efficiency of processing, and accuracy in data collection. Training includes, but is not limited to, classroom training, on-the-job training, the production and use of user guides, and the update of specific company guidance.

Workforce Planning. Changes in business practices and the introduction of new computer systems and software, which may require new job skills, may affect the nature of work in the new project effort. The Change Management Team (CMT) usually consists of a group of three or four people whose responsibility it is to identify changes to workload and workforce planning issues. Working with management, the CMT will facilitate a review of the impact that implementation may have on employee skills and assigned duties in order to develop a plan to address any proposed workforce changes.

Evaluation. In order to assess success, the CMT should use several evaluation methods. On a continuing basis, the efforts of the CMT will be evaluated and measured for success based on established performance measures and critical success factors. These performance measures and critical success factors will correlate with those established for the other parts of the project. A critical success factor might include workforce acceptance of best practices and use of the system. Conventional methods for evaluation and measurement to be used will generally include strategically planned surveys, questionnaires, interviews with appropriate personnel, and other activities for feedback from those affected by the new or changed system.

For any change management process to work, one must recognize that the greatest risk to the successful implementation of an enterprisewide system is the failure to take into consideration major aspects of change management. Poor communications, training, and workforce planning lead to a lack of acceptance of business changes and poor performance at the end-user level. In some cases, failure to provide for adequate change management planning results in the loss of millions of dollars in failed or delayed implementation. Ensure the project management team understands the need for a substantial chage management effort and has devoted the necessary fiscal and human resources to it.

1.11 Business Requirements Oversight Committee (BROC)

The BROC is established in order to meet, review, approve, and coordinate major projects that affect all enterprise business units and to establish project implementation schedules coordinated with other related enterprise project activities. The SPMO serves as facilitator of these meetings. The meetings are staffed by business leaders designated and empowered from the various segments of the company. The BROC has final review, approval, and disapproval authority for all proposed projects. Any proposed projects generally must meet all of the following criteria:

1. The project must be correlated to a business need that requires such an application's integration or installation effort in order to perform this function.

2. The project must positively impact corporate systems and users. Products or tools used for external customers or for revenue generation are not usually within BROC scope.

3. The project must exceed a preset dollar limit, which will vary by enterprise. In most cases for mid- to large-sized companies, this amount is $50,000. The project must also provide services to a specific, defined business process or function.

4. Internal corporate application systems are also placed under the same level of scrutiny and must submit to the BROC prioritization process for any of the following when costs exceed the preset limits:

   - Application version upgrade (major new release/upgrade)
   - New application to replace existing legacy system
   - Major new functionality in existing system(s)
   - Customization of standard application code

Although the BROC reserves the right to review other system changes, it does not normally review or prioritize bug fixes, patches, or minor enhancements/configuration changes to systems already in production. Generally, normal internal support processes are followed for these types of changes. The primary functions of the BROC are to gather and review new project requests.

All new application project requests that fall within the scope of the aforementioned criteria should be submitted to the BROC for review and approval. The project proposal submitted should follow the basic guidelines of the SEP methodology and, at a minimum, must include the following:

- High-level business requirements
- Proposed scope
- Proposed schedule
- Business unit budget for project
- Justification

The BROC is also expected to review, prioritize, and approve projects. As projects are submitted for approval, they are reviewed for cross-functional integration between business units, along with determination of application architecture for enterprise systems.

All approved projects are to be given a priority for implementation. The BROC is responsible for determining project dependencies and risk. It is also required to review and approve internal IT-initiated projects as stated in Item 4 of the project criteria listed above.

1.12 BROC Roles and Responsibilities

The BROC Sponsor is usually the head of a business division or organization. He or she makes a commitment to name a representative, who is empowered to speak on his or her behalf at all BROC meetings. This designee is empowered to sign documents and approve requests, plans, or other project-related documents. This is necessary to prevent endless meetings where attendees are required to run back and forth to their managers to seek permission to go to the next step. It prevents delay tactics from being used by organizations within the enterprise that are jockeying for project priority. In other words, it ensures that all seats at the table are represented equally and empowered to act in the best interests of the business.

1.12.1 BROC Sponsor Role

The BROC Sponsor is responsible for the following tasks:

- Appointing a BROC representative for his or her business unit
- Ensuring the BROC is supported by the business unit
- Approving projects requiring funding in excess of the signature authority of the BROC members
- Resolving prioritization conflicts that cannot be determined by BROC members

1.12.2 BROC Member Role

The BROC members are responsible for the following tasks:

- Presenting new project requests to the BROC for their business unit
- Prioritizing the projects driven by their business unit

- Preparing and presenting project proposals for BROC review, prioritization, and approval.
- Objectively reviewing all Project Request Forms and establishing project prioritization equally for all business units

All BROC members should have director-level purchasing approval authority. Each BROC member must be fully empowered to represent his or her functional area. This involves gathering business requirements, understanding the business unit needs and priorities, and making needed decisions at the meetings.

1.12.3 SPMO Role in the BROC

The SPMO is responsible for the following tasks:

- Facilitating BROC meetings
- Providing BSM and Project Manager assistance to BROC members preparing project proposals
- Assigning an advisory Project Manager to provide SEP guidance and oversight to business unit Project Managers on all projects with an anticipated IT budget that falls below the corporate-established spending limit
- Assigning a senior Project Manager to plan and manage large cross-functional integrated projects with an anticipated budget at or over the corporate-established spending limit
- Assigning a BSM to project teams to facilitate development and documentation of business requirements, acceptance criteria, and solution recommendations

Before we get into the specifics of each phase, it is important to understand that somewhere around the early 1990s, people began to question the significance of the Software Development Life Cycle (SDLC), and much discussion evolved in private and government sectors regarding the advantages of using SDLC approaches to mitigate cost and reduce risk. This thought revolution led to the implementation of the Information Technology Management Reform Act of 1996 (ITMRA), which is sometimes known as the Cohen Bill[7].

1.13 The COHEN Bill of 1996

Formally known as the Information Technology Management Reform Act of 1996, this law became effective on August 8, 1996. It places strong focus on the life cycle management processes used in IT and on the processes supporting a given technology, rather than simply on the processes and procedures used to acquire IT technologies. Although it applies mostly to federal development and government-contracted efforts, the act emphasizes the management of IT as a "capital investment" and establishes new requirements related to the management of IT resources, including the following:

- Developing and using performance metrics that measure how well the IT resources used or acquired by an agency support their respective programs
- Determining whether the functions supported by the IT resources should be performed by the private sector
- Reviewing planned IT initiatives to ensure that
    - High-risk projects receive closer scrutiny and more points of review and evaluation
    - Out-of-date, ineffective, or inefficient procedures and work processes are not automated
    - They proceed, on a timely basis, toward agreed-upon milestones within the system life cycle, meet user requirements, and deliver intended benefits

The ITMRA also emphasizes requirements previously established in the Paperwork Reduction Act of 1995 (PRA) and implemented by the Office of Management and Budget (OMB) in revisions to OMB A-130. These requirements include the following:

- *IT Planning:* establishing and maintaining a strategic IT management plan that is linked to an agency strategic plan (required by the Government Performance and Results Act [GPRA], Public Law 103-62), this ensures that IT resources support the achievement of mission goals
- *Cost-Benefit Analysis:* preparing an analysis for IT initiatives to demonstrate how the IT resource will meet mission requirements, support ongoing management oversight processes, maximize return on investment, and minimize financial and operational risk

- *Security Plan:* preparing a plan for the IT initiative to meet security requirements and controls for all information collected, processed, transmitted, stored, or disseminated by the proposed IT resources

This law is significant for individuals in the private sector in that much effort in government migrates into the private sector over time. As processes are developed within government, they frequently find their way into mainstream thinking through cross-pollination of ideas, publications, and individuals transferring from government to private-sector positions. Historically, much of the evolution of the software industry has followed government impetus in areas where funded research has taken place. A good example of this is seen in some of the work coming out of the Software Engineering Institute (SEI) at Carnegie-Mellon University. Through government funding, many novel and innovative ideas transition into the private sector.

So far, we have covered the fundamental aspects of an SPMO operation, albeit at a very high level. As we progress through each of the eight phases of the SEP process, we will go into much greater detail about what actually gets done by the Core Team at each stage in the process. At this point, let's go to the next chapter, where we begin our discussion of the SEP Phase 1 roadmap and review the initial responsibilities of the Core Team during the kickoff meeting.

1.14 Chapter 1 Review

1. What are the key roles in an enterprise SPMO?
2. Describe the major service areas of an SPMO.
3. What are several benefits of project performance reporting?
4. List the five key components of project performance reporting.
5. Cite five to seven elements a project performance report should include.
6. Why is financial management important in an SPMO environment?
7. What are several benefits of effective vendor management?
8. List the key components of vendor management.
9. What is the purpose of a CCB?
10. What are the main components of quality management?
11. Define change management as it pertains to an SPMO.

2

SEP Phase I: Initiation

The purpose of this chapter is to have the project Core Team members focus on what is or is not going to be important for this particular project. All of the details of the SEP guidelines for project initiation are discussed in the following paragraphs. This section should be familiar to all members of a Core Team. The kickoff meeting is always a good time to review the SEP guidelines so everyone has an understanding of the environment in which work will be done.

Figure 2.1 *SEP Phase I: Initiation Roadmap.*

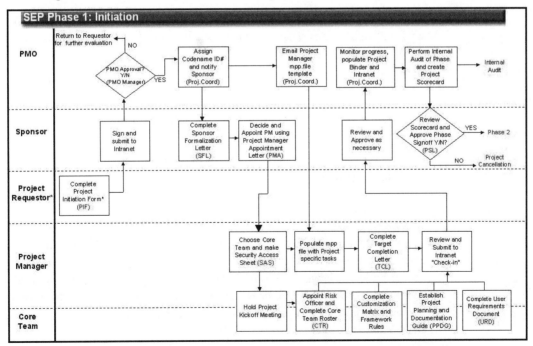

As seen in the SEP Phase I roadmap (Figure 2.1), this phase is actually where the entire project development process starts. As mentioned previously, it all begins with the submission of a Project Initiation Form (PIF, shown in Figure 2.2) to the SPMO. The user completes the PIF, entering basic information regarding the user, sponsor, funding source, a brief description of the project, and so on. All of this information is used by the SPMO to begin the process. Once the form has been submitted, the SPMO enters the data into a project database and makes some preliminary reviews against business needs, objectives, and so on. If the request is determined to meet the needs of the business, the SPMO will assign a project code name and an SPMO Project ID number.

Generally, the task of completing the PIF is handled by a Project Coordinator working within the SPMO. The Project Coordinator will also be tasked to generate a Sponsor Formalization Letter (SFL) and arrange for a meeting with the Project Sponsor. During this meeting, the Sponsor will be asked to sign the initiation document to approve any future work on the project. Key points in the SFL are statements of commitment from the Sponsor, such as the following:

- I will be the representative for the project to peer/upper management.
- I will appoint a Project Manager to manage the project.
- I will be the focal point for decisions beyond the Project Manager's scope of authority.
- I will approve/disapprove the scope and objectives, including schedule and budget.
- I will provide strategic direction, as well as approve any project changes.
- I will apply resources to the project as deemed necessary by the Project Manager.

Once the Sponsor has signed the letter making a commitment to all of these items, this letter is placed in a project binder and kept for future reference by the SPMO. The SPMO will coordinate with the Sponsor to identify a Project Manager. When that person has been identified, a letter generated by the SPMO on behalf of the Sponsor will formally appoint that person as the Project Manager. A sample of the text needed in the appointment letter follows:

Figure 2.2
Project Initiation Form.

PROJECT INITIATION FORM		
ROUTE TO: <Enter your Enterprise name, address, and contact information here>		
E-MAIL: <enter your email address here> (Subject = Project Request)		
Request Date: December 19, 2001	**Project ID # (to be assigned by PMO):**	
Requestor: John Rittinghouse	**Phone:**	
Functional Group:	**Business Unit:**	
Sponsor:	**Phone:**	
Sponsor Priority (1 high-5 low):	**Funding Source(s):**	**Est. Budget:**	**Requested Completion Date:**
Project Description (Brief description of what you are trying to accomplish – Please attach any applicable supporting documentation):		
Business Benefit (Briefly describe the business drivers behind this request - Briefly describe other benefits your business unit will receive from the project):		
Current Environment and Risks of Not Moving Forward (Briefly describe how the function is currently being provided, if at all. What is the impact to the business if the project is not completed?):		

Letter of Appointment

Effective 29 March 2003, <insert Project Manager Name> will serve as Project Manager (PM) of <insert Project Code Name> Project. The PM will continue to report to <insert current supervisor name here> during this assignment.

I will sponsor this project and the PM is authorized by me to coordinate and manage this work. He/she is also authorized to issue directives relating to the project. His/her full responsibilities and authorities are outlined in the attached memo titled "Project Manager's Job Description."

Project team members in your departments will be responsible for managing their project activities so they are completed under PM direction within the agreed-to scope, schedule, and resource commitments. It is their responsibility to inform the PM if they forecast that schedule, cost, or deliverable agreements will not be met. This must be done continually and communicated as early as possible so that adaptive actions can be developed and implemented.

Please join me in welcoming the PM to his/her new assignment. I know you will give your full cooperation during all phases of this project and the support required to successfully complete the effort.

Sincerely,

<Sponsor Name>

As you can see, the Project Manager appointment letter is empowering. The main point of this letter is that this appointee has been given the authority to act on behalf of the Sponsor within the guidelines and scope of the SPMO and the Project Manager job description, which will vary by organization. A copy of this letter is also placed in the project binder kept by the SPMO for anyone to reference should the need arise. Having a letter of appointment minimizes confusion about who is running the project, and it publicly announces the undertaking of a project to the organization.

Another important point to remember is that it is extremely important to communicate a project to the organization from the very start. This communication elicits interest from other interested parties that may be unaware of the initiative and, in many cases, it allows the Project Manager to obtain resources from other areas of the organization.

2.1 Forming a Core Team

It is the Project Manager's responsibility, once he or she has been assigned to a project, to coordinate with the SPMO and choose from among many people in the organization who will be representatives on the Core Team. The Core Team should be made up of key representation from all affected areas of the business. It is a mistake to select all of the team members from a single part of the organization. For example, you should select someone from IT, Finance, Quality, Sales, Marketing, and so on, for a large, cross-functional project. The general rule is that any organization that will be affected in any way with the implementation of this project needs to be involved.

Each team member selected for the project will have his or her name added to the Core Team Roster (CTR). This roster of names will also be added to the project binder. The following is a sample CTR:

Name	Title	Role (s)	Organization	Phone Number	Fax Number	Email Address	Location
John Doe	Manager	Core Team	IT	X71605	X71833	Email address here	Bldg. 2

2.2 Security Access

The project data in any corporate project must be protected. The first step in protecting corporate information is to develop and maintain a Security

2.2 Security Access

Access Sheet (SAS). As you can see in Figure 2.3, this sheet specifies the dates for which access will be granted, to whom it will be granted, and what that person's role is on the Core Team. Access to the centralized project database, the SPMO database, the SPMO intranet, and the project binder can be granted or withheld by specifying Y/N in the columns provided.

2.2.1 Project Kickoff Meeting

Once the Project Manager has identified the Core Team and specified access rights to the project, it is time to have a kickoff meeting. The purpose of this meeting is to get all of the Core Team members in the same room and to develop some framework rules for all future activities. This is also the time when any Core Team members who are unfamiliar with software program management should be trained. During SEP Phase I: Initiation, the Core Team is responsible for several key deliverables. These include developing a Framework Rules Document (FRD), revising the CTR, customizing the project deliverables checklist, developing a Project Planning and Documentation Guide (PPDG), and completing the User Requirements Document (URD). We will discuss each step in turn in following sections.

2.2.2 Risk Officer Appointment

When the Core Team meets initially, one of the first activities that should be completed is the appointment of the Risk Officer. It is this person's responsibility to play devil's advocate. Question everything! Ensure that sound reasoning and logic surround all decision making within the Core Team. This role is often unpopular and often meets with great amounts of criticism. The Project Manager is responsible for ensuring that the Core Team appoints someone strong enough to stand his or her ground on tough issues. The Risk Officer does not have the job of stopping progress, but rather of recording and informing the team about concerns that arise during the scope of the project. In reality, group consensus should guide deci-

Figure 2.3 *Security Access Sheet (SAS).*

Start Date	End Date	Name	Role	Proj DB Access	PMO DB	PMO Intranet	Project Binder

Enterprise — Program Management Office — Intranet

sion making. If the Risk Officer objects strongly to proceedings and feels like the issue is being ignored, he or she is authorized to go directly to the Project Manager or even to the Project Sponsor with concerns. The process of managing risk is covered in greater detail in Chapter 10.

2.2.3 Core Team Roster Revision

During the initial kickoff meeting, the Core Team members will most likely identify folks in the organization who were not selected initially, but should be on the Core Team. This is very often the case in large, cross-functional projects. There is a balance between involving everyone and being crippled by indecision with in a large Core Team. The Project Manager has the final say, of course, in the composition of the team. In general, he or she should include at least one representative and one backup from each functional business unit in the organization. For example, just taking one person and a backup from Sales, Finance, IT, HR, Operations, Call Center, and so on can quickly increase the size of the team dramatically. As you can see, with just these few units, 12 people are already involved. Whatever the final selection results are, the initial CTR must be revised and updated. Any future changes require that an updated roster be turned in to the SPMO as a matter of record. The same rule applies to the SAS as well. One should not be changed without review of the other.

2.2.4 Project Customization Matrix

The Project Customization Matrix is created and reviewed by the Core Team to make inclusion/exclusion decisions about specific areas that are often overlooked at the beginning of an initiative. It is up to the Core Team members to make such decisions based on their knowledge of the company and what is significant or considered relevant to business need. It is folly to assume that everything on the matrix is relevant to every project. Likewise, it is just as much an error to assume that nothing on the matrix applies. Items may be added or deleted from the matrix, but the key issue to remember is that a team of capable, knowledgeable business representatives has taken the time to review and make such decisions about the direction the project will take.

An added benefit of having the Core Team make these decisions before work start is that they gain an awareness of both the scope and magnitude of the initiative, and the Core Team members will begin to appreciate the complexity of the task they have inherited. A sample Customization Matrix is shown as Figure 2.4.

2.3 Project Framework Rules Document

A Project Framework Rules Document (PFRD) defines agreements made by the project team as to how the team will operate. It should clarify the expectations of the project participants and ensure that important decisions are made early in the process and documented. The Core Team should participate in drafting and finalizing the PFRD. The decisions made in this meeting do not need to be unanimous; however, when gridlock occurs, the Project Manager casts the deciding vote. Some of the questions for each major area of consideration that should be answered in the PFRD are listed in the following sections.

2.3.1 Planning Decisions to Be Made and Documented

Development

- Who is responsible for developing the project plan?
- If more than one person is responsible, who should be involved?
- What are the specific roles and responsibilities of each participant?
- What does the plan include?
- Does it meet customers'/management's needs?
- What product or service life cycle will it follow?

Figure 2.4 Customization Matrix.

Area or Task to Review	Excluded or Included	Decided by/Date
Fundamental Problem to be solved		
Tasks/functions the tool will perform		
Benefits/Savings/Cost Justification		
Economic		
Productivity Gains		
Contribution to management goals		
User's current mode of operation, including		
Current software tools in use		
Current hardware tools in use		
Current manual tasks		
Forms in use		
Environment		
Ease of use		
Hardware/Software		
Information/Data that will be included		
Publication Media		
Quality		
Performance Requirements		
Security		
Compatibility/Migration		
International		
Service and Support		
Pricing/Licensing		
Publications		
Standards/ISO Compliance		

- Will meetings be needed to define the project plan?
- When and where should they be held?
- Who will attend?
- Who needs to be informed of decisions made? How will they be kept informed?
- Will a list of terms be distributed for better comprehension?
- Is there a plan to improve management of the project?
- Is there past experience on similar projects? How can we use it?

Planning Output

- What are the outputs from the planning process?
- In what format will they be presented?
- How detailed should they be?
- Who needs to receive them?
- Who is responsible for them?
- How will we know that each output is completed?
- Who will assess the quality of each output?
- Who needs to approve and sign off at the completion of each output?
- How will we know that each output has been signed off on?

Project Tools

- What project management tool(s) are we going to use?
- What equipment is required to support the tool(s)?
- Will all subprojects use the same tool?
- Who will operate the chosen tool?
- Who will enter planning and tracking information?
- Who will need training to operate the tool?
- Who will provide technical support for the users of the tool?
- What additional software do we need in order to support the project management tool?
- If additional software is needed, is it for financially related issues or for action items, follow-up, documentation, and so on?

2.3 Project Framework Rules Document

2.3.2 Tracking Decisions to Be Made and Documented

Tracking

- How will we assess progress?
- How will we get data from the project team to others about the progress of each activity?
- How often will we get this data?
- At what level of detail will we track the project?
- Who will assess the impact of each variance?

Progress Review Meetings

- What types of meetings will we hold (e.g., general, top-level, activity-specific)?
- Where will they be held?
- How often will they be held?
- What is the process for calling an emergency meeting?
- Who will define the strategy and method for managing meetings effectively?
- Who will run these meetings?
- Who will produce an agenda to be distributed before each meeting?
- How will the meetings be run?
- Who should be included in each type of meeting?
- In what format should the meeting information be presented?
- Who will keep minutes of the meetings?
- Who will produce them?
- To whom should they be distributed?

Reporting

- What project reports will be generated?
- Who will generate, analyze, and distribute them?
- To whom should they be distributed?
- What content is appropriate for each audience?
- How detailed should status reports be for each audience?

- What formats (tabular, narrative, graphic) communicate best to each audience?
- What criteria will we use to define an exception for exception reporting (e.g., deviation, spotlight, urgent action)?
- Who initiates these reports?
- Who will receive and analyze exception reports?

2.3.3 Best Practices Decisions to Be Tracked and Documented

The Project File
- What should the project file contain?
- How will all project information be kept?
- Who will create the project file?
- Who will update and maintain it?
- Will changes to the file be allowed? If so, by whom?
- Has a filing system been set up for all documents?
- Where will the file be located (e.g., online, paper copy, library)?
- Who will have access to the file (e.g., to update, change for information only)?
- For how long will the file be kept after project completion?
- Who will keep it after project completion?
- How will it be used?
- Where will it be stored?

Managing Change
- When will the plan baseline be frozen?
- Who will make the decision to freeze the plan?
- What will the decision to freeze it be based on?
- What criteria define change (e.g., design, baseline, or schedule changes)?
- Who will define the change management process we will use?
- Who will maintain the change log?

2.3 Project Framework Rules Document

- Who will have change approval authority?
- What documents will be presented for change approval?
- How will we document approved plan changes?
- How will we assess the impact of changes?
- Who will set adaptive actions?
- How will we track the effectiveness of these adaptive actions?
- How will we decide whether to update the baseline plan?
- How much deviation from the plan are we willing to accept before doing a total reschedule?
- How will we link revision to the change management process?

Continuous Improvement/Project Assessment

- Will a project assessment meeting be held?
- Who will attend?
- What subjects will be addressed?
- How often during the project life will an assessment be done?
- How will we document project assessment so others can learn from our experience?
- What information should be kept to provide a historical basis for continuous improvement?
- What is the release plan process for this project?
- Is the product release part of this project?
- Who owns the release plan?
- When should the plan be fully defined?
- Who has the authority to approve it?

2.3.4 Relationship Decisions to Be Tracked and Documented

Ownership

- What departments will we need to interact with during the life of the project?

- What are the roles and responsibilities of each organization (e.g., reviewer, approver, creator)?

Communication

- How do we communicate among ourselves? With others outside the team?
- How frequently do we need to communicate?
- How will we keep people informed of deliverables, dates, changes, problem areas, and so on?
- Are there specific communication milestones, dates, or intervals?
- What information will or will not be exchanged?

Escalation

- What process will we use to resolve disagreements?
- What is the conflict resolution process?
- What is the standard decision-making process?
- What escalation process will we use for making decisions?
- Who has final decision-making authority?
- Who decides when to escalate a problem?

As you can see, this decision-making process is not a quick and easy task. The team must be encouraged to find solutions to these questions by relying on the resources of the SPMO. Many of the previously listed questions are answered by using processes that are defined within the SEP framework; however, it is very important for project success to have the Core Team take the necessary time to review **all** of these questions and decide among themselves how to handle each and every issue. In doing so, the team will begin to appreciate the sheer magnitude of the task, and its members will better understand the overall scope of the project to which they have been assigned. They will begin to understand that doing the job correctly it will take considerable time and effort. They should also understand that the SPMO is their first, best, and most reliable resource in going forward with a project.

2.3.5 Target Completion Notice (TCN)

The TCN is sent by the Project Manager to the Sponsor. This letter notifies the Sponsor of when the User Requirements Document (URD) is due to be completed by the Core Team and presented to the Sponsor. The selection of a target completion date, of course, should be a mutual exercise between the Project Manager and all of the Core Team members. A sample memorandum as follows displays exactly what the TCN should look like for the sample project with the code name *Marvel*.

```
Memorandum of Record
March 29, 2003
From: <Click here and type Project Manager's name>
To: <Click here and type all recipients by name>
Subject: Marvel User Requirements Document Target Completion
Notice


The User Requirements Document (URD) will be completely finished
and delivered for sponsor sign-off on [Mar 29, 2003]. <Click
here and type Project Manager's name> will serve as Project Man-
ager of the project codenamed Marvel and will be responsible for
ensuring that the URD is completed on time.


Sincerely,

_____

Marvel Project Sponsor
CC: <Click here and type all involved department heads, listed
by name>
```

2.4 The Requirements Gathering Process

The first step is to define the problem. Normally, management perceives a problem with a particular work process that supports or is an integral part of accomplishing the organization's mission. It may be taking too long to process requests, action items may not receive proper attention, or there may be too many mistakes being made in processing. The problem should be documented in a manner that clearly defines it for everyone involved in finding a solution. Sometimes the problem may be that the process has been done a particular way for so long that it is time to see if there is a better way of doing it. In SEP, the Project Objective Statement is used to accomplish this goal.

2.4.1 Evaluate the Work Process

The next issue that needs to be addressed is whether the organization should be performing the function/work process where the problem, actual or potential, has been identified. The first question to ask is whether the function needs to be performed at all. Does it contribute to the accomplishment of the organization's primary mission? The next question is whether the function should be performed by your organization. Could this function be combined with another function to increase the efficiency and/or effectiveness of the organization? Would it be more appropriate for another organization to perform the function? Would it be more appropriate to outsource the function? The answer to all of these questions should be documented thoroughly.

The second issue that needs to be addressed is whether the work process can be performed more efficiently or more effectively. Many systems were developed to support work processes before some of the current technology was available. The work process needs to be reexamined with a view toward utilizing the latest technology to develop a system that will allow management to restructure the work process to increase the efficiency and effectiveness of the process. The work process also needs to be examined to determine if the conditions that existed when the process was established have changed enough to reexamine the utility of the current process. The results of that analysis should be documented. The work process analysis can range from a quick review of a simple work process to a full Business Process Reengineering (BPR) project.

2.4.2 Define the IT Requirements

After a decision has been made to continue to perform the function in the original organization and the work process has been evaluated, the next step is to define the IT requirements for the current or proposed work process. Defining the requirements has been done for many years using haphazard approaches. SEP is intended to formalize this process and help organizations integrate it into their SDLC activities. Requirements must be clearly and fully defined. Some of the factors used to determine information requirements are as follows:

2.5 User Requirements Document (URD)

- Information that is currently being received in the organization
- Information that is needed, but is not currently being received
- Information that needs to be provided to or obtained from other organizations
- Sources that are available to obtain the needed information
- Information relationships and outputs (reports)
- Requirements for validation, integrity, accuracy, completeness, and reliability of the information to be processed or stored
- Quantity, timeliness, location, and format of information required
- Requirements for accessibility, privacy, and security of the stored information
- Functional processing requirements

Detailed guidance will be provided throughout this chapter as we proceed to explain the SEP. The lack of such detailed guidance may be part of the reason why requirements have not been defined well in the past. Next, we elaborate on the User Requirements Document (URD), which is where all of the information cited previously needs to be placed to document actions and decisions made during the course of meetings and discussions between the user community and the project team.

2.5 User Requirements Document (URD)

The URD is intended to document the intent of the system from the user perspective. It should address as many issues as necessary to enable a detailed design process to occur. At a minimum, the sample outline, shown below, should be used as a guide for the Core Team in creating the URD:

```
1      Introduction
       1.1    Purpose of This Document
       1.2    Copyright
       1.3    Intended Audience
       1.4    Inputs to this Document
       1.5    Outputs from This Document
       1.6    Distribution List
2      Executive Overview
```

2.1 Project Objective Statement
2.2 Fundamental Problem to Be Solved
2.3 Product Summary
2.4 Financial Summary
2.5 Project Schedule
  2.5.1 Beta Release Date
  2.5.2 Software Production Release (SPR) Date
3 Background
  3.1 User's Current Mode of Operation
  3.2 Related/Dependent Projects
4 System Requirements
  4.1 General Features
    4.1.1 Key Features
    4.1.2 Environment
    4.1.3 Ease of Use
    4.1.4 Performance
    4.1.5 Quality
    4.1.6 Compatibility/Migration
    4.1.7 Service and Support
    4.1.8 Standards/ISO Compliance
    4.1.9 Product Integration
  4.2 Software
    4.2.1 Minimum Software Configuration
  4.3 Hardware
    4.3.1 Minimum Hardware Configuration
  4.4 Architecture
    4.4.1 Security
    4.4.2 Internationalization
5 Financial
  5.1 Business Case
    5.1.1 Benefits/Savings
    5.1.2 Return on Investment (ROI)
  5.2 Project Budget
6 Productization
  6.1 Publications
  6.2 Packaging

```
            6.3   Additional Components
            6.4   Technical Support
            6.5   Competitive Offerings
            6.6   Pricing/Licensing
```

2.6 Project Planning and Documentation Guide (PPDG)

The PPDG contains a high-level overview of the contents of each of the documents that make up a company's SEP. It is, in essence, the master plan. The information contained in this document can be used as a reference point for the information that can be found in each of the SEP documents. As the work is completed throughout each phase of the SEP, the deliverables are validated against the recommendations found in the PPDG and added to the project binder. A detailed outline of the PPDG is shown below. This outline is intended to help the Core Team stay focused on the various elements of each phase of the SEP. This outline also serves to standardize the software program management approach used in the delivery of systems throughout the enterprise. Note the close correspondence between the SEP roadmaps and the structure of the PPDG. It is not an accident.

```
        0     Introduction
              0.1   Purpose of This Document
              0.2   Copyright
              0.3   Intended Audience
              0.4   Inputs to This Document
              0.5   Outputs from This Document
              0.6   Distribution List
        1     Phase 1: Requirements Evaluation and Proposal Phase
              1.1   User Requirements Document Target Completion Notice
                    (TCN)
              1.2   User Requirements (URD)
              1.3   Project Organization Documents (POD)
                    1.3.1 Sponsor Formalization Letter (SFL)
                    1.3.2 Letter of Appointment (LOA)
                    1.3.3 Core Team Roster (CTR)
              1.4   Framework Rules (FR)
              1.5   Framework Rules Document (FRD)
```

2   Phase 2: Analysis and Detailed Planning Phase
       2.1   Project Definition Document Notebook (PDDN)
             2.1.1 Project Objective Statement (POS)
             2.1.2 Flexibility Matrix (FM)
       2.2   Data Analysis Document (DAD)
             2.2.1 Data Risk Analysis (DRA)
       2.3   Technical Analysis Document (TAD)
             2.3.1 Software Reengineering Assessment (SRA)
             2.3.2 Technology Analysis (TA)
             2.3.3 Technical Risk Analysis (TRA)
             2.3.4 In-House/Contractor Analysis (IHCA)
             2.3.5 Lease/Purchase Analysis (LPA)
       2.4   High-Level Solution (HLS)
       2.5   Bids/Proposals (BP)
       2.6   Funding Documentation (FD)
             2.6.1 Project Budget (PB)
       2.7   Project Schedule (PS)
             2.7.1 Critical Path (CP)
             2.7.2 Task Duration Estimates (TDE)
             2.7.3 Dependency Diagrams (DD)
             2.7.4 Optimization Tradeoff Plan (OTP)
             2.7.5 Resource Histogram (RH)
             2.7.6 WBS Dictionary (WBSD)
       2.8   Risk Analysis
             2.8.1 Risk Management Matrix (RMM)
             2.8.2 Risk Assessment Matrix (RAM)
       2.9   Change Management Process (CMP)
       2.10   Status Reports (SR)
             2.10.1 Variance Reports (VR)
             2.10.2 Adaptive Action Plan (AAP)
       2.11   Review Package (RP)
             2.11.1 Meeting Agenda (MA)
             2.11.2 Project Definition Document (PDD)
       2.12   Documents from Review Meeting (DRM)
             2.12.1 Waiver/Exception to Required Standards (WERS)
             2.12.2 Project Continuation Approval (PCA)

2.6 Project Planning and Documentation Guide (PPDG)

        2.12.3 Project Team Review Minutes (PTRM)
        2.12.4 Approval Letters (AL)
3   Phase 3: Detailed Design Phase
    3.1   Product Requirements and Specifications (PRSpec)
        3.1.1 System Infrastructure Requirements (SIR)
        3.1.2 Software Requirements Specification (SRS)
        3.1.3 Interface Requirements Specification (IRS)
        3.1.4 Performance Requirements Specification (PRS)
    3.2   Data Development Plans
        3.2.1 Content Pipeline Document (CPD)
        3.2.2 Data Distribution Plan (DDP)
    3.3   Marketing Communication Plan (MCP)
        3.3.1 Marketing Rollout Schedule (MRS)
        3.3.2 Marketing Rollout Signoff (MRSO)
    3.4   Contracts/Agreements (CA)
    3.5   Project Transition Letter (PTL)
    3.6   Software Development Plan (SDP)
        3.6.1 Database Conversion Plan (DCP)
        3.6.2 Quality Assurance Plan (QAP)
        3.6.3 Human Factors Plan (HFP)
    3.7   Test Plans
        3.7.1 Stress Test Plan (SsTP)
        3.7.2 Integration Test Plan (ITP)
        3.7.3 Software Test Plan (STP)
        3.7.4 Product Assurance Test (PAT)
        3.7.5 User Acceptance Test (UAT)
        3.7.6 MIS/Outside Certification Plan (MISCP)
4   Phase 4: Construction Phase
    4.1   Product Deliverable
        4.1.1 Source Code (SC)
        4.1.2 Software Executable (SE)
        4.1.3 Database Conversion Scripts (DCS)
    4.2   Product/Project Signoff and Certification Letters
        4.2.1 Product Assurance Signoff Letter (PASL)
        4.2.2 Functional Certification Letter (FCL)
        4.2.3 MIS Certification Letter (MISCL)

                4.2.4 Data Certification Letter (DCL)
         4.3   Product Manuals
                4.3.1 Software User Manual (SUM)
                4.3.2 Software Installation Manual (SIM)
                4.3.3 Training Manual (TM)
                4.3.4 Operations and Maintenance Guide (OMG)
5.   Phase 5: Testing Phase
         5.1 Create Test Log (TLS
         5.2 Execute Test Cases
                5.2.1 Compile Bug Tracking Reports (BTR)
6   Phase 6: Implementation Phase
         6.1   User Training Plan (UTP)
                6.1.1 Training Roster (TR)
                6.1.2 Training Schedule (TS)
                6.1.3 Training Signoff (TSO)
         6.2   HW/SW/NW Equipment Installation Plan (SIP)
         6.3   Rollout Plan (ROP)
                6.3.1 Rollout Schedule (RS)
                6.3.2 Rollout Signoff (RSO)
7   Phase 7: Customer Support Phase
         7.1   Software Transition Plan (SWTP)
                7.1.1 MIS Software Handoff Acceptance Letter (SHAL)
                7.1.2 MIS Hardware Handoff Acceptance Letter (HHAL)
                7.1.3 Hardware Life Cycle Management Plan (HLMP)
                7.1.4 Help Desk Support Questions (HDSQ)
8   Phase 8: Completion Phase
         8.1   Closeout Documents (COD)
         8.2   Archive Project
         8.3   Closeout Ritual

As you can see from the outline, the PPDG constitutes a fairly comprehensive approach to project management in an organization. The Intranet software available with this book has a complete set of sample documents to illustrate each deliverable shown. It is of critical importance to understand the relationship between the SEP, the roadmaps that illustrate the various tracks, and deliverables each entity in the process is responsible for delivering, and the living document—the Bible of the project—the PPDG. This relationship cannot be taken for granted. It is precisely this relationship that defines a software program management function. The SPMO is tasked with responsibility to ensure a methodical execution of these processes that enable a corporation with effective Software Program Management capabilities.

When the Core Team has finished the URD, it is submitted to the SPMO and checked in for final review. It will be reviewed by the Project Sponsor, and, if it is approved, it will be placed in the project binder. The SPMO will then perform an internal audit of the Phase I process and create a project scorecard rating how well the team has done. The scorecard will then be reviewed by the Project Sponsor, and this is when the Phase I signoff should occur.

We have covered all significant aspects of Phase I of the SEP, Project Initiation, in this chapter. In Chapter 3, we delve deeper into the SEP, going into the SEP Planning Phase, where we discuss each of the many deliverables required to take a project from the planning to the design stage. The planning stage is crucial because mistakes made here can have huge impacts in later phases.

```
Ponder this: "What is the biggest secret to successful project
management? Don't ever charter a big project!" According to Bob
Lewis, any project lasting more than nine months or requiring
more than 12 people on the Core Team is doomed from the start. He
states the following reasons:

1.    Big projects cannot be estimated.
2.    Big projects mean no urgency.
3.    Big projects reduce personal accountability.
4.    Big projects mean big overhead.
5.    Big projects mean big risk.
```

The next time you start a project initiation phase, take a moment to review these thoughts and contemplate the effect of your actions. For more detail on these reasons, the reader is encouraged to consult Lewis's book[8], *IS Survival Guide*.

2.7 Chapter 2 Review

1. What happens when a PIF is submitted to the SPMO?
2. What are the key points in a Sponsor Formalization Letter (SFL)?
3. Who is responsible for establishing a project Core Team?
4. Describe the role of a Risk Officer.
5. Who completes the Project Customization Matrix?
6. What is the purpose of a URD?
7. What is the PPDG? What is it used for?

3

SEP Phase II: Analysis and Detailed Planning Phase

Let's begin by taking a look at the SEP Phase II roadmap (Figure 3.1). For the three tracks of SPMO, Sponsor, and Project Manager, the tasks accomplished between phases 2 and 7 are redundant. The SPMO basically monitors progress, continues to ensure that all required steps are completed, and assembles documents into the project binder with deliverables as they become finished products. The SPMO will also perform internal audits or work with the Internal Audit Team of the organization, if it exists, and

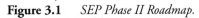

Figure 3.1 *SEP Phase II Roadmap.*

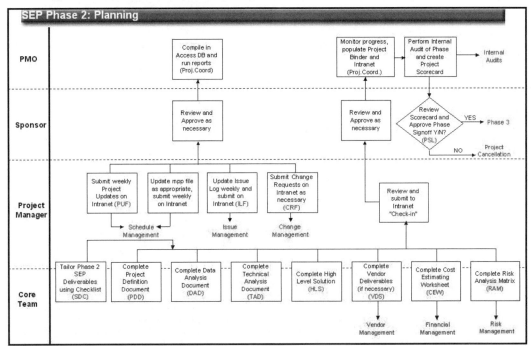

develop project scorecards at the end of each phase. The Sponsor will review progress using the scorecards and provide approvals or guidance as needed.

The Project Manager is much more involved with the Core Team and plays the role of administrator, providing updated project files to interested parties, creating budget and progress reports, monitoring the issue status log, and so on. We will concentrate on the work done by the Core Team, because this is where all the action is from this point forward. This phase of project development will be focused on providing the framework for the entire project life cycle. Each step of this phase addresses important planning and documentation considerations that will affect all future project work and ultimately play a leading role in dictating the project's critical path.

Did you know that the best-run projects use some common approaches to managing the effort? These common approaches include the following:

- Planning and executing project tasks in staged deliveries
- Having the progress of the project tracked by both senior management and the user community
- Having open reviews of the project status (good and bad news) conducted on a recurring basis

In order to complete this phase, we must complete the following checklist:

	Project Objective Statement Completed
	Project Definition Document Completed
	Flexibility Matrix Completed
	Project Definition Document Notebook Completed
	Data Analysis Document Completed
	Technical Analysis Document Completed
	High-Level Solutions Document Completed
	Bids/Proposals Document Completed
	Project Schedule Completed
	Risk Analysis Completed
	Change Management Process Standard Completed

	Status Reports Completed
	Review Package Completed
	Review Meeting Documents Completed
	Project Budget Worksheet Completed
	Capital Equipment Request Form(s) Completed
	Phase II Completion Approval Signoff Completed

3.0.1 Project Objective Statement (POS)

The POS states what work you are going to do (the scope), by when (the schedule), with how many or how much (the resources or cost). It provides clarity and focus for the project team. It should be fewer than 50 words in length and stated in clear, concise, unambiguous terms. The Core Team should draft this statement.

3.0.2 Project Definition Document (PDD)

The PDD is a high-level summary of the project. It should document information in the following order: description, purpose, strategic alignment, completion criteria, project start, customers, dependencies, and hardware/software requirements. For **each** of these topic areas, you need to address, at a minimum, the items listed:

- *Description and purpose:* This is the 40,000-foot view of the project and why it is needed.
- *Strategic alignment:* How does it align with business goals?
- *Quick wins and long-term strategy:* Why is this good?
- *Target customer(s):* Who are the users of this project deliverable?
- *Dependencies:* What are committed dates and commitments to/from other projects?
- *Staffing:* What is required, both in terms of skills and balance of experience?
- *Risk of doing versus not doing the project:* Provide an impact assessment.
- *ROI analysis:* What is the return on investment? Does it make fiscal sense to do this?

- *Assumptions made:* Are you making calculated assumptions or taking unneeded risks?
- *Implementation constraints:* What limiting factors would hinder success?
- *Contingency plan:* What happens if the plan goes all wrong?

3.0.3 Flexibility Matrix (FM)

This is a matrix to help the team decide and prioritize the tradeoff between scope, schedule, and resources (Figure 3.2).

Figure 3.2 *Flexibility Matrix.*

	Least Flexible	Moderately Flexible	Most Flexible
Schedule			
Scope			
Resources			

For each of the three items in the left-most column—schedule, scope, and resources—determine which level of flexibility is most applicable. Is the schedule fixed and are you tasked to drive the project to a date? If so, mark an X in the Least Flexible column for schedule. Is the project scope subject to change or is it set in stone? If scope makes no difference, then mark the appropriate column, indicating most flexible. Repeat this for resources and your flexibility matrix will quickly reveal your program priorities.

3.0.4 Project Definition Document Notebook (PDDN)

The PDDN is a binder containing the PDD, the POS, and the Flexibility Matrix. This notebook should also contain a formal presentation that can be used as an overview of the project for any visitors or other interested parties. The standard project binder should also contain PowerPoint templates designed for standardization of formal project presentations.

3.0.5 Data Analysis Document (DAD)

The DAD is a detailed study that is performed to determine if the data requirements presented in the URD can actually be implemented with the data currently available from sources obtained in-house, from commercial off-the-shelf (COTS) sources, or through an impending, near-term deliverable. Let's examine each of these sources in turn.

3.0.6 In-House Analysis

Performing the in-house analysis requires that the Core Team ask several questions regarding the availability and completeness of information. The team must determine whether the information available will meet all of the user requirements or not. If not, the team needs to determine how many of the total requirements are met by the information available. Furthermore, it must ascertain where the additional information required will be obtained. When examining the data, the team must ask if the data is appropriate for release in its present form and format or determine if it will have to be reworded or reformatted. What is the sensitivity of the data? Are there special confidentiality or security concerns that must be addressed?

3.0.7 Commercial Off-the-Shelf (COTS) Sources

An examination of commercially available data sources is required. This includes knowledge brokers and data aggregators; however, the same process of examination for in-house evaluation needs to be performed for each candidate reviewed. The Core Team must ask several questions regarding the availability and completeness of COTS information. The team must determine whether the COTS information will meet all user requirements. If it will not, the team needs to determine how many of the total requirements are met by the COTS information. It must ask where any additional information required will be obtained and determine the availability of such information.

3.0.8 Near-Term Deliverables (NTD)

In many organizations, large initiatives depend on completion of sub-projects or other initiatives within the organization. These types of deliverables are called near-term deliverables (NTD). Once again, the same process of examination for in-house evaluation needs to be performed for each deliverable used in a project. The Core Team will need to ask several questions regarding the availability and completeness of NTD information. The team must determine whether pending NTD information will meet all of the user requirements. If it will not, the team needs to determine how many of the total requirements are met by NTD information. Once again, it must also ask where any additional information required will be obtained and determine the internal availability of such information.

3.0.9 Data Risk Analysis (DRA)

The DRA is a subjective assessment regarding the likelihood of not achieving project data objectives because of the availability of information, the delivery of information, any data-formatting issues, sustainability, feasibility, and security of data. If the information is difficult to obtain or it is questionable as to whether the information will be made available for the project, the risk to the project increases significantly. If the data is formatted so that much additional work will be needed to make the information usable, there is a significant risk involved. There may not be a choice in the matter, but the DRA will bring these matters to light *before* the issue arises and save the Core Team much time and effort in defending decisions after the fact.

Sustainability refers to the duration of the validity of the data. The team must ask itself how long this data will be usable to the project. If a project is built around data that is transient in nature, that increases the risk of success and should be known before commencement of work. Finally, does the data proposed for use in a project constitute a security risk to the business? If so, then the Core Team must question the wisdom of using such data and the risks of proceeding. There may be a need to proceed with such sensitive data, and the team incurs a responsibility to provide mechanisms for data protection during the course of the project. The answers to these questions provide varying degrees of risk to the success of the project. The Core Team needs to understand all such implications before proceeding with a project.

3.0.10 Technical Analysis Document (TAD)

There are five key components of a basic TAD. These components are as follows:

1. Software Reengineering Assessment
2. Technology Analysis
3. Technical Risk Assessment
4. In-House Contractor Analysis
5. Lease-Purchase Analysis

The ultimate purpose of a TAD is to save time and money in the execution of a project. Exploring each of the following components will help the

Core Team make decisions that enhance the probability of the project being executed in a manner that is most cost-effective and timely. Each of the five key components is explained in detail in the following paragraphs.

Software Reengineering Assessment (SRA)

The purpose of an SRA is to assist the Core Team in making a sound, informed business decision that will determine whether it is practical to reengineer legacy software. It is often much less expensive to make changes to existing legacy packages than to rebuild or replace them from scratch. A formalized analysis of the issue is often the best method of obtaining a clear picture of what the proper course of action for the project should be. The Core Team should first ask if the current software can be modified to meet the new requirements. To answer this question, the team should conduct a cost-benefit analysis. In performing the cost phase of this analysis, it is important to understand what cost analysis entails.

Cost Analysis is defined as any cost associated with the operation of the existing system on an annual basis and includes the following:

- Computer costs
- License and maintenance fees
- Dedicated computer equipment costs
- Data storage costs
- Data communication and distribution costs
- Maintenance costs (excluding maintenance fees)
- Main computer utilization costs
- Personnel costs
- Computer systems operations personnel
- Training costs
- Supply costs
- Miscellaneous costs
- Rental of floor space
- Office furniture costs

Next, you should estimate costs associated with developing the proposed solution using the current system. It is a good idea to also describe the techniques that were used to derive the cost estimates.

When evaluating benefits for this analysis, for each tangible benefit, the team should quantify the dollar value of the expected reductions in operating costs or increased revenues. Identify the projected payback period associated with the changes. For each intangible benefit, describe the added values associated with the system's implementation and provide the appropriate justifications, where necessary. In performing the benefit phase of this analysis, the following items should be considered:

Tangible Benefits

- New sources of revenues
- Increased profits
- Cost avoidance (staff)
- Reduction in maintenance costs

Intangible Benefits

- Improved service
- More accurate and timely information
- Improved control
- Greater flexibility
- Competitive edge
- Improved employee morale

Once all of the cost and benefit factors have been identified and quantified, the Core Team should prepare a formal recommendation and provide written justification for the decision. This becomes a part of the overall TAD. This information should be stored in the project binder once reviewed and approved by the Core Team.

Technology Analysis (TA)

The TA is a study to determine if a technology requirement can be implemented with the current technology available (hardware and software) in house, COTS, or through an NTD from another project currently being executed within the organization. The TA should provide a detailed analysis of what is available and state whether such technology is feasible within the current operational or organizational environment (e.g., hardware/software requirements, operating system requirements, File, Print, Database or Applications Server-specific requirements, networking or Internet requirements, client requirements, browser-specific requirements). The TA should contain a matrix of technology and associated functions with weighted requirements that match directly to specific user acceptance requirements as part of the recommended solution.

Technical Risk Analysis (TRA)

The TRA is a much more subjective assessment. It is one of the Risk Officer's responsibilities to ensure that this TRA is completed. The TRA reviews the known or expected risks regarding the likelihood of not achieving the project's technical objectives due to any of the following factors:

- Technology assessment/availability
- Key issues with technology beyond team control
- Programmatic issues that may arise
- Support issues that would be outside the control of the Core Team
- Feasibility of implementation
- Security issues
- Alternative approaches
- Strategy integration

3.0.11 In-House/Contractor Analysis (IHCA)

This study is used to determine the feasibility of developing software in-house. It evaluates the benefits of doing internal work as opposed to contracting the requirements for software development to outside sources. It should take into account each of the five following factors:

1. In-house availability of resources
2. Knowledge of implementation team
3. In-house costs compared to outsourced costs
4. Contractor availability, knowledge, and prior track record
5. Recommendations from contractor references

Lease/Purchase Analysis (LPA)

The LPA is a study to determine the feasibility of leasing versus purchasing equipment and/or software. To accomplish this study, it is quite common to invite vendors to make presentations to your team, to visit other sites or organizations that are already using the package (vendor references), or to install packages in your environment for a trial period (referred to as a pilot program). When performing the LPA, it is recommended that the following items be included:

- Costs of systems modifications required to satisfy the key user requirements
- Costs of additional hardware configurations to support the new package
- Costs of additional software configurations to support the new package
- Costs of additional networking configurations to support the new package
- Training costs for hardware systems administration
- Training costs for the user community
- Training costs for support personnel
- Data conversion costs
- Maintenance costs
- Documentation costs
- Operating costs
- User support costs

3.0.12 High-Level Solution (HLS)

The HLS is an initial response from the Project Manager to the problems and needs presented in the URD. This document is not intended to describe the end solution or final product in great detail. It is meant only to provide a 40,000-foot view (hence the name high-level solution). The information contained within the HLS provides fundamental direction to all groups that will be part of creating the product solution. This document is typically about one-tenth the size of the Product Specifications Document—the fully detailed solutions document. The HLS should present, at a minimum, the following items for review:

- Overview of the proposed solution
- Is/is not lists (detail what is and is not part of the solution)
- Deviations from requirements (exceptions from requirements are noted here)
- Audience (user, support, systems, administration, etc.)
- Functions (high-level and subfunctions needed to meet basic requirements)
- Ease of use (in terms of accessibility, graphical user interface [GUI] standards, etc.)
- Architecture (technical, data, hardware, and software)
- Hardware supported/required
- Software supported/required
- Information and data to be included/excluded
- Performance requirements (hardware, software, network, etc.)
- Publications (used, generated, or needed)
- Standards/ISO compliance
- Reliability
- Serviceability
- Compatibility/migration
- Internationalization/localization requirements (will other language deliverables be needed?)
- Pricing/license agreements
- Packaging requirements and plans
- Security issues
- Future enhancements

As you can see from this list, addressing each of these issues from a high-level perspective at the beginning of a project will save much grief later in the project. Such issues are often overlooked and kludges are made after the fact to remedy an omission. This creates additional maintenance and development costs and could even cause budget overruns. Taking the time to review and decide on each of these items beforehand is crucial to project success.

3.0.13 Project Deliverables

Many deliverables are necessary to have ready at the final stages of SEP Phase II. Some of these deliverables are intended to go outside the organization to vendors, and some are exclusively for in-house consumption. In general terms, the deliverables intended for in-house use are project management oriented, whereas those used for vendor management most often pertain to billing, contracting, and dollar-related activities. We review some of the more significant deliverables in the following paragraphs.

3.0.14 Bids/Proposals (BP)

If the In-House/Contractor Analysis determines that the best solution for your project is to use outside resources to complete the project, a bid or a proposal should be submitted by each vendor for consideration. This bid should be in response to a Request for Proposal (RFP) that the Core Team sends out to each vendor. The structure of the RFP is covered in the next section. The RFP should be sent to several potential vendors, which are narrowed down by the Core Team from a larger list of many potential candidates. The list may be obtained by reviewing directories or catalogues specializing in software packages or from a review of various computer and trade magazines. Hardware vendors often supply lists of software vendors whose products run on their processors. Finally, the Core Team may consult with professional user groups that can provide software directories for their members (such as IEEE or ACM).

3.0.15 Develop a Request for Proposal (RFP)

This document is intended to be used by the SPMO when the Core Team has found it necessary to solicit outside parties to provide assistance in project execution. It is the official request from your organization to one or more vendors, asking them to submit to your SPMO a written proposal describing how the vendor would satisfy each of the stated requirements in the URD. The RFP would further require the vendor to state how it intends to accomplish all of the objectives stated in the HLS. At a minimum, the RFP sent out to the vendor by the SPMO should contain the following items:

   I. Cover letter
   II. Title page

III. Table of contents
IV. Structure of the RFP
V. Situation of the system
VI. System requirements description
VII. Functional and data requirements
VIII. Operational requirements
IX. Miscellaneous requirements
X. RFP reply format and evaluation criteria
XI. Appendix of additional info that might enhance the comprehension of the request for proposal (flow diagrams, entity relationship diagrams, etc.)

Once the vendors have submitted their responses, the Core Team should develop a standard list of selection criteria that will be used to evaluate the vendor proposals. The selection criteria should be weighted (i.e., is it essential, important, or just nice to have?). A numeric value should be assigned to each weighting factor.

Next, the Core Team must rate and rank the selection criteria to determine if it satisfies the system requirements perfectly, if it satisfies the system requirements except for a few minor items, if it satisfies the system requirements in general (although some important characteristics might be missing), or if it does not satisfy several important aspects of the requirements or does not satisfy the requirements at all.

During the final evaluation process, all of the criteria are numerically rated and then ranked from high score to low score according to how well the systems requirements are met. A final numeric score is produced for each criteria from each vendor. The vendor that attains the highest average aggregate score is usually chosen to be the contractor for the project. Sometimes additional factors, such as vendor cost, are added as criteria with numeric ranking assigned based on high, average, or low rankings. The key is to consistently and fairly evaluate each vendor based on the same criteria and make an informed, balanced decision based on objective data.

3.0.16 Funding Documentation (FD)

The funding documentation should contain all of the documents needed in your organization to request capital and/or expense dollars for the project.

The funding documents generally go to the Project Sponsor first. If the dollars requested exceed the spending level the Sponsor is allowed to authorize, the funding documentation may need to be prepared to go up the management chain for final approval. The funding package should contain an explanation of the costs to sustain current operations, any savings to be realized, and a calculation of the return on investment (ROI) or economic value added (EVA). Usually, your organization's finance team will provide instructions on how to calculate ROI or EVA. If there is no available information in your organization, there are many excellent texts on ROI/EVA models at your local bookstore.

The funding package should include any project development costs for hardware, software, data formatting and/or conversion, and programming. Project implementation costs such as training, publications, rollout costs, costs of sustaining the product after delivery, maintenance fees, and support costs are included in the funding documents. Finally, the funding documents should disclose funds that have already been budgeted for this project. An appendix should contain any copies of outstanding and/or approved Capital Expense Requests (CERs), Purchase Orders (POs), and vendor invoices (paid and unpaid) that have been received to date. The funding document should provide a complete picture of the costs (now and in the future) for the project. A Cost Estimate Worksheet (CEW) is often the best tool to gather and present this information. A sample CEW is shown as Figure 3.3 on the following page.

3.0.17 Project Budget (PB)

The Project Budget is simply a financial tracking document used to account for all expenses associated with the project. This will be maintained by the Project Manager and kept in the project database. A spreadsheet (see Figure 3.4) which is aslo known as The Project Budget Template is placed in the standard project binder should be used to record both internal time sheets for employees as well as other expenses required by the project. Here are some examples of such expenses:

- Original CAR/expense amounts
- Committed/allocated funds
- Invoiced amounts

Figure 3.3 *Cost Estimate Worksheet.*

	A	B	D
	Enterprise Program Management Office		**Intranet**
2	Insert Project Name/ ID# / COST ESTIMATING WORKSHEET		
3	Project Name/Date/Revisions		
5	Enterprise IT PMO Cost Worksheet	Resource Hours	Extended Cost
6	Internal/Hourly Costs:		
7	Initiation Phase	0	$0.00
14	Planning Phase	0	$0.00
21	Design Phase	0	$0.00
26	Construction Phase	0	$0.00
31	Testing Phase	0	$0.00
35	Implementation Phase	0	$0.00
41	User Support Phase	0	$0.00
46	Completion Phase	0	$0.00
50	Total Hours	0	$0.00
51	External Costs:		
52	Hardware Costs/External	$0.00	$0.00
53	Software Costs/External	$0.00	$0.00
54	Vendor Costs/External	$0.00	$0.00
55	Administration Costs	$0.00	$0.00
56	Miscellaneous Costs	$0.00	$0.00
57	Total Costs (Hours and External)	$0.00	$0.00

Figure 3.4 *Project Budget Template.*

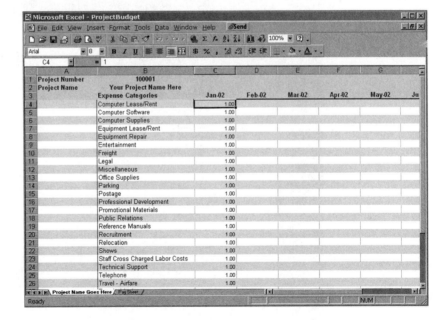

3.1 Project Schedule (PS)

A display of project time allocation, the Project Schedule is usually represented by a Gantt chart. It should include task name, duration of task, start date, finish date, dependencies of tasks, predecessor tasks, and, while the project is underway, it is recommended that the software used show the percentages complete for each task. The Project Schedule must also adhere to the organizational Standard Definitions for Development Activities that are included in the project binder maintained by the SPMO. Figure 3.5 is a sample Gantt chart.

3.2 Critical Path (CP)

The critical path is a calculated result of interdependent activities of a project that determines the shortest total length of the project. The critical path of a project may change from time to time as activities are completed ahead of or behind schedule. This is most frequently conveyed as a filtered list of critical path elements taken from the project Gantt chart.

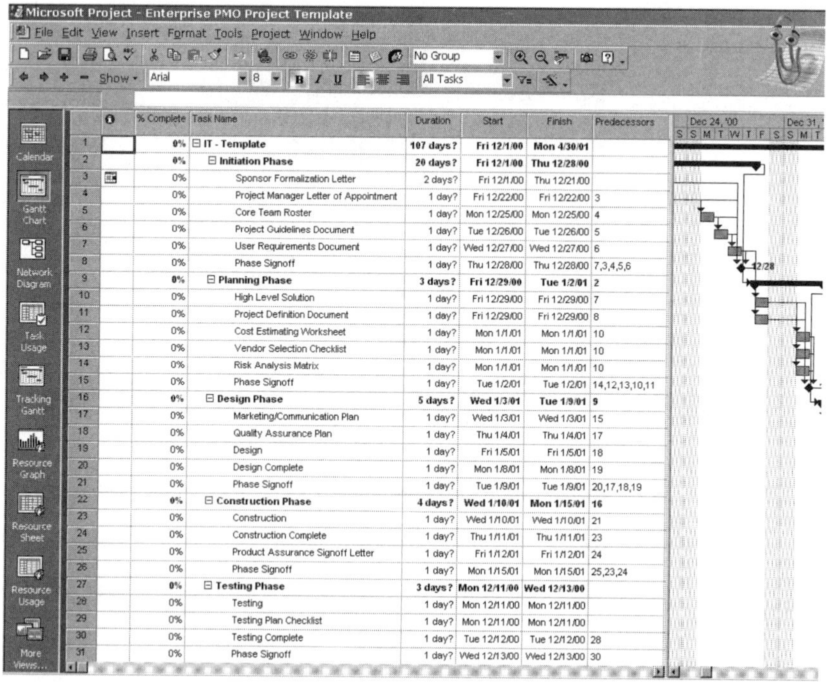

	% Complete	Task Name	Duration	Start	Finish	Predecessors
1	0%	⊟ IT - Template	107 days?	Fri 12/1/00	Mon 4/30/01	
2	0%	⊟ Initiation Phase	20 days?	Fri 12/1/00	Thu 12/28/00	
3	0%	Sponsor Formalization Letter	2 days?	Fri 12/1/00	Thu 12/21/00	
4	0%	Project Manager Letter of Appointment	1 day?	Fri 12/22/00	Fri 12/22/00	3
5	0%	Core Team Roster	1 day?	Mon 12/25/00	Mon 12/25/00	4
6	0%	Project Guidelines Document	1 day?	Tue 12/26/00	Tue 12/26/00	5
7	0%	User Requirements Document	1 day?	Wed 12/27/00	Wed 12/27/00	6
8	0%	Phase Signoff	1 day?	Thu 12/28/00	Thu 12/28/00	7,3,4,5,6
9	0%	⊟ Planning Phase	3 days?	Fri 12/29/00	Tue 1/2/01	2
10	0%	High Level Solution	1 day?	Fri 12/29/00	Fri 12/29/00	7
11	0%	Project Definition Document	1 day?	Fri 12/29/00	Fri 12/29/00	8
12	0%	Cost Estimating Worksheet	1 day?	Mon 1/1/01	Mon 1/1/01	10
13	0%	Vendor Selection Checklist	1 day?	Mon 1/1/01	Mon 1/1/01	10
14	0%	Risk Analysis Matrix	1 day?	Mon 1/1/01	Mon 1/1/01	10
15	0%	Phase Signoff	1 day?	Tue 1/2/01	Tue 1/2/01	14,12,13,10,11
16	0%	⊟ Design Phase	5 days?	Wed 1/3/01	Tue 1/9/01	9
17	0%	Marketing/Communication Plan	1 day?	Wed 1/3/01	Wed 1/3/01	15
18	0%	Quality Assurance Plan	1 day?	Thu 1/4/01	Thu 1/4/01	17
19	0%	Design	1 day?	Fri 1/5/01	Fri 1/5/01	18
20	0%	Design Complete	1 day?	Mon 1/8/01	Mon 1/8/01	19
21	0%	Phase Signoff	1 day?	Tue 1/9/01	Tue 1/9/01	20,17,18,19
22	0%	⊟ Construction Phase	4 days?	Wed 1/10/01	Mon 1/15/01	16
23	0%	Construction	1 day?	Wed 1/10/01	Wed 1/10/01	21
24	0%	Construction Complete	1 day?	Thu 1/11/01	Thu 1/11/01	23
25	0%	Product Assurance Signoff Letter	1 day?	Fri 1/12/01	Fri 1/12/01	24
26	0%	Phase Signoff	1 day?	Mon 1/15/01	Mon 1/15/01	25,23,24
27	0%	⊟ Testing Phase	3 days?	Mon 12/11/00	Wed 12/13/00	
28	0%	Testing	1 day?	Mon 12/11/00	Mon 12/11/00	
29	0%	Testing Plan Checklist	1 day?	Mon 12/11/00	Mon 12/11/00	
30	0%	Testing Complete	1 day?	Tue 12/12/00	Tue 12/12/00	28
31	0%	Phase Signoff	1 day?	Wed 12/13/00	Wed 12/13/00	30

Figure 3.5 *Project Gantt Template.*

3.2.1 Task Duration Estimates (TDE)

This is an estimate of the amount of time each task will take to be completed. The task duration estimate should consider both effort and required wait time (i.e., two hours to code a report and four hours to run it equals six hours duration). While somewhat subjective in nature, making a best guess at the duration of each task is both a good exercise in learning to determine overall project scope and, more importantly, it requires that some thought go into what is actually put into the plan. An important thing to remember is that these estimates can be revised as new or better information is obtained. They are to be used as a tool in making a best guess at the time for task completion.

3.2.2 Dependency Diagrams (DD)

These are simply diagrams illustrating which tasks are dependent on the start or completion of other tasks. The diagram focuses exclusively on logical dependencies, not resource dependencies. These project dependency diagrams are most often seen as PERT charts of the project. They are used to display a visual representation of project dependencies.

3.2.3 Optimization Tradeoff Plan (OTP)

The OTP outlines a process for identifying issues, solutions to issues, and tradeoffs for each solution. The OTP assists in selecting the best solutions based on real project information and incorporating it into your project plan and project schedule. The final deliverable implementing the OTP is an optimized project plan and schedule.

3.2.4 Resource Histogram (RH)

The resource histogram is a display of the number of resources required as a function of time on a graph. Individual, summary, incremental, and cumulative resource curve levels can be shown. Such histograms are autogenerated in many project management software packages and are useful in performing resource allocations and load balancing against multiple projects.

3.2.5 Work Breakdown Structure Dictionary (WBSD)

The WBSD is a task-oriented breakdown of activities that organize, define, and graphically display the total work to be accomplished in order to achieve the final objectives of a project. The WBSD lists every project task, its WBS code, the task owner, and its completion criteria. The astute Project Manager will realize that using the WBSD is a quick means of tracking task assignments and following up on task completions.

3.2.6 Risk Analysis (RA)

The Risk Officer appointed by the Project Manager at the beginning of the project is responsible for delivery of both the Risk Management Matrix and the Risk Analysis Matrix as part of the overall risk assessment provided at this phase of the project. All of the risk deliverables should be reviewed by the Project Manager and the Core Team in a meeting specific to risk analysis where the Risk Officer can formally present his or her findings. Any disagreement over the findings should be resolved at this time by the Project Manager. Once the team agrees on the level of risk, the formal, revised findings are presented to the Project Sponsor.

The Risk Management Matrix (RMM) identifies key risks and their probability of occurrence. This plan also identifies preventive actions and contingencies. The Risk Analysis Matrix (RAM) is a formal review, examination, and recommendation of all known project risks based on the findings of the Risk Officer. A sample RAM is shown as Figure 3.6 below.

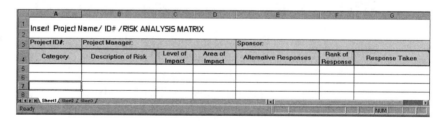

Figure 3.6
Risk Analysis Matrix.

Change management is used by the organization to manage product change requests. The process should identify the problem affecting a change, describe the change needed to correct the problem, the impact making the change will have, the consequences of making the change, and the reasons for approval/rejection of the change. Minimal change management forms should contain the following elements:

- Project name (code name)
- Change control number (assigned by the SPMO)
- Name of person requesting change (same person who approves the change)

- Date opened (date assigned by the SPMO, not the date reported)
- Title of the change (name it something all Core Team attendees will relate to)
- Requested close date (requestor specifies a proposed fix date)
- Description of the change (be as specific as possible here)
- Justification for the change (why the change is needed)
- Person assigned to make the change (tracked by a member of the Core Team)
- Impact assessment (SPMO generated)

3.2.7 Status Reports (SR)

Status reports are produced in the design, development, and implementation phases of the SEP project life cycle (regarding the current status of project tasks) before conducting the review meeting. The report should be written specifically for the intended audience (e.g., management, project team, customer) and should include, at a minimum, the two following sections:

Project Management Tasks

- Accomplishments
- Budget slippages
- Concerns/issues
- Gains
- Planned activities
- Scope impact/changes
- Timeline slippages
- Variances

Data Development Tasks

- Accessibility
- Availability
- Documentation
- Human factors information
- Program coding status

- Technical tasks
- Training status
- User acceptance

3.2.8 Variance Reports (VR)

Variance reports indicate areas where the project has varied from the approved baselines. These reports should be generated from the corporate project management software tool. The reports should be compiled upon request of the Core Team or Project Sponsor, or at minimum, at the end of each of the eight SEP project phases. Variances are recorded for schedule and project scope changes and for resource and cost changes. The reports should include reasons for variances.

3.2.9 Adaptive Action Plan (AAP)

This is a plan for systematically responding to each variance or change in the project in order to remain focused on achieving all of the project objectives. AAPs should include all issues with a list of solutions for each issue. The plan should discuss benefits and costs or tradeoffs for each solution proposed.

3.2.10 Review Package (RP)

This package is prepared by the Project Manager and the SPMO for review by the Project Sponsor. The package should contain all documents produced in a particular phase of the SEP project life cycle. This includes all project and vendor deliverables as explained previously. This package is sent out usually three to five days before the review meeting and includes all documents produced from the current phase. The review meeting should be held at least once during a phase, before the closeout of the phase, and should conscientiously review the progress made during the phase.

Care should be taken during the review meeting to identify potential risks in the development process and to ensure that the Project Sponsor is comfortable with these risks and the steps taken to mitigate them. The last person you want to be surprised by an outcome of a project is the Sponsor. This person is your advocate and must be kept informed of *everything*. This relationship builds trust between the Sponsor and the SPMO and the Project Manager. Make sure your folks understand the value of that relationship.

3.2.11 Meeting Agenda (MA)

The meeting agenda is a list of meeting participants and items to be addressed during the meeting. The agenda should be followed closely during the meeting, and one person from the Core Team should be designated to ensure that the meeting actually follows the agenda. That person should be empowered to interrupt the meeting if the topic strays from the agenda and remind the team of the purpose of the *current* meeting.

3.2.12 Documents from Review Meeting (DRM)

Notes or minutes taken from the review meeting, along with any instructions from the Project Sponsor, approvals or denial letters, and so on are all review meeting documents. They should be incorporated into the project binder and distributed to interested parties following the conclusion of the meeting.

3.2.13 Waiver/Exception to Required Standards (WERS)

This is a written authorization to accept a configuration item or other designated items that are found to depart from specified requirements but are considered suitable for use "as is" or after rework by an approved or designated method. An authorization to depart from the SEP should document the following:

- Form to record waiver/exception
- Explanation of what the deviation from the standard is
- Explanation of why is it needed
- Appropriate signoff (usually by the Sponsor)

3.2.14 Project Team Review Minutes (PTRM)

Minutes should be taken at each review meeting that is conducted by the SPMO. This is particularly necessary during the review/approval cycle of each phase of the SEP project life cycle. The minutes should contain at least the following key information:

- Team name

- Purpose of meeting
- Topics discussed
- Decisions/agreements made
- Action items assigned

3.2.15 Approval Letters (AL)

This document is simply a letter sometimes also called a Project Continuation Approval (PCA) Letter verifying that the Sponsor or his or her designee has reviewed and approved all project documentation, project funding, and/or any particular course of action needed during the review/approval cycle of each phase of the SEP project life cycle. The approval letter is placed in the project binder kept by the SPMO.

The PCA is a letter or document signed by the Sponsor or his or her designee indicating that the project has been approved for continuation into the next stage. A sample PCA is shown as follows:

Phase Completion Approval Signoff

```
Every phase of Project <enter project code name> requires
approval before it can continue to the next phase of develop-
ment. This document must be reviewed by all affected parties or
their representatives and signed to signify approval. I have
reviewed the deliverables and documents associated with this
phase and verified that all necessary work has been completed. I
hereby authorize work to begin with the next phase of the
project.

SEP Phase Number and Title:
_____


Signed: ____<insert Project Sponsor name> _____
Date: _____
```

It should be quite obvious by now that the planning phase of a project can be quite detailed and take considerable time. Studies abound about how the amount of time spent here will save money and effort in later phases of the project life cycle. As a Program Manager, it is your responsibility to ensure that all projects are executed with proper planning and guidance. The function of the SPMO is to provide such a framework for each team to use.

In the next chapter we transition from analysis and planning to design and start building documents that detail how things get done in a project. So far, we have covered what is needed and why. We have covered a formal process that allows a team to *understand* what needs to be done. The purpose of the design phase is to communicate precisely and exactly how and what is to be done to those tasked to actually go do it in order to achieve the goals outlined in the URD.

3.3 Chapter 3 Review

1. Why is the POS necessary?
2. What is the PDD?
3. What is the purpose of a Flexibility Matrix?
4. Why should a Data Risk Analysis be completed?
5. List five key components of a technical analysis document.
6. Who is responsible for the completion of the TRA?
7. What is the High-Level Solution Document?
8. When is an RFP used?
9. What basic elements should a funding package contain?
10. Who manages the project budget and schedule?
11. What are dependency diagrams used for?
12. When are variance reports necessary?

4

SEP Phase III: Detailed Design Phase

Figure 4.1 depicts the SEP Phase III roadmap. The steps outlined in the Detailed Design Phase are centered around detailing every aspect of the project. From the original analysis and planning performed in Phase II, the Project Manager should direct his or her team through a guided process of generating exact specifications to meet product requirements. The resulting

Figure 4.1   *SEP Phase III Roadmap.*

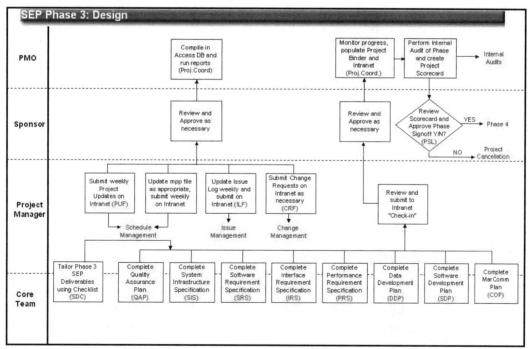

77

specifications documents should be verified with the user in a review process before to the next project phase is initiated.

4.0.1 SEP Deliverables Checklist

The deliverables checklist (Figure 4.2) below is reviewed by the Core Team to help decide which deliverables, by phase, are required for a particular project. You may have noticed that the left-most column seen in Figure 4.2 represents those deliverables that are required for any project. The column to the right of that allows the Core Team the flexibility to choose whether a particular deliverable is relevant to the project it is working on. This customization matrix allows for a high degree of flexibility in project execution, but it also enforces a high degree of consistency in projects underway throughout the SPMO environment. Such consistency ultimately saves money in an organization and creates efficiencies that allow for faster execution and better understanding of project methodology.

4.1 Quality Assurance Plan (QAP)

The QAP defines, tracks, and measures both product and process quality goals throughout the project development process. QAPs ensure the completion of defect removal activities. They require high-level design inspections, low-level design inspections, and project code inspections. All of these types of inspections that occur before the beginning of the development phase will save the organization time and money by discovering errors and omissions at the beginning of a process rather than at the end. The better a problem is known and understood before work is begun to solve it, the better the solution will be. QAPs allow the Core Team to work with pre-defined conditions for each development activity. These conditions include having an entry point, an implementation process, an exit point, and specific-defect removal goals. Satisfying each of these conditions for each development activity will ensure that a quality process is enforced.

4.2 Human Factors Plan (HFP)

The HFP is a researched document used for conducting human factors studies within the project environment. Human factors planning ensures that the team does not build a work environment that is not suitable for the workers or users of the project deliverables. For example, a test bench is fabricated to exact specifications of 54" in height. Later, it is discovered that

Enterprise Program Management Office **Intranet**

SEP DELIVERABLES CHECKLIST Insert Project Name /ID#

Req.	Complete		
		• **Phase 1: Initiation**	**Comments:**
☒	☐	Project Initiation Form	
☒	☐	Sponsor Formalization Letter	
☒	☐	Project Manager Appointment Letter	
☒	☐	Core Team Roster	
☒	☐	Project Guidelines Document	
☒	☐	User Requirements Document	
☒	☐	Phase Signoff Letter	
		• **Phase 2: Planning**	**Comments:**
☒	☐	Project Definition Document	
☐	☐	Data Analysis Document	
☐	☐	Technical Analysis Document	
☒	☐	High Level Solution	
☒	☐	Cost Estimating Worksheet	
☒	☐	Vendor Selection Checklist	
☐	☐	Vendor Resume(s)	
☐	☐	Vendor Reference Questions	
☐	☐	Vendor Selection Matrix	
☒	☐	Risk Analysis Matrix	
☒	☐	Phase Signoff Letter	
		• **Phase 3: Design**	**Comments:**
☐	☐	System Infrastructure Specification	
☐	☐	Software Requirements Specification	
☐	☐	Interface Requirements Specification	
☐	☐	Performance Requirements Specification	
☐	☐	Data Development Plan	
☐	☐	Software Development Plan	
☒	☐	Marketing/ Communication Plan	

Figure 4.2 *SEP Deliverables Checklist.*

the average height of the test team is 5'6" and the test bench is level with most test-team members' collarbones!

Many other facets of testing are a part of the overall HFP. Such user-oriented testing must occur in conjunction with requirements testing, integration testing, platform testing, media tests, and so on. It is generally a good idea to have a dedicated team exclusively devoted to the human factors process. Some organizations even believe it is best to have outside consultants come to work for them to explore these types of issues. Their reasoning for this is that outsiders do not have preconceptions about the internal workings, environment, or operation of the product and can provide the best objectivity. Following is a list of some other human factors to consider:

- O/S suitability tests
- Code testing
- User input testing
- General performance testing

- User feedback
- Graphics suitability
- Performance
- Functionality

4.3 Human Factors Report (HFR)

The HFR is a final report derived from the human factors study (outlined in the HFP). This report is used to identify any relevant issues that need to be resolved before implementation. The report also recommends any changes needed to make the product more user-friendly or to improve the overall application ergonomics. These include, but are not limited to, the following four areas:

1. User-interface issues
2. Documentation issues
3. Usability test results
4. Product or service ratings

4.4 Product Requirements and Specifications (PRSpec)

The PRSpec encompasses a set of required deliverables that describe in great and exacting detail precisely what the customer will receive when the completed product is made available. Every single function, command, screen prompt, dialog, and other user-interface-related item is documented in this group of specifications. Much of the information in this document can be expanded from the High-Level Solutions Document. The four key specifications documents required at this stage include the following:

1. System Infrastructure Requirements
2. Software Requirements Specifications
3. Interface Requirements Specifications
4. Performance Requirements Specifications

4.4 Product Requirements and Specifications (PRSpec)

The various requirements specifications documents listed are intended to ensure that a well-conceived and copiously detailed breakdown of the proposed solution is completed by the various Core Team members and other participants of the project development process.

In the course of gathering and building a requirements document, it is often necessary to review existing documentation/software. A Requirements Analysis Team may be tasked to analyze the problem domain and conduct customer interviews or even to conduct one or more user surveys. The Requirements Analysis Team must identify and evaluate reusable system components and work with the local IT or MIS organization to determine the type of host platform required. The team must also determine what platform features will be used to implement security safeguards. Additionally, the following are some other general areas to take into consideration for analysis when deriving user requirements.

- Architecture
- Audience
- Commands
- Compatibility/migration
- Competitiveness
- Deviations from requirements
- Ease of use
- Functions
- Future enhancements
- Hardware supported
- Information/data to be included
- Internationalization requirements
- Packaging
- Performance
- Pricing/license agreements
- Publications
- Reliability
- Screen layout

- Security
- Serviceability
- Software supported
- Standards/ISO compliance
- User interfaces

In the following paragraphs, we cover each of the four key specifications documents and discuss why each is important in the project execution process.

4.5 System Infrastructure Requirements (SIR)

The SIR document specifies the exact infrastructure requirements needed to support the final product. Infrastructure requirements refer to the physical features of the hardware and software environment, as well as the physical surroundings these environments exist in. An example would be the addition of a piece of hardware requiring a SCSI cable in a non-SCSI environment. The infrastructure requirement might be to simply adapt the non-SCSI environment to accommodate new SCSI devices. It may also be something less technical, such as having an electrical outlet converted from 110V to 220V.

In general, every input and output adapter of every device within the physical environment should be reviewed to ensure compatibility or upgraded to meet the requirements of the new system. Most importantly, this document should be reviewed by the local IT or MIS representative (who should be a Core Team member) to catch any unrealistic assumptions or misconceptions early. What follows is a recommended table of contents for any of the various requirements documents generated. The particulars of each section may change, but the general format remains the same. Note also that this document is distinctly different from the format of the User Requirements Document (URD) covered previously.

Requirements Document Table of Contents (recommended)

Document Management Issues

    Revision History

    Introduction

    Purpose of This Document

4.5 System Infrastructure Requirements (SIR)

        Intended Audience
        Inputs to This Document
        Outputs from This Document
        Distribution List
Executive Overview
        Vision Statement
        Fundamental Problem to Be Solved
        Product Summary
        Financial Summary
        Schedule
        Beta Release Date
        Software Production Release Date
        Background
        User's Current Mode of Operation
        Business Case
        Related/Dependent Projects

System Requirements
        General
        Key Features
        Environment
        Ease of Use
        Performance
        Quality
        Compatibility/Migration
        Service and Support
        Standards/ISO Compliance
        Product Integration
        Software
        Minimum Software Configuration

        Hardware
        Minimum Hardware Configuration
        Architecture
        Security
        Internationalization
        Y2K (Year 2000) Support

Financial
        Benefits/Savings
        Project Budget

Productization
        Publications
        Packaging
        Additional Components
        Product Integration
        Service and Support
        Competitive Offerings
        Pricing/Licensing

Appendix A
        Standard Definitions for Development Activities

As you can see, the purpose of such precise documentation is to cover as much detail as needed to explain who needs it, when they need it, why they need it, what it will do when they get it, how it benefits the organization or team, and what it requires in terms of time, cost, and materials.

4.6 Software Requirements Specification (SRS)

The SRS document specifies the exact functional specification for each and every item mentioned in the URD. Sometimes, these requirements are referred to as a Computer Software Configuration Item (CSCI). There may be more than one functional specification for each item mentioned in the URD. The URD should be viewed as the high-level, broad-brushstroke view of the user's requirements. The SRS is sometimes referred to as a Functional Specification Document (FSD). Whatever the name, SRS or FSD, this document is the epicenter of design for each requirement stated by the user as necessary to satisfy his or her business needs.

These requirements are often included in a document called a Requirements Traceability Matrix (RTM). In this document, requirements are cross-checked against all of the design documents, test plans, and so on. Each requirement mentioned in the URD is or should be found in the RTM, along with any new requirements uncovered by the Core Team along the way. This matrix is used by test teams, development groups, and so on to keep them focused on what they are striving to achieve. Figure 4.3 shows a sample RTM.

4.7 Interface Requirements Specification (IRS)

The IRS document should translate all required user functionality into an elegant user-interface (UI) description. Each level of the UI should be detailed, including function keys, hot keys, user dialogs, and so on. As much as possible, all of the UI development should follow preestablished standards for the systems environment into which the deliverable will be placed. It is not a good practice to drop functionality into an existing systems infrastructure that operates with a UI that is quite different from the UI found in existing applications in the organization. Therefore, the design of the UI should be reviewed by the Core Team and signed off on by the Project Sponsor to ensure adherence to prescribed systems standards. Of course, the exception here is if the organization has decided to change from

Figure 4.3
Requirements Traceability Matrix (RTM).

one UI standard to a new one, and this project would be in the vanguard of such an effort.

4.8 Performance Requirements Specification (PRS)

The PRS specifies performance needs and details the implementation decisions that will ensure compliance with these needs. For software products, performance needs include response time, hardware access time, network jitter, and so on. Each item should be carefully considered in terms of how it is measured and how it is used. Ideally, these performance requirements should be benchmarked against other existing systems in the production environment.

4.9 Data Development Plan (DDP)

The DDP consists of two documents. The first of these two documents is the Content Pipeline Document (CPD), which describes the process by which data to be delivered by the product will be channeled to those responsible for sustaining the content management. A minimal CPD should do the following:

- Identify content authors
- Define content flow process and content correction process
- Define data format
- Define data publication tool assignments
- Generate reports
- Collect data
- Format data

The second part of the DDP is the Data Distribution Plan (DDisP). This plan describes the process by which information contained within the product will be distributed to the target audience as requested by the user. The DDisP should identify target audience content, define distribution and/or dissemination processes, define all data formats, define other potential tools in which to incorporate this data, identify the timing of information delivery, define all reports to be generated by the system, and finally, identify data assignments (i.e., who is responsible for procuring, processing, and producing this data?).

4.10 Contracts/Agreements (CA)

Once the bid/proposal (or RFP) process has been completed, the contractor you have chosen will need to submit a formal contract before beginning work. Your organizational guidelines for contract processing should be closely followed, but here are some items that you should ensure are present in any agreement:

- *Terms:* Make sure all contract terms are written in clear, simple language; if you cannot easily understand the terms in a contract, it should probably be rewritten. There is nothing that says complicated legal wording is necessary.
- *Cancellation policy:* Be sure one is included because this is often overlooked.
- *Pricing:* Ask for a summation page with all pricing indicated and stipulate that in the event that there are any discrepancies in prices on other pages, pricing will defer to the price found on the summation page.
- *Licensing:* Be sure to get all license information reviewed by your users to ensure that the license procured is what is needed to satisfy requirements.
- *Patents and trademarks:* Ensure that any infringements on patents or trademarks as a result of contractor work will require the contractor to provide legal protection and/or defense to your organization.

4.11 Software Development Plan (SDP)

The SDP is a generalized description of a group of specifications and plans for conducting a software development effort. The term *development* is meant to include the creation of new items, incorporation or update of existing items, or a combination of these approaches. Not all of these specifications and plans are applicable to every project. It is the Core Team's responsibility to work with the requirements requirements analysis team and data analysts and development and/or engineering team leaders to determine the proper level of detail and the scope of effort that is required to complete the SDP. The followign are some items that should be considered for inclusion in the SDP:

- Architectural system design standards
- Data conversion strategy
- File and database backup/recover/reorganization strategy
- Functional data model
- Functional process model
- Physical data model
- Physical data storage estimates
- Physical process model
- Program file/database access patterns
- System control requirements
- System job flowchart
- System Administration Manual table of contents
- System processing load estimates
- Testing strategy

Remember, the purpose of this book is to describe what is needed to run an effective SPMO in an organization. For our purposes, it is not necessary to go into great detail on the specifics of how to calculate physical storage requirements, determine load estimates, and so on. It is assumed that such resources are available to the project team to get the work done. It is only necessary that a Project Lead or Program Manager knows when it needs to be done in the SEP process and finds resources to do it.

4.12 Database Conversion Plan (DCP)

The DCP is used to define existing application files that need to be converted, specify the new files that need to be created, identify the volume of data that is to be converted, and stipulate which organizational entities are to be involved in defining the conversion process, target dates, data integrity, and so on. This document is an end-to-end flow for data placed in and retrieved from the system. In most instances, existing data from legacy systems will be integrated with new systems data and data structures. To successfully accomplish this task, much data analysis needs to take place. A Data Analysis Team is required to determine the need to convert data from one internal machine representation to another.

4.12 Database Conversion Plan (DCP)

Part of the responsibility of a Data Analysis Team is to evaluate all of the various data elements originating from several files and databases and validate the content of the fields. It is often necessary for data analysts to merge different fields from different files or databases into a single data file. Part of the data analyst's job is to establish relationships or dependencies among different data fields currently stored in different files and/or databases and to synchronize several files and databases concurrently. He or she must decide to expand or shorten the size of data elements and reorder the records or place data elements in a different sequence to accommodate new data structures. Sometimes, data analysts must modify the contents of the data field itself.

Data analysts are required to analyze the high-level data requirements of the new system and identify the primary domains of change that exist between the current and new system data architectures. They must examine the overall quality and integrity of the data presently stored in manual and automated files and databases belonging to the current system. The analysts must identify existing or special software tools and facilities or hardware and networking equipment that will be required to support the data conversion process.

After all of this work is completed, the Data Analysis Team will derive an optimal strategy to perform a well-defined data conversion effort in the context of the project scope. The magnitude of this conversion effort is directly related to the complexity of the existing and new system data architectures, the volume of data involved in the conversion process, and the degree of change associated with the application to be installed. The Data Analysis Team must walk through the preliminary system data conversion strategy. These analysts are required to evaluate the scope of change between the old and new systems and to identify all existing application files that need to be converted, along with a brief description of the records and data elements involved in the process. The new files that must be created from scratch need to be identified, along with a brief description of the data elements that must be loaded into these files. For each file, the estimated volume of data that needs to be converted to accommodate the new system data requirements should be documented.

During the data conversion process, systems developers may be called on to provide unique data conversion programs, data validation programs, or file comparison facilities that assist in converting the existing files and databases efficiently. They may be asked to produce reports needed by the users to validate the results. For these reasons, it is very important that the major objectives and scope of the conversion process, along with the major issues to be addressed by the development team and the users, be explained at the beginning of a data conversion process. The roles and responsibilities assigned to each user and systems group involved in the conversion process should be identified.

The description of the files and databases that must be converted in association with this particular release of the system should be documented and distributed to all interested parties. This documentation should provide a section that details the type of conversion that will be performed against each affected file or database:

- Automated-to-manual conversion (not desirable but often necessary)
- Automated-to-automated conversion
- Fallback procedures in case something goes wrong during the conversion process
- Manual-to-automated conversion
- Manual-to-manual conversion (the worst way to go)
- The type of reports required by users to verify the results of the conversion
- The type of reports required by users to analyze the quality of the data
- The particular sequences in which the files will be converted
- The dependencies that exist among the files

The major business units of the organization that should be involved in the conversion process are, at this point, required to identify possible constraints that might be imposed on the conversion process. The Data Analysis Team must provide them with expected target completion dates. They should stipulate any special handling of highly sensitive data and identify any dependencies with other systems and, if needed, state the necessity to construct interfaces to them.

During the data conversion process, the Data Analysis Team most often needs to ensure availability of the files to the users (i.e., the current production files must remain available for the users 23 hours a day, 5 days a week) and to create an availability schedule for public dissemination. During the conversion process, representatives from the business owners should periodically examine the level of quality of the data currently stored in the existing files. Ultimate responsibility for ensuring the success of the conversion and the integrity of the data lies with the users.

4.13 Marketing Communications Plan (MCP)

The purpose of this document is to communicate to the appropriate Marketing Communications organization all of the information required to develop a Marketing Communications (MARCOM) Plan. The information provided by the Project Manager in this document should include the following data:

- Barriers to success
- Business objective (refer to the POS)
- Distribution process
- Distribution medium and format
- Expected delivery date
- Interprogram dependency
- Key messages (usually two or three key statements)
- Marketing budget
- Measurement standards
- Project name (not the internal code name)
- Project Manager name
- Release timing
- Target audience
- Timeline dependencies
- Value proposition

4.14 Marketing Rollout Schedule (MRS)

The MRS is a schedule determined by the marketing team. It is used for indicating the timeline for rolling out product announcement information associated with the product. This schedule is used by the project team to update project indicators regarding deliverables and release timing. Once the marketing team has a firm, committed date, it is the responsibility of the rest of the Core Team to ensure that this date is met. It is ill-advised to have dates publicized by Marketing that subsequently cannot be met by the project team (for any reason, because it causes the organization to appear to be out of touch with reality). Equally importantly, the marketing team must understand project schedules and timings to ensure the right date is publicized.

4.15 Marketing Rollout Signoff (MRS)

This is a completion document. It comes from the marketing team and is used to indicate that the marketing information was successfully rolled out. It is basically a notification that the marketing team has completed their part of the project work.

4.16 Project Transition Letter (PTL)

This letter is meant to describe the transition of a project from the planning phase to the tracking phase. Remember, work will still continue on the project, but the SPMO is basically beginning the process of tracking such work at this stage of the game. Software developers are now busy developing, test plans are being written, and so on. All project baseline schedules have been set in stone at this point. Every group working on every facet of this project has been given hard target dates to meet for the project to be delivered on time. This letter should be drafted by the Project Manager, and it should dictate the specific activities involved in tracking the project from this point forward.

This letter signifies the completion of the Initiation, Planning, and Design Phases of the SEP process. Project development activities will transition from the Core Team to the development group headed by <insert Team Lead name here>. This transition requires Project Sponsor approval before the project can continue to the next phase in the SEP process. This document must be reviewed by all affected parties or their representatives and signed to signify approval. A sample letter is shown below.

Project Transition Approval Signoff

```
I have reviewed the deliverables and documents associated with
this phase and verify that all necessary work has been com-
pleted. I further understand that work will transition from the
planning and design phase to the build/development phase. I
hereby authorize work to begin with the next phase of the
project.
```

```
Core Team Member Name and Title:
_____<insert name here>_____
Sponsor Name and Title:
_____<insert project sponsor name here>_____


Signed: _____
Date: _____

CC: <insert name of all parties affected here>
```

At this stage, all the hard work in preparation, planning, and design by everyone involved in the project has been completed. The work that has been completed has been reviewed and approved by the Project Sponsor and reviewed by all interested parties. A formal transition of the work effort has been made, and the development work begins in earnest. In the next chapter, we cover the construction phase of the SEP and examine all the tasks required to take a well-conceived concept from paper to reality.

4.17 Chapter 4 Review

1. What is a QAP?
2. What are some factors to consider in building a Human Factors Plan?
3. List the four key specifications documents required in the Design phase.
4. What is an SRS?
5. User-interface requirements are detailed in which specification document?
6. Which two components are found in the DDP?
7. List the basic elements of a DCP.
8. What is the purpose of a DCP?
9. What is an SDP?
10. What is the Marketing Communications Plan used for?

5

SEP Phase IV: Construction Phase

During this phase, the development or engineering team executes project plans according to the detailed specifications generated in the previous phase. It is here the Alpha and Beta versions of the product are released. Let's look at the SEP Phase IV roadmap (Figure 5.1).

The first step in the roadmap requires that the Core Team review the SEP Phase IV deliverables checklist. As you can see in Figure 5.2, there is not a lot of mandatory work to be done; however, you should not be fooled

Figure 5.1 *SEP Phase IV Roadmap.*

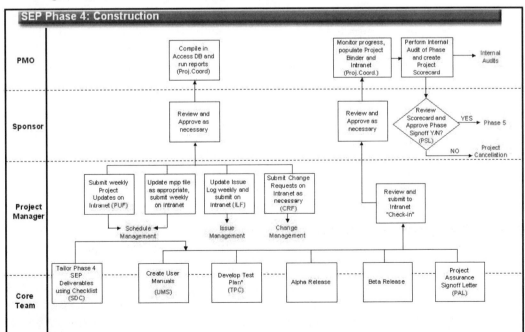

Figure 5.2
SEP Phase IV Deliverables Checklist.

		• Phase 4: Construction	Comments:
		User Manuals	
☒		Project Assurance Letter	
☒		Phase Signoff Letter	
		• Phase 5: Testing	Comments:
☒		Test Plan Checklist	
		Test Logs	
		Bug Tracking Reports	
☒		Phase Signoff Letter	

by this. Remember the Project Transition Letter. The project was turned over to the development/engineering team for continued work, and they have a much more work-intensive process underway at this point in the project.

As we follow the path of the roadmap for this phase, the next step in the process is creating all user manuals. Based on specifications documents and concurrent development, work on all product manuals should not be saved until the completion of development. Manuals should reflect all changes processed through the Change Management Process (CMP).

5.1 Software User Manual (SUM)

The SUM is a basic instruction manual intended for the end user. It is written as a fundamental learning tool for the project deliverables. In order to help the user in learning the basic program features, the SUM should list all product entities the user would possibly see in the operation of the product. This includes any keyboard commands and input device controls. The SUM should instruct the user on printing and viewing system reports, customizing the application, and performing troubleshooting actions.

The SUM should be the first point of reference for a user and should be comprehensive enough to prevent the user from needing to pick up the phone and call for support. Taking the time to prepare a SUM properly will ultimately save the organization in support costs and, in many instances, provide a higher degree of satisfaction for users.

5.2 Software Installation Manual (SIM)

The SIM is used by systems administrators to give step-by-step instructions for installing the application. It should include server installation procedures as well as client application installation procedures. The SIM should list all system requirements and provide exact, verified installation instructions. All control codes should be specified within the document. It should list all default control settings.

5.3 Training Manual (TM)

The TM is to be used when conducting training on the new product. Like any good training material, it should provide a formalized, well-planned introduction to the material that covers the product deliverable. A suggested TM outline is as follows:

I. Introduction
II. Lesson(s)
III. Objectives
IV. Lesson Details
V. Practice Sessions
VI. Workbook Exercises
VII. Lesson Summary
VIII. Glossary

Each student should be given a copy of the TM, and the instructor should follow it exactly. This ensures that all students are trained according to the guidelines developed by the Core Team and that the instructors deliver consistent content. In a large organization with many large systems, it is a huge cost consideration to train people. Having consistency across training programs helps reduce costs and leverage efficiencies across applications. Do not develop the TM from scratch for each application; consistent format and presentation are important factors in a successful implementation process.

5.4 Operations and Maintenance Guide (OMG)

The OMG describes the technical operation and maintenance specifications for the finished product. It should include installation procedures, product features, specifications, and troubleshooting steps. This guide is the handbook used by systems administration personnel to maintain the system during its production life cycle. The OMG provides continuity when personnel change from job to job and serves as a quick reference material for administrators responsible for maintaining 30 to 40 applications on average in an enterprise. Without such references, there will be much chaos when a systems administrator departs an organization.

5.5 Development Process for Test Plans (TP)

This is the stage where all product development plans and specifications will be scoured, and test criteria will be gleaned from each specifications document for inclusion in a series of test cases as part of the overall master test plan. This includes data from the System Infrastructure Requirements (SIR) document, the Software Requirements Specification (SRS), the Interface Requirements Specification (IRS), and the Performance Requirements Specification (PRS).

Test cases are generally constructed to cover materials from each unique specifications document or plan, but they are not limited to just those documents. For example, if the IRS states that a common Windows-like interface will be used, there may be a specific set of test cases developed that test common Windowing features such as maximize, minimize, scroll up, down, left, right, and so on. During the test case construction process, the test manager should instruct the test case developers as to how to build reusable test cases. Properly designed, well-confined test cases can be reused for maximum organizational efficiency. They are also reused for regression testing as the software progresses through its life cycle. The best reference to explain how best to go about properly constructing a test plan is the ANSI/IEEE Standard 829-1998 for Software Test Documentation[9]. This standard recommends the following outline format be used for documentation purposes when building a test plan:

I. Contents
II. Scope
III. Definitions
IV. Test Plan
V. Test-Design Specification
VI. Test-Case Specification
VII. Test-Procedure Specification
VIII. Test-Item Transmittal Report

5.5 Development Process for Test Plans (TP)

IX. Test Log

X. Test-Incident Report

XI. Test-Summary Report

As you peruse the format of the recommended contents, you can see that Sections I through III are fairly self-explanatory. We focus on Sections IV through XI in our coverage of test planning. The purpose of the test plan is to provide an overview of the testing effort needed for the product delivery to be successful. It is common for all of the unique test plans developed for product testing to be placed into a single planning document that is broken into multiple sections. The master test plan is a centralized repository to be used for all documentation relating to the testing effort. Each section of the master test plan would contain a specific type of test plan (e.g., SIR, SRS, PRS). Some organizations choose to create many separate documents and maintain each individually, but from an SPMO perspective, this is a less efficient method of document handling.

The test plan should contain a test plan identifier. This is a combination of alphanumeric characters that os most often used to cross-reference test results data in a database. An example may be something like SIR–*NN-NN-NNN-DDD*, where SIR would be the abbreviation for System Interface Requirements and *NN-NN* would represent the Product Major and Minor Revision ID numbers. The next set, *NNN*, could represent three digits that are the requirement ID number taken from the SIR document, and *DDD* could represent the Julian date on which the test plan was last modified or even the last date on which the plan was executed. The sample number might look something like this: SIR-02-01-054-167. Note that each set of alphanumerics between the dashes could be a sort field in a test database. It would be possible to develop a query for SIR (or SRS, IRS, etc.) or all specifications containing the Major Revision ID of 02, and so on. This is, of course, highly subjective and easily modified to meet organizational needs. The purpose of the identifier is to easily find results data as it relates to indexed plans.

Each test plan constructed should have an introductory section. In this section, it is often necessary to explain or cross-reference any relevant organizational policies and standards. The introduction should also give a high-level overview of the product being tested as it relates to the specific plan.

The next section of the test plan should cover the test items. Test items are references to software modules, features, control functions, interfaces, and so on. Each significant feature of the software should have a corresponding test item. All of the items relevant to the plan should be listed in this part of the plan. Furthermore, each item should be cross-referenced back to the design plan or specification that it came from. It is common to assign each test item a numeric ID for future reference.

Your test plan should stipulate which features of the product are to be included or excluded from the testing process. The plan should also cover the approach used in testing the product. This approach would include any tools, techniques, processes, people, and so on that are used in the testing process. For each of the test items mentioned previously, there needs to be a section that defines pass or fail criteria and explains how a tester would make such a pass/fail determination. If a test needs to be halted and subsequently resumed, a corresponding procedure should explain the process. For example, if there is a massive power outage or network outage, does the test resume from the last successful test item, from scratch, or from somewhere else?

The test plan should itemize all of the deliverable documents that will be produced from the testing process. It should explain what deliverables are required, when, and to whom they will be presented. All preparation, execution, and closure tasks need to be identified, do any special environmental conditions or settings that may need to be set up in advance or during the testing. This may include placing network load factors onto the production environment for testing, specific lab conditions, and so on.

All participant responsibilities should be clearly outlined in the plan. Staffing requirements and training needs should be addressed in the plan and coordinated in advance of the testing start date. A schedule of testing needs to be produced and coordinated with all internal and external parties interested in the testing process. Finally, when all of these things are completed, someone (usually the Project Sponsor) must approve the test plan before it can be executed.

Section V of the recommended Table of Contents for IEEE Standard 829-1998 covers test design specification. This section explains *how* a test item will be tested. According to the standard, each test design specification should contain a test design specification identifier. The features that are to be tested need to be documented in this section. Any refinement to the overall approach needs to be explained here. You should list the specific test case ID number that is associated with each of the features to be tested. Itemize the pass/fail criteria for each test case and explain the method of determining pass or fail for each of the criteria.

5.5 Development Process for Test Plans (TP)

Section VI of the Table of Contents for IEEE Standard 829-1998 is the place where a test case is actually defined. It should include a test case specification identifier. The test case specification should include the test items to be covered in this test, and it should list any input and output specifications or environmental needs. If any special processing requirements are needed to conduct the test, they should be listed in this section. Finally, if there are any dependencies on other test cases, they should be explained in this section of the document.

Section VII of the Table of Contents for IEEE Standard 829-1998 outlines the exact procedure for executing a test case. The test procedure specification should contain a test procedure specification ID number, a short section on the purpose of the test procedure, a section to list any special requirements necessary for executing the test procedure, and, most importantly, a section that contains all of the steps involved in the procedure. The procedure steps should contain logging requirements, setup, start, execution, measurement, and shutdown procedures. Details for restarting a procedure, stopping a procedure, closing out a procedure upon successful completion, and contingency actions should also be included.

In Section VIII of the Table of Contents for IEEE Standard 829-1998, the Test Item Transmittal Report is presented. The Test Item Transmittal Report is used when software is submitted to the test group for testing. It should include a transmittal report ID number and a list of all items being submitted for testing. For each item, the location (e.g., file path and/or associated application directory structure) should be stated clearly. The status of the items being submitted for testing should also be stated in the report. The status should focus on what has changed since initial submission for testing. Finally, the approval for turning materials over to the test group should be completed by the development or engineering team lead and signed off on by the Project Manager.

During the testing process, you should keep a log of all tests conducted. Standard 829-1998 requires a test log ID number and a description of the test. For each activity noted in the log, there should be entries for execution descriptions, procedure results, environmental information, unexpected events, and incident report ID numbers. Incident reports, or problem reports, should also follow IEEE Standard 829-1998 guidelines. This calls for an incident report ID number, summary, input, expected results, actual results, anomalies, date and time of the incident, the procedural step, the environmental conditions, and attempts to repeat or re-create the problem, names of the testers and observers, and the impact the incident had on the test plan or specifications.

After all testing has been completed, Section XI of the IEEE Standard 829-1998 requires submission of a Test Summary Report. This is an explanation of the testing process, environment, results, and so on. It should contain a Test Summary Report ID number and a section summarizing the results of testing, explaining any variances in the testing process. An assessment of the level of comprehensiveness of testing is required. The summary of results section should discuss what problems occurred during testing and what was done to solve them. A section providing an overall analysis or evaluation of the process should be in the report. Finally, the report needs to summarize all activities from all tests, and it should be signed off on by the Test Group Manager, the Project Manager, and the Project Sponsor.

As you can see from this discussion, the conduct of testing is a rigorous and detailed process. Ensuring that this process is conducted with the best methods and by the best people improves the odds that the organization will benefit from the process. The SPMO should ensure all of the sections of the recommended standard are adhered to throughout the process. In the following sections, we cover what are considered minimum essentials for a complete testing process.

5.6 SPMO Recommended Test and Certification Plans

Test plans should thoroughly consider how to effectively evaluate every single aspect of the product's functionality. For software products, each step in the testing phase should include both white and black box testing (or equivalents) in order to ensure stability from the inside out. Formal execution of test cases for the project deliverables will occur in SEP Phase V. Your overall project test plan should cover, at a minimum, six major areas:

1. Stress Test Plan
2. Integration Test Plan
3. Software Test Plan
4. Product Assurance Test
5. User Acceptance Test
6. MIS/Outside Certification Plan

5.7 Stress Test Plan (SsTP)

The Stress Test Plan is designed and executed to ensure that the product will perform exactly as expected in the user production environment. This test includes such items as placing a maximum data load on the environment, pushing the limits of each known boundary in software, hardware, and so on. The whole point of this process is to find the breaking point (if there is one) in testing and make it known *before* any real users are allowed to begin using the system. This stress test process includes both hardware and software and should be one of the key milestones in project execution. Gloss over this step at your peril!

5.8 Integration Test Plan (ITP)

The ITP describes the overall test approach. It identifies the tests to be performed and provides schedules for test activities. In large, multisystem environments, such tests often need to be coordinated and orchestrated in conjunction with downtime or completed during off-hours to avoid interruptions in business operations. The ITP will describe how to test interfaces between the various programs of the system, validate any manual-to-automated interfaces of the system (e.g., screens, reports), test external interfaces with other systems, and verify all functional and nonfunctional specifications of the system. It should also include testing of the following areas:

- System interface
- Control
- Conversion
- Security
- Backup, recovery, and restart
- Screen dialogue
- Volume
- Performance
- Stress
- Usability
- Documentation
- Storage

- Maintainability
- Compatibility

5.8.1 Software Test Plan (STP)

The STP describes the software test approach, identifies the tests to be performed for each module, and provides detailed schedules for test activities. It ensures correctness and accuracy of the program's internal logic and validates interfaces among the various modules of the program. The STP should be designed to check proper execution of all the procedural statements contained in the program modules. The STP must be written to exercise the internal logic of the program. While not all-inclusive, the following list outlines several test variants that certainly need to be included in a well-designed STP:

- Statement coverage tests
- Branch/loop coverage tests
- Value sampling tests
- Boundary value coverage tests
- Program interface tests
- File-handling tests
- Error message tests
- Error-prone tests

5.9 Product Assurance Test (PAT)

The PAT verifies that the total system solution performs as expected. This test is performed by executing a series of test cases that have been specifically constructed to demonstrate to the users that the system works properly in a production environment. The PAT is usually designed from taking material from the system operations documentation. The PAT should validate performance and data storage requirements for production operations. The PAT should encompass a complete processing cycle in production. Things to consider in this production cycle are monthly closings, cutovers, and any other conditions in the organization that you feel would bring additional load onto the system and stress its performance. At a minimum, production mode testing should consist of at least the following components:

- Job control statements
- Files/databases/datafeeds (streaming, non-streaming)
- Hardware/software/networking configurations
- Documentation of the system

5.10 User Acceptance Test (UAT)

The purpose of the UAT is to verify the total system solution and ensure that it satisfies the original business requirements. It should verify that all of the automated and manual components of the system work properly. Users (ideally, the most knowledgeable representatives from within the user community) should write most of these test plans. These users will often contract outside sources to help them develop a solid UAT. The SPMO must ensure that the outside sources develop such deliverables in conjunction with the guidelines established by the SEP guidelines and the SPMO. The UAT construction team should take into consideration each of the following areas:

- Automated processes with their input/output requirements
- Backup, recover, and restart processes
- Compatibility issues
- Control issues (e.g., user, system, data environment, outside sources)
- Conversion issues
- Documentation issues
- External system specifications and related nonfunctional specifications
- Functional tests
- Interfaces with other systems
- Manual procedures
- Performance expectations
- Screen dialogue (e.g., form, aesthetics, language, symbols)
- Security issues
- Storage issues
- Stress testing (should dovetail the Stress Test Plan)

- System interface tests
- Usability issues
- Volume (defaults, min, max)

5.11 MIS/Outside Certification Plan (MISCP)

This is a formal plan for the organization's IT or MIS group to use during the certification process. It should include written installation procedures, test procedures, system/software handoff procedures, target delivery dates, and any other procedures or documentation necessary for the IT or MIS team to successfully test, approve, and accept delivery of the application.

5.12 Product Deliverables

Concurrent with the development of the test plans, an engineering or development team should be focused on creating the product software deliverables. These deliverables include source code, software executables, data conversion scripts, and so on. Many times, software scripts must be written to support a data conversion effort. These data conversion scripts convert data from one internal machine representation to another or validate the content of the fields. They may be used to integrate various data elements originating from several files/databases or to merge different fields that are located in different files/databases. Such scripts are also used to establish relationships or dependencies among different fields currently stored in different files/databases, synchronize several files/databases at the same time, expand or shorten the size of a data element, reorder the records or data elements in a different sequence, or modify the contents of the field. Each of these functions generally saves considerable time and effort when the alternative of manual action is considered. They have become a fairly standard approach to delivering code and are a very important part of the project deliverable.

5.13 Product Signoff and Certification Letters

After the development or engineering teams have completed their work and are ready to pass the torch to the implementation teams, the SEP methodology requires the SPMO to assist in completion of some certifications and letters. These certifications are necessary to formalize the transition of project work from the design and build phase to the test phase. They formally allow one team to conclude its efforts and another team to pick up the torch and carry on with the work of getting the deliverable into production. This requires the following:

I. Product Assurance Signoff Letter
II. Functional Certification Letter
III. MIS Certification Letter
IV. Data Certification Letter

5.14 Product Assurance Signoff Letter (PASL)

This is a letter from the user (generally the Executive Sponsor) indicating that the total system solution satisfies the original user business requirements and that all of the automated and manual process components of the system work properly together. This is done after successful completion of the PAT.

5.15 Functional Certification Letter (FCL)

This is a letter from the customer or the functional business representative that documents his or her satisfaction or areas of concern with the functional performance of the system. Generally, this person is the Core Team representative from the functional business unit he or she has represented over the course of the project.

5.16 MIS Certification Letter (MISCL)

This is a letter from the MIS team indicating that the software has been tested and approved by MIS and is ready for implementation. Generally, in ideal situations where an MIS representative has been on the project Core Team from the beginning, this is a rubber-stamp process; however, some organizations may require the vice president of MIS or IT to sign off before formal acceptance of responsibilities.

5.17 Data Certification Letter (DCL)

This is a letter from the user representative (usually the Executive Sponsor) indicating that the data sources contained within the product have been validated, and approved and are ready for publication. This step is very important because corrupted data could cost the organization many, many dollars. The importance of having knowledgeable users validate the data in a new system cannot be overemphasized. It is the Project Manager's responsibility to ensure that this occurs, and the SPMO should verify this before any letters are presented for signature.

All of these certification letters are completed whenever product deliverables are moved forward in the life cycle process. This means they should be done for each phase of the development process. It starts with Alpha releases, Beta releases, Release to Test (RTT) candidates, or Release to Manufacturing (RTM) releases. Each iteration through the development process cycle should generate a new set of documents that are placed in the project binder. One of the subtle advantages of this approach is that over time, members of the organization will come to depend on the cyclic redundancy of the process. It will become an ingrained part of their understanding of how the SPMO works, further propagating understanding of the SEP and the advantages of using it. This maturity in process is exactly what CMMI is trying to achieve.

As we return to the SEP Phase IV roadmap, once the Alpha, Beta, and RTT phases are completed, the formal handoff to testing occurs. That is where the final versions of the certification and signoff letters are completed. It is good practice to have cyclical testing occur formally from the Alpha phase forward through Beta and in mock trials and smoke tests to ensure that the actual cutover process is ready when RTM or production delivery actually does occur. Next, in Chapter 6, we transition to the formal testing phase.

5.18 Chapter 5 Review

1. Why is the SUM written?
2. Who uses the SIM?
3. Why should training manuals be standardized?
4. What is an OMG?
5. Test cases should be constructed in accordance with which standard?
6. What is the purpose of a test plan?
7. What is a master test plan?

5.18 Chapter 5 Review

8. What is the Test Summary Report used for?
9. Name four to six major areas that a test plan should contain.
10. What is an STP?
11. What is the purpose of the PAT?
12. What is the purpose of the UAT?
13. Who completes the Functional Certification Letter?

6

SEP Phase V: Testing

This chapter explains the cyclical process of testing a product, returning it to the development team for further modifications, and beginning a retest sequence. It covers the management aspects of conducting a formalized test process. It does not cover detailed procedures for the testing process. Material in this chapter will help both the Test and Program Managers to understand what areas of testing need to be addressed and what types of test cases need to be built to adequately cover the most common aspects of a product

Figure 6.1 *SEP Phase V Roadmap.*

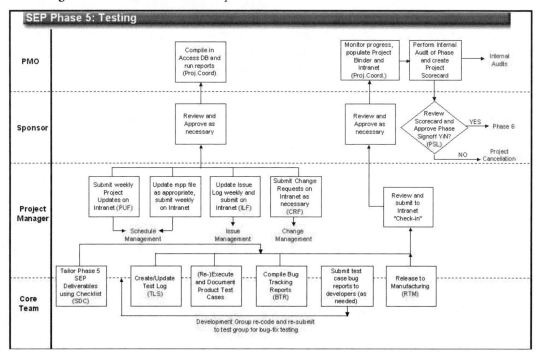

release. It will help managers learn to ask specific, targeted questions about each aspect of the testing process and ensure that they focus their teams on performing proper testing.

As we begin to review the testing phase, let's take a look at the SEP Phase V roadmap (Figure 6.1) for this phase. The roadmap shows only a few steps needed to be accomplished by the project team members; however, do not be deceived by its simplicity. The amount of work needed at this point is highly focused and concentrated solely on completing test execution and the associated materials needed to document such testing activities.

The roadmap also shows an iterative process of executing test cases and reporting bugs. The test group executes test cases and documents bugs found in the testing process. The bug reports are reviewed by the developers. The development group then attempts to correct the bugs and resubmits the recoded modules for retest. This iterative process generally continues until all modules have passed all appropriate test cases. It does not, however, guarantee that the program is bug-free.

Testing in this phase ensures that all test cases are executed and work as advertised. Bugs found elsewhere in the system are documented and placed in a hold status until proper classification can occur. These bugs may require new test cases, additional development work, and so on. The main point here is that they are documented and addressed before final delivery is made.

In most organizations, quality processes guide this iteration sequence. Modules are rejected in the test process. The development team receives a notice that something failed. It looks up the details of the failure in the bug tracking or configuration management software. Generally, the lead developer will work with his or her team to fix the problem and validate the fix to their team leader. The team leader will approve the release of the module back into the testing group for retest and subsequent pass or fail status.

Now, back to the roadmap. Once again, the first step in this phase is to review the deliverables checklist for the testing phase. As you can see in Figure 6.2, all of the boxes for this section of the checklist are mandatory. Let's take a look at the first item in Figure 6.2, the Test Plan Checklist.

Figure 6.2 *SEP Phase V Deliverables Checklist.*

			Phase 5: Testing	Comments:
☒			Test Plan Checklist	
☒			Test Logs	
☒			Bug Tracking Reports	
☒			Production Delivery or RTM Certification	
☒			Phase Signoff Letter	

6.1 Review the Test Plan Checklist (TPC)

This step requires that the Core Team conduct a thorough review of the Test Plan Checklist (TPC). Once the review of the TPC has been completed, it should be reviewed by the Project Manager and the Project Sponsor. Once approval to proceed with the checklist has been obtained, the Test Team should be directed to begin the prompt execution of all of the test cases prepared within each of the respective test plans that were previously completed in Phase IV of the SEP.

It is not uncommon for the Project Manager to appoint someone independent of the Test Team as a Test Monitor. This person is responsible to observe the Test Team and ensuring that the tests are conducted and documented in a professional, logical manner. Appointing a Test Monitor is not something the Test Team should construe negatively. The constant presence of a representative of the Core Team only emphasizes the importance that is placed on the testing effort. When negativity is sensed from Test Team members, it is a good idea to convey to them how important their efforts are to the success of the project and to let them know the Test Monitor is a liaison between them and the Core Team.

6.2 Test Plan Checklist

Testing Team Considerations

- Has a Test Lead and/or Team been established?
- Have vendor responsibilities for testing been established and agreed upon?

Stress Test Plan Considerations

- Are maximum system stress levels compatible with the user environment?
- Will existing system stress levels impact performance?

Integration Test Plan Considerations

- Are all interfaces for the various programs identified and functioning properly?
- Are manual-to-automated interfaces functioning properly?
- Are external interfaces with other systems functioning properly?

- Is data conversion complete and accurate?
- Is security of the system adequate?

Software Test Plan Considerations (where appropriate):
- Is internal logic correct and accurate?
- Do all modules interface correctly in the program?
- Has internal logic of the program been exercised in the following areas:
  - Statement coverage tests
  - Branch/loop coverage tests
  - Value sampling tests
  - Boundary value coverage tests
  - Program interface tests
  - File-handling tests
  - Error message tests
  - Error-prone tests

User Acceptance Test Plan Considerations
- Can the user navigate unassisted through the program?
- Are screen dialogue, volume, and overall usability acceptable to a user?
- Is all data desired by the user obtainable?

Testing Plan Quality Considerations
- Have all functions of the product been tested?
- Have all problem areas been addressed?
- Have all user problems or complaints been identified and addressed?
- Have all issues regarding testing been resolved?

The Test Plan Checklist not only requires that the Test Team conduct reviews of the four recommended test plans (i.e., Stress Test Plan, STP, ITP, and UAT) that were created in the previous phase of work, but it also asks for an introspective look at the Test Team and the quality of the test plan. This review helps the team focus on more than just going through the motions of completing a test case; it asks the Test Team members to take responsibility for the validation of the product.

The overall test process should be driven by a quality assurance frame of reference. The Core Team should work carefully with the Test Team to ensure that each test plan designed is properly executed and documented. Ultimately, the SPMO and the Project Manager will have final say on the test execution process because they are accountable to the Project Sponsor for the success of the project.

6.3 Test Logs and Incident Reports

The next two items on the deliverables checklist, test logs and incident reports, are completed by the Test Team during execution of the tests. Chapter 5 described what a test log should contain. As a brief recap, each log entry should contain the following information:

- Execution descriptions
- Procedure results
- Environmental information
- Unexpected events
- Incident report ID number

Figure 6.3 (following page) is a recommended template for creating an incident report. Incident reports should follow the IEEE Standard 829-1998 guidelines. These guidelines call for the following items to be present in a test report:

- Incident report ID number
- Summary
- Input
- Expected results
- Actual results
- Anomalies
- Date and time of the incident
- Procedural step at which the incident occurred
- Environmental conditions

Figure 6.3
Incident Report.

```
Enterprise    Program                    Intranet
              Management Office
                                         January 11, 2002

              Insert Project Code Name
              PROJECT INCIDENT REPORT

INCIDENT REPORT ID NUMBER: _____
SUMMARY: _____
_____
_____

INPUT: _____
EXPECTED RESULTS: _____
_____
_____

ACTUAL RESULTS: _____
_____

ANOMALIES: _____
DATE AND TIME OF THE INCIDENT _____
PROCEDURAL STEP _____
ENVIRONMENTAL CONDITIONS _____
ATTEMPTS TO RECREATE THE PROBLEM _____
NAME OF THE TESTER _____ OBSERVER: ___
IMPACT _____
```

- Documentation of any attempts to repeat or re-create the problem
- Names of the testers and observers
- Impact the incident had on the test plan or specifications

> *"Today, there is no question that if a software product has not been tested, it will not work. It is equally true, however, that once a program has been tested, the odds that it will work correctly under all conditions are only moderately improved. We should think of testing like weeding a garden: individual bugs can be found with tests but more powerful methods are needed for the thickets.*[10]*"*
> *—Watts Humphrey*

6.4 Test Domains

An excellent reference on the subject of software testing, *Testing Computer Software*[11] by Cem Kaner, contains 12 appendices describing some specific areas of testing (or testing domains) that a dedicated Test Team should

6.4 Test Domains

always focus its time and effort on. Those 12 areas recommended by Kaner are as follows:

- User-interface errors
- Error handling
- Boundary-related errors
- Calculation errors
- Initial and later states
- Control flow errors
- Errors in handling or interpreting data
- Race conditions
- Load conditions
- Hardware errors
- Source, version, and ID control errors
- Testing errors

Professional testers generally create a series of test cases specific to the new application that will cover each of the test areas listed. Of course, the level of testing is usually constrained by both time and resources. Many times, some of these test domains are omitted in lieu of basic functional testing. Although I do not recommend omitting any of these areas, the reality of a corporate environment is that deadlines more often than not drive the delivery schedules, and these organizations frequently pay dearly for the tradeoff between a more thorough testing process or faster project delivery.

Instituting an SPMO in an organization and subsequently implementing SEP as part of a software program management initiative will help prevent such mistakes. Effective software program management will enable the organizational project teams to begin establishing more realistic, process-driven schedules. In the long run, instituting this change will make a big difference on the organization's bottom line. Now, let's begin with a review of the testing domains that should be a part of any product test plan. Remember, the purpose of this section of the book is to help you, as the Program Lead, be aware of all of the test issues and areas that could cause a program initiative to fail. What follows in the next few sections is not intended to be a crash course in formal testing of a product.

6.5 User-Interface Errors

Anything the user can see or do with the deliverable can be classified in the User Interface domain. Kaner has broken this domain into several sections. The Project Manager and Test Manager should ask some key questions regarding each of these areas to ensure that the tests are built to adequately suit the needs of the business.

6.5.1 Functionality

- *Does the system function as advertised?* There are few things more irritating to a user than to have an expectation for the application to do something and find out that it does not. Even worse, the application interface indicates that it does one thing when it actually does something else.

- *Is it proper for the task it supports?* In this case, think about the old adage of using a sledge hammer to drive a needle. Does it take four menu selections to change the color of the text? If you hit the back key, does the action erase a character, a line, or a paragraph? Watch for overkill here.

- *Is there anything wrong or missing?* What? There is no print feature for your Report Generation Program? Oops! You can just imagine the level of irritation that oversight would cause. Users are very unforgiving about such mistakes. Take nothing for granted when reviewing designs and imagine you are sitting in the user's work space, trying to get your job done. Visualizing the work effort from the user's perspective will help in catching these types of errors.

- *Does the user have to do anything extra to make it work?* To print a file, imagine having to select a printer, select a paper type, select the paper tray, verify printer communications, and so on, rather than having a default printer established for all of your applications. It really used to be that way!

- *Does it do what the user expects?* How many times have you heard a user state, "I thought it would do X, but when I pressed that key the program did Y," or words to that effect? A good application should not surprise the user by doing something unexpected.

- *Is the functionality excessive or superfluous?* Are there menu items in your application designed to make your name appear in sparkly text every time you see it in a report? Does the program allow users to waste time simply by trying to use features that are not listed as requirements in your project documentation? Development groups are notorious for leaving their mark on an application. Be sure this situation is brought under control quickly if you find such things occurring in your organization.

6.5.2 Communication

- *Is information missing from the system?* Does the entire online help system consist of a copy of the table of contents from the cellophane-wrapped user manual sitting on your desk?

- *Is online documentation available to support the application?* Worse than incomplete help, having no help at all for a software deliverable can really get a user into a negative frame of mind! The first thing most of these users do is pick up the phone and burden your internal support with more work.

- *Does the product have any undocumented features?* Does pressing the Ctrl-Alt-Left key sequence in your application show several animations of bears dressed as hillbillies line dancing outside their shack? Or does it show something even more ridiculous? An even worse scen-ario to consider is something like a developer adding some special reporting features to a program that users could really benefit from, but not enabling those features until a requirement is submitted asking for them. Where is the logic in that?

- *Does the program present incorrect, misleading, or confusing information?* A good example here would be a menu item indicating use of a hot-key sequence. When the user presses the hot-key sequence, the menu item immediately below the one on the menu the user saw and selected is activated.

- *Is the help documentation adequate?* A well-known computer manufacturer once used to brag about its product documentation being delivered in terms of linear feet of paper stacks. Can you imagine trying to find out how to do something by sifting through four linear feet of paper? Or even worse, how about having the four linear feet of documentation all being made available online, without any hyperlinks, indices, or cross-references?

- *Are there spelling or typographical errors in the online documentation?* Does it make sense to you? It would be **emburrassing** to find such blatant errors in online documentation, wouldn't it?

- *Are there bugs in the program display?* When your mouse hovers over a command button, does the program lock up or do something unexpected? Does the text overrun the display area? Are the colors funky? All of these display issues can really undermine user satisfaction with a deliverable.

- *Is the display layout correct?* Does it correspond to what the design and requirements documents have stipulated? If not, why would it be acceptable to a user? This situation is preventable. Design reviews allow the user to look at mockups of the displays and approve or disapprove before the layouts are coded.

- *Would any areas of the program be considered useless?* Consider scenarios such as having an option for directing the printer output to a flatbed plotter and subsequently realizing that your company does not even own a plotter! The solution to the situation here is not to go out and buy a plotter!

- *Are the menus organized logically?* They should be organized along standardized recommendations. Were they developed in a vacuum? Did the users stipulate a menu organization that defies logic? Did the developers try to implement cute menus for something different to do? Sanity checks on this before and during the coding process are advised.

- *Do the menus have adequate wording, spelling, shortcuts, and so on?* An example here would be a File | Print menu option being referenced as the **File | Direct output to printer/fax** or some other unexpected wording.

- *Should missing commands be added?* What? Are you sure you really want to save your work? After only spending two hours working on that manuscript? Sanity checks during design reviews prevent calamities such as this (it has happened before, really!).

- *Is the program too rigid?* The program should not make the user feel like it is "my way or the highway" when trying to get something done. Situations like this occur as a result of bad design and should be corrected as soon as they are discovered.

- *Can the user tailor the interface?* Still don't like the funky colors? Okay. Just ensure that the user does not also encounter something like "press F6 and reboot" to change colors when he or she is trying to tailor the interface. Sometimes, programmers think very little about what a user will experience when working on a system. I have found many of these issues are resolved by having programmers occasionally work side-by-side with users in order to gain a new perspective on what it is like to actually sit down and use their work.

- *Is the tailorability too much or too little?* Can I change the color of each of the 32 labels on my display to my liking? Is it really necessary for a report to contain sparkly text or marching ant borders? Sometimes, sanity checks performed in a design review will prevent the occurrence of such overkill.

- *Is command-line input supported, and, if so, is it documented?* Consider the following actual output from the Microsoft Windows 2000 operating system[13], then ask yourself if a command-line sequence is absolutely necessary or not. In today's computing environment, this type of input should be rare and used sparingly:

```
COPY [/V] [/N] [/Y | /-Y] [/Z] [/A | /B ] source [/A | /B]
  [+ source [/A | /B] [+ ...]] [destination [/A | /B]]

  source       Specifies the file or files to be copied.
  /A           Indicates an ASCII text file.
  /B           Indicates a binary file.
  destination  Specifies the directory and/or filename for the
               new file(s).
  /V           Verifies that new files are written correctly.
  /N           Uses short filename, if available, when copying a
               file with non-8dot3 name.
  /Y           Suppresses prompting to confirm you want to
               overwrite an existing destination file.
  /-Y          Causes prompting to confirm you want to overwrite
               an existing destination file.
  /Z           Copies networked files in restartable mode.

The switch /Y may be preset in the COPYCMD environment variable.
This may be overridden with /-Y on the command line. The default is
to prompt on overwrites unless the COPY command is being executed
from within a batch script.

To append files, specify a single file for destination, but
multiple files for source (using wildcards or file1+file2+file3
format).

C:\WINNT\SYSTEM32>
```

- *Are command-line input sequences too complex?* See the previous example once again!

- *Is the system performance acceptable?* Did it take 30 seconds to change the color of each of the 32 labels? When your users save work, does it take inordinate amounts of time for them to be sure the program has saved the work? Is the system so slow that operations times are referenced by the C&D method (i.e., come back after two cups of coffee and a donut)?

- *Does the output generated by the system meet user expectations?* It is sometimes difficult for a developer to understand why a senior executive does not like to read 6-point font on a 20-page report. Many developers like to work with very large monitors and often state that the report looked great when they looked at it. You get the idea. To meet user expectations, the developers should exit the trenches and go see what the user has to work with. That can often save a lot of headaches.

6.5.3 Command Structure and Entry

- *Does the program support a consistent, understandable command structure?* Inconsistencies in an application lead to user frustration. This can create an unfavorable impression of the entire project effort. Be sure to validate the use of common command structures across all segments of the application and ensure that these command structures adhere to some known standards.

- *Does use of the command structure save or waste time?* If it takes 11 keystrokes to execute a command on a menu, there is likely going to be great dissatisfaction among users of your product. Old mainframe applications were often composed of nested screen displays. To move from one part of the program to another meant going from screen to screen to screen until you got to where you wanted to be; however, if you knew from the first screen you wanted option 1, option 4 on the second screen, and option 7 on the third screen, the menu at the top of the first screen would allow you to type something like this: =1,4,7. The system would immediately go to the result of option 7 on the third screen. If this does not sound so hot to you, remember that back in those days, sharing time on a computer often produced quite a delay going from screen to screen. It became the *de facto* method of navigating mainframe menu structures because it saved time.

- *Are the menus adequate for navigation of the complete system, or are there dead-end paths from the menus?* Does the menu structure have frivolous commands embedded within it? Every menu item should correspond to a destination in the program. Likewise, each destination should allow you to return to the menu that brought you to that point.

- *Is the keyboard used logically?* At first glance, this may seem like a stupid question; however, consider a key sequence of Shift | Alt | $ being used to execute a report. Okay, so the report is an income statement. Get it? Income? $? Now, you know where the programmer's head was at when this system was devised. These types of design issues can be caught and avoided in user review sessions and usability studies. Do not leave it up to the programmer to decide how or what the user should do to execute an option. Go back to the users to find out what they want. Try not to let these things slip through the test process. Great frustration and ridicule will be vented upon the project team for simple issues like this.

6.5.4 Missing Commands

- *Does the user get locked into a state where he or she cannot transition from one part of the program to another?* There is nothing quite so terrible or damaging to the credibility of a development team as having a user hate your application because it sends him or her into dead zones. *Always* ensure bidirectional traversal in menu structures.

- *Are there means imbedded into the system to prevent disaster, and does the system support error handling by the user?* An example of this would be something like printing a quarterly sales report and suddenly noticing that the printer has run out of paper. Obviously, you would hope the program would notice too, but alas, all 200 pages of your quarterly sales report must spool out before the program regains control. There was no facility in your application to stop the current print job because it was not part of the basic requirements document. Imagine how frustrating a situation like this could be to your end users, who are trying to get a report out to the Sales VP to roll up numbers for the quarter. Situations like this beg for design reviews to catch the problem before it happens. Fixing this at the time of development is trivial, but recovering from the damage that is caused by not catching it until after a user reports the problem is certainly no trivial matter. Credibility will certainly have been destroyed.

- *Are there nuisance issues to deal with?* Imagine a situation where every time you wish to read that quarterly sales report on-screen you must change the background and foreground colors to make the text readable. Programmers had no requirement for setting text and background colors and sent the output to a standard display; however, on your particular monitor the colors appear funky. You can muddle through, of course, but you find it much better and easier on the eyes if you can change the colors and make the text more readable. Now, imagine a situation where there are no options in the application to allow you to change the funky colors! Additional damage to your team credibility occurs.

- *Can the user quit when he or she decides it is necessary?* It is definitely hell week. You press the F3 key to return to the previous menu; however, because you could not change the funky colors on your display, you did not notice the foreground text, which was only one shade of color different from the background text—you know, that text that said press Esc to exit. You press F3 again and again. After a few minutes both you and the terminal you were working on have become unplugged!

6.5.5 Program Rigidity

- *Can the user tailor the program to suit his or her needs?* Think about the funky colors again. This topic does, however, go well beyond colors. Report format changes or output customization, menu selections that are most frequently used being more accessible, selection of a different printer, and so on should all be considered before getting out of the design review.

- *Can users feel as if they are in control of the session?* If the program operates such that users are made to feel as if they are on a Death March every time they try to use the system, design specifications have probably failed to achieve desired usability goals. Users are most happy when they feel as if they are masters of their universe. Ensure that you take steps to let them rule their domain by providing them with the ability to do exactly what they need and exactly what they want to enhance productivity. Look for ways to improve on existing environments or use new, standardized, time-tested interfaces that will deliver the desired results.

- *Is the system hostile to experienced users?* The best example of this situation is having a user who is starting to learn a new application. The design team was thorough enough to think to include pop-up help for every option, button, and dialog that was viewed during use. This was great the first few times you used the application, but after you have seen the pop-up help shown 400 times this week after pressing the print button, I am willing to bet that you do not care to see it again—at least not today. Am I wrong?

- *Are there repetitious steps?* You select a menu item from the main menu of your application. A dialog box pops up. Hit F1 to continue. Another dialog box pops up again. Hit F1 to continue again. Ad infinitum. Get on with it already!

- *Are limits imposed on the user that are unnecessary or ridiculous?* You select the print option to print your report. The printer spits out page one. A dialog box pops up. Hit F1 to continue. The printer spits out page two. Another dialog box pops up again. Hit F1 to continue again. *Ad infinitum.* You get the idea. If not, after about the 25th page, you will.

6.5.6 Performance

- *Is the program too slow, is responsiveness sluggish, or does the program bog down and die a slow death when load is placed on the system?* Performance degradation can be caused by a variety of factors. It is the design team's responsibility to set performance standards in the design documents and the Test Team's responsibility to check them. On new systems, this testing of performance standards usually occurs and the system often initially works with flying colors; however, after being in production for a month or so, users begin to notice wait times. Perhaps testing failed to account for the additional load placed on the database server during monthly report generation times or during the monthly close of the corporate books. This happens more often than you would think and can be prevented by taking more time in the beginning of the design phase to understand how and when the application will be used.

- *Does the application support process optimization features like type-ahead or macros?* Most users salivate at the thought of having and using any type of system shortcut or time-saver they can to make their work easier. Conducting pre- and postimplementation usability studies can help ensure you have happy users on your system.

- *Is the system overloaded with graphics or features that make performance suffer?* The golden rule here is to always be conscious of the time a user needs to spend in accomplishing any given task on a system. Impeding progress by throwing up multimedia that is superfluous to accomplishment of the task is almost always viewed negatively. Do not forsake completion of basic program actions in lieu of cute graphics or helpful animations. First of all, most users will readily agree that getting the desired results tops their priority list. Second, if they lose time by allowing aesthetics to hinder the delivery of their desired results, most will tell you to forego the aesthetic changes. The best course of action is to provide users with a mechanism to choose how to prioritize their time. Then, if it takes a bit longer because they like looking at a dancing dog, they will not complain about it to you.

6.5.7 Output

- *Can all desired data be output, and can the output be directed to where the user wants?* Imagine how frustrating it would be to have a weekly commissions report generated, and you, as the Sales Manager, are looking to see who your top performer for the week is going to be. When the report generates, however, you find that sales representative names have been omitted from the report. A lot of good that report will do! Let's take this a bit further and suppose that the names were present on the report. You are so pleased with the results that you want to print it out in color and include it as part of your slide deck for the weekly meeting with your VP. What? No option for printing to a color printer? This stupid program cannot do anything I want! Helpful Hint: Remember this stupid example during the design review!

- *Is the output format adherent to a standard, or is it proprietary?* There are many standards out there to choose from: XML, RTF, SGML, HTML, and so on. Don't try to create another one without ensuring that one of these will do the job for you.

- *Is the output generated appropriate for the audience?* Use different report formats for various levels of the organization. Ideally, find a one-size-fits-all type of solution suitable for all audiences, but don't get caught asking yourself if you are absolutely certain your CEO will enjoy seeing your departmental icons embedded in his or her up-channel reports. He or she will probably *not* want to see that kind of material in reports!

- *Can output layout be changed or controlled?* In many instances, users need only a few columns of data from a report. If at all possible, design the application so users can choose which columns appear in the report and save those features to prevent having to define the same report each time they want it printed.

As you can see, there are quite a lot of factors to consider when beginning the testing process, for an application. Ideally, these considerations were first made in a design process and the Test Team is not discovering each of these examples during initial prerelease testing. If that is the case, be assured, your costs are going to skyrocket, and you will likely not hit your budget targets for this project.

So far, one of the most important points I have tried to drive home in this chapter is to make sure you and your team spend enough time during the design process to avoid these types of errors. We have only discussed User Interface type errors at this stage. Now that you know what to look for in the interface domain, let's take a look at some other types of errors and see what else we can do to salvage our project budget.

6.6 Error Handling

In this domain of testing, there are three key factors to consider: prevention, detection, and recovery. Taking adequate steps to prevent errors will certainly help ensure that you have a happy user community, but how do you prevent errors if they cannot be detected by the program before the user suffers the consequences? Have you and your team taken the time to investigate and account for every possible keystroke, input, and data type that a user could enter? Really think about this while you are still in the design phase and again during the initial development of the test plans, because it can come back to haunt you for many, many build and retest iterations. Finally, if an error does occur, what can be done to get the program back to the state of usability it was in before the error occurred?

Most of the errors found in this domain are the result of inadequate design, poor programming practices, and poor testing. Poor programming practices include coding only the method of achieving the desired results without accounting for user error, mistakes in input, validation errors, and so on. All programmers know how to develop data validation checks and usually try to put them off until they get the code working. Making data validation a requirement bumps the priority of doing this work up a notch on the list of things the programmer has to do. Poor testing is epitomized by Test Teams failing to account for these types of factors in the design and construction of the product test plans and test cases.

6.7 Boundary-Related Errors

When a program executes, the program cursor moves from one part of the program to the next, executing the coded instructions sequentially. The transition from one area to the next in the program is defined by the exit from one boundary condition and the entry into the next. This transitional state, or boundary, can include numeric, text, and operator boundaries. If the user is asked to enter a number from 1 to 99 in a program, what happens if the user enters the letter B or types in 123 instead? What if the user enters the number 84, and the system says the number is too large, prompting the user to try entering a number from 1 to 99 once again? Does the program fail to validate the input and attempt to process bad input? Have all possible boundary conditions been accounted for in design and test? Really?

6.8 Calculation Errors

An infinite number of conditions can cause calculation errors. The programmer logic may have been in error or his or her formula for the calculation may be coded incorrectly. Rounding or truncation errors can significantly alter desired results. A good design process should incorporate pseudocode for any and all calculated results to show how these formulas are intended to be implemented or used in production. Code reviews would check to see that they are indeed implemented as designed. Test cases would execute all boundary conditions against the code and verify the implementation is as rock solid as it can be before turning it over to production for general use.

6.8.1 Initial- and Later-State Errors

When a program executes subroutines and uses variables, these variables must be initialized with a default value. If this is not done specifically by the developer, it is anyone's guess as to what the value of that variable will be when first called. Remember, all of these types of errors are a result of programmers not doing the job correctly. For instance, let's assume that in the previous example there has been no variable initialization when a routine calls for a variable to increment. The program processes 50 records, incrementing the value of the variable each time the routine is executed. When the value is output at the end of processing, it should be equal to 50; however, the uninitialized variable had a value of 122 (or some other random number) and the output shown to the user is 172. This describes what constitutes an initial-state error.

To demonstrate later-state errors, consider the same situation, but instead of passing the expected value of 50 to another module to use for processing, the value of 172 is passed along. These errors are a bit harder to detect because the output from the called module is where the user thinks the error occurred. Programmers assigned to debug this problem have to trace through the execution path and follow the changing state of the variable until it is discovered to be a problem in the calling module, not the called one. The result of this is that a great deal of time and effort go into discovering a problem that was avoidable. If the user reports this from a production system, project team credibility would once again take a hit. As a program manager, you must ensure that these types of situations are prevented by facilitating adequate, in-depth discussion in the design phase.

6.9 Control Flow Errors

Previously, we stated that when a program executes, the program cursor moves from one part of the program to the next, executing the coded instructions sequentially. Some execution instructions force the program to jump from one routine to another. This movement in execution is referred to as program or control flow. When a program does something wrong in control flow, it is generally a problem with the program logic or a programmer error in coding the design. Such logic errors are often uncovered during code reviews in the implementation phase. Sometimes, in testing they are discovered by building test cases to validate program flow based on the design specifications built in the design phase and the test plans built in the implementation phase. Any of these types of errors discovered by a user when a system is in production reflects a failure of the Test Team to adequately test the product. As a Project Leader, you are ultimately responsible for preventing this situation. Try to work with the Design Team and test case developers as early in the process as possible to set proper expectations for the type of testing and the level of thoroughness you expect.

6.10 Errors in Handling or Interpreting Data

There are many ways data can become chock full of errors in a development process. Almost all of these myriad ways data can go awry are attributed to human error. These types of errors can be a result of miscalculation, errors in logic, parameter passing errors, use of incorrect data types, and so on. Almost anything a programmer can do to make a mistake can cause an error in data. The best means of preventing such errors is a continual check of logic, review of expected and actual values, review of input and output data, and so on. This is an ongoing process that involves both the user and developer.

From a user perspective, the data should be benchmarked against current means of producing the data. The user should continually review the results of output to ensure something has not run afoul and corrupted data. From the developer perspective, basic coding discipline should be enforced; range and boundary conditions need to be checked, parametric values need validation, data type validation must occur, and use of test data must be validated to be of the right format, current and in sync with production data, and usable for production output. It is always good for Team Leads to reinforce these concepts with developers and ensure that periodic code reviews take place. It is essential to team success.

6.11 Race and Load Conditions

A race condition is best defined as one event preceding another. The trick is making sure the first condition should be first or the last condition is supposed to be last. Few programmers think about or even check for race conditions. These conditions are sometimes identified only after great labor has been expended in doing traces into executable code, step by step, to see what is happening. When you hear the word *irreproducible* as testers are talking about this type of bug, interpret it to mean a possible race condition and ask if they have checked for it.

Load conditions are common and are the result of putting more work on the computer than it can bear. A simple point of illustration is having a computer process millions of records. It is the perfect job for a computer, but when the time to process each record is more than a few milliseconds, the million records to be processed can take a great deal of time. For example, let's assume an ideal situation where your application does some complex validation necessary to properly process a record and that it takes 10 milliseconds to process each of these records in a perfectly managed test environment. This translates to a processing rate of 100 records per second. Not bad, but when you divide 100 into 1 million records, you quickly find out that this job will take 10,000 seconds or 2.7 hours to run to completion. Again, this is acceptable in most cases, except that you must remember the machine is completely tied up with processing. No reports can be produced, no queries can be run, and so on. In today's modern computing environment, this is not acceptable.

Let's take another view where real-world conditions are applied. In a test environment, where the 10 milliseconds are ideal computing conditions, we will compound the problem with user interaction and system overhead. Let's look at record retrieval times and factor them into the equation. Your 10 milliseconds are now 14.5 milliseconds per record. User queries and other user interactions could easily add another 10 or so milliseconds per activity, and now we are at 25 milliseconds of processing time for just a single record. We are now looking at 6.75 hours to run the same job that ran in 2.7 hours in the test lab. The point here is that testing should account for such load conditions before release into production. If users know before kicking off a production job that it will take 7 hours to run, they can go off and do other things or run the job at night; however, if they *expect* is a 2.5-hour job, they will always be dissatisfied with performance because it is not what they expected.

6.12 Hardware Errors

Hardware issues are among the most frustrating a user can encounter. An example would be having a user choose to print a report and watch it scroll by on the screen, at a million words per second. The printer device was not specified correctly or not specified at all. The user assumed a printer would print the report, but device errors or lack of device handling caused this situation. There are many types of devices that a programmer must account for, and the testing process needs to account for user interaction on all of them. Aside from the condition cited, programs can send the wrong codes to the right device, overrun the device with data, and so on. Programmers and testers are responsible for ensuring that these conditions are accounted for and tested before the user community is exposed to them. All these types of errors can do is give you a bad mark in credibility as your users rate your performance.

6.13 Source, Version, and ID Control Errors

These types of errors are generally caused by poor configuration management and an internal lack of enforcement of existing configuration management policies and procedures. An example of this is having a new programmer insert a Beta version of code into a production stable release for a normal bug fix and then not telling anyone a change has been made in that module. Normal testing of the maintenance release will likely not catch the problem, and it may go unnoticed for several subsequent releases.

As another example, this situation could be something as insidious as a data error that shows up only when quarterly financials are produced. When there is no reason to be found as to why the company balance sheet is off by several hundred thousand dollars, much effort is expended in having senior developers perform code traces to find a problem. Someone will eventually discover that there is some Beta code in a production module that has errantly rounded everything to the nearest dollar or some other similar stupid mistake. Good intentions aside, the best cure for these types of problems is good programmer discipline for configuration management and having strong policy enforcement ingrained into an organization's corporate culture.

6.14 Testing Errors

Even testers make mistakes. They can interpret the logic of a test case improperly, misinterpret test results, fail to report glitches, and so on. Testers may forget to execute test cases or report bugs that really don't exist. These folks are human too. That means their results are also subject to questioning. When your teams have worked hard to develop something and the test results come back skewed badly one way or another, question the test process.

6.15 Test Plan Reviews

A formal review process, with participation from the users, developers, systems analysts, data analysts, and testers, will help mitigate many of these situations. According to authors Freedman and Weinberg[15], it is best for all concerned if the formal test review includes the most experienced users and developers present in an organization. Some users may not have the proper experience with a system to correctly identify problems before they occur, and this added experience can only benefit a review process. Ensure that participation in a formal test plan review is based less on the availability of user and developer personnel and more on the contributions the best-qualified developers and users can bring to the table.

This chapter has covered the testing process from the perspective of a manager having overall responsibility for the results of the testing effort. This chapter has tried to provide a big-picture overview of the most common areas in testing where deliverable systems can go awry. It has attempted to provide an arsenal of ideas and thoughts related to testing—a beginner's guide to what to look for in testing.

In the next chapter, we go beyond the testing process and delve into the next phase of the life cycle—implementation. This is where the proverbial rubber meets the road in the world of software program management. Your efforts so far have gone from the requirements stage through testing, and throughout the process you have tried to cover all the bases and do things correctly. The next chapter will give you some ideas about how to ensure you get good traction on your implementation and show you how to get off the line and deliver a winner!

6.16 Chapter 6 Review

1. Describe the cyclical process of testing.
2. What is the purpose of the Test Plan Checklist?
3. Test log entries should contain what minimal information?
4. List several types of test domains.
5. What is the most important preventive measure a Core Team can take to avoid test errors?
6. Name three key factors to address error-handling issues.
7. What is a control flow error?
8. What is a load condition?
9. Who should be included in a Test Plan Review?

7

SEP Phase VI: Implementation

The SEP Phase VI roadmap (Figure 7.1) starts with a review of the deliverables checklist. We cover the details of the deliverables checklist in the next section. For now, let's focus our attention on the roadmap. In this phase, the Core Team is responsible for developing training plans and rollout plans. What is not shown on this roadmap is the actual process of getting the system installed, started up, and into a production mode. At this point, most of the work of standing a system up falls into the hands of the IT or

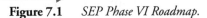

Figure 7.1   *SEP Phase VI Roadmap.*

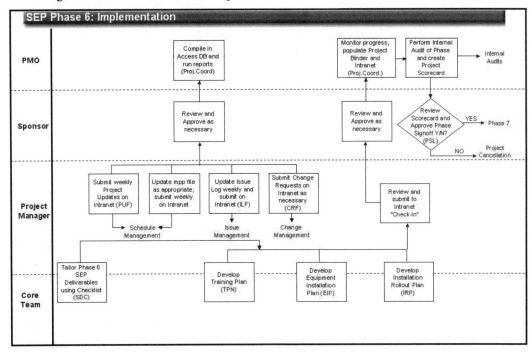

135

Figure 7.2
SEP Phase VI Deliverables Checklist.

			Comments:
☒	☐	• **Phase 6: Implementation**	
☒	☐	Training Plan	
☒	☐	Installation Rollout Plan	
		Phase Signoff Letter	
		• **Phase 7: User Support**	Comments:

MIS organization, whose responsibility it is to ensure the hardware is in place and operational. The software deliverable is usually handed off from the development and test teams to the IT organization for installation on the company premises or company-designated locations. The focus of this chapter is not on the details of the physical implementation of hardware and software, but on handling the user aspects of training and implementation at an organizational level, such as installing a new Sales Force Automation tool into the sales organization.

7.1 Review SEP Deliverables Checklist

As you can see, there is not a lot of detail in this checklist (see Figure 7.2). Three mandatory items—the Training Plan, the Installation Rollout Plan, and the Signoff Letter—are what the Core Team is responsible for accomplishing; however, do not let yourself be lulled into a false sense of security by the simplicity of this checklist. Many, many programs fall down at this point in the process. It is important to understand that the Implementation phase is a precursor to formal product handoff. During this phase, the Core Team will work with one or more predetermined rollout sites to define and implement all of the required plans for training and software transition to production status.

7.2 Develop the User Training Plan

The User Training Plan details the activities required for getting all system users trained on the new application and understanding the new work flow procedures. The plan should identify personnel training needs, and this is also where you must finalize the description of the detailed training specifications. The Core Team should develop test cases that will be used to verify the training subsystem. There should be time set aside to have all of the relevant business leaders walk through the detailed system training strategy so they are appraised of what their organization is facing when training is delivered.

The Core Team should also develop a cost-benefit analysis for the training, highlight the benefits that will result from effective training, and try to

7.2 Develop the User Training Plan

quantify them so they can be presented during the business leader walkthrough of the training program. The business leaders will certainly want to know what the estimated costs of training are and how the numbers were derived. The team should also develop a training program that is designed to evolve with the inevitable changes in the system. Finally, the Core Team will need to develop a detailed system training strategy, covering the following for each targeted audience:

- Scope and objectives
- Training methods
- Training delivery
- Training facilities
- Training materials development
- Timing, duration, sequencing, and dependencies
- Training estimates
- Hardware/software requirements

7.2.1 Scope and Objectives

Ask yourself, Who is the target audience for this software? Who will need to be trained? In most instances, the business owner can readily identify the users in his or her organization, but there are others you may want to consider. These include data analysts assigned to the project, support and administrative personnel, newcomer needing orientation, and so on. An answer must be provided to the question of whether every user in every area should be trained or just selected users in major business segments who, in turn, will train other users. This is really a question of cost.

Training is a costly proposition, and you should be aware of that fact. To train some or all users internally or externally is a calculated tradeoff between the quality of training the user will receive and the time and cost of having specific training for each user. Consider the different categories of users in your program and how many people per user category must be trained. Ask yourself if the training should be tailored to suit the specific needs of each category of user or if one training curriculum will satisfy all users. Next, ask what the level of training should be: basic, intermediate, or advanced.

7.2.2 Training Methods

Which type of training method is recommended and by whom? You have identified the audience(s) and the proper level of training for each audience. What method will be used to deliver the training? Does the method of training vary by audience? Is a hands-on approach suitable for administrative personnel or best suited for the sales team? Is the classroom approach with hands-on exercises or a self-study approach best? Should this training be done with some on-the-job coaching? If so, who should coach? What type of audiovisuals should be included in the training? How many materials are needed and what quality of production is required for these materials? Should the training be given in a formal presentation format? As tutorials? Seminars? Interactive computer-based training? Should some mechanism be put in place to obtain constructive feedback on the effectiveness of the training materials? Defining the training methods to be used helps the training team clarify what is to be done and helps members focus their efforts on delivering the right material to the right audience in the right facilities with the right equipment. When you can answer these questions about training methodology for your program, you are ready to define training delivery.

7.2.3 Training Delivery

With any system you are introducing to the user community, you should ask yourself; who should deliver the training? Your question should also ask who will give the training for the various audiences, such as the development team, the users, and other internal departmental personnel. Should the training be delivered by an internal training department or by a specialized, external training firm? Should that firm be the vendor that is supplying a commercial package? Especially in large systems, the vendor is often more than willing to charge exorbitant costs to provide such training. In many cases, this training is well worth it. As a business leader, you should decide whether the benefits of incurring such costs are appropriate for the package and the audience who will receive it. It is always wise to look to third-party training organizations that specialize in training for the package you are implementing and have your internal group develop delta coverage of what is not covered in the general training given by these third parties or software vendors. It usually works out that a hybrid solution gives the best results.

7.2.4 Training Facilities

As part of the Training Plan, the Core Team should decide what type of physical facilities will be needed to deliver the training. They should determine if these facilities are suitable to the training of staff, users, or both. The plan should outline where people will be trained. Will training be conducted in-house or given outside the organizational facilities? Will the training require the students to be in a general-purpose classroom or in a dedicated training center? Will they be in their own working environment? How many people can attend a single training session? What type of office equipment will be required to support the training process? Will other equipment be required? An overhead projector? A 35-mm slide projector? Video equipment? Whiteboards? Flip charts? It is important to be thorough and plan every detail of training. The students will represent the training you give them across the entire organization.

7.2.5 Training Materials Development

The Core Team is tasked with asking what exactly must be developed at this point to conduct the proper level of training. It is important to understand what type of documents are going to be required to train the staff. Find out if any special forms are needed. Will preassignment booklets be utilized? What type of documentation will be provided to the trainees during or after a course? Does the training require presentation transparencies, classroom notes, or other materials? Will the new user operating manuals be used during the training sessions? If so, have they been validated against the actual system implementation? Will they be printed and available for training before the system is implemented?

7.2.6 Timing, Duration, Sequencing, and Dependencies

It is important to communicate not only *how* but also *when* the training sessions will be scheduled. Determine if it is during the normal workday, weekends, after work, or whatever. If it is conducted during the normal day, who will do the work while the people are attending training? How can people be pulled from the job to train without having special accommodation for their absence made in advance? In planning for people to attend training, ask what will be the duration of the training sessions and in what sequence. Will the staff be trained at one physical location at a time? One region at a time? All at once? Do special transportation arrangements need to be made? Are there any special or unusual training dependencies between the various releases of the system?

7.2.7 Training Estimates

The Core Team must determine the total number of people to be trained and calculate an estimated level of resource consumption utilized to deliver the training. This means they must account for things like how many computer systems, training manuals, and so on will be needed. It also includes how many meals or coffee cups must be provided during training sessions. It all depends on the type and level of training provided. Other things to think about are how many people will be needed to conduct the training session, how many machine resources will be consumed, and what provisions should be made during training times for a guaranteed system response time while training people. All of these items require advanced planning and coordination. It is not as simple as throwing people in a room and preaching words of wisdom in their general direction. Real training takes real effort.

7.2.8 Hardware/Software Requirements for Training

Knowing what type of hardware equipment or software facilities are required to support or conduct the training session is essential to your success. It is crucial to know and understand what, if any, special hardware equipment will be required to train the staff. Imagine having the need for dedicated terminals, printers, plotters, automated teller machines, large-screen computer projection systems, microcomputers, or other such equipment and not having it ready when the trainees show up for class!

Equally important is the software used for training. Ask about software requirements, and determine if you need to buy software for training, or ascertain whether the new system will be used to train the staff. Will help screens be provided with the new system? If so, will the help screens be a part of the training curriculum? Would a prototype model suffice for training purposes? Does the software package offered by the vendor include a training subsystem that can be used? Is it usable or suitable to the type of training you want to give? Can some portions of the old training material be used with minor modifications? Remember that just because the vendor provides it, that does not mean it is good or adequate for your training purposes. Vendors often offer superficial coverage of items to meet contractual obligations more than to ensure you have a happy user community. It is your responsibility to get it right, so take input from all sides and make informed decisions, but make sure you make the call because of a real, valid, documented business reason and not because someone can do it for you.

7.2.9 Training Roster (TR)

The Training Roster is simply a list of all users who need to be trained. It should include their organization and a list of product modules they will be most likely to use. The Training Roster should be completed well before training is actually given and should be used as a validation of receipt of training. It is important for an organization to know who has had training because training equates to dollars. You want to help ensure the organization does not waste money training those who will not benefit or do not need training. Likewise, it is imperative to train all of those in the organization who need and will use the training. Having untrained personnel causes the organization to incur costs in terms of lost productivity, and it does not take very long for those costs to add up to a large sum of money.

7.2.10 Training Schedule (TS)

This schedule lists the occurrence of training classes for the new product. Separate schedules should be maintained for users, administrators, executives, and so on. Tailor each schedule to the needs of the audience receiving the training. Post the schedule as far in advance as possible, work with the different business organizations to pre-enroll trainees, and have the business leaders work with you to ensure that the training on the new product gets the proper level of attendance.

7.2.11 Training Signoff (TSO)

Signoff at this point is simply a letter or document from users indicating they have all been trained on the product. It is basically intended to be a formal certification that training was received. It can be used to validate training completion to business owners wanting to know who has received the training and who needs to be trained. It can also be used to help calculate final training costs. To derive this cost, you can easily divide the total cost of training by the total number of people who were trained to get a cost-per-head figure for training. This data can be useful in follow-up releases and future budgeting exercises. It can also be used as a basis of comparison for decisions about whether to have third parties conduct the training for you. It will be a benchmark for negotiations because you already know what your in-house cost for training will be.

7.3 Equipment Installation Plan (EIP)

This section describes plans for installing hardware, software, and networking equipment at user locations and training sites, and it should also include the plans for converting equipment from old systems to the new system. The Core Team should review and finalize the detailed list of the existing hardware, software, networking facilities, and equipment that will be required to develop and operate the new system in the production environment. It should conduct a formal review and finalize the list of hardware, software, networking facilities, and equipment that needs to be acquired and installed to develop and support the new system.

The task of placing orders for new hardware, software, networking equipment, and facilities required for the new system is next in this process. After the order is ready to be placed, the Core Team should finalize the acquisition strategy, place the order, and concentrate on an installation strategy. This will require a walk-through of the plan, during which the entire Core Team should comment on and try to poke holes in the strategy. It is better to do this at this stage rather than later in the process.

The Core Team will next complete a detailed description of all the major and minor hardware, software, and networking items, along with their unique characteristics. For each particular site, finalize the list of equipment and facilities that must be installed in the test or production environment. For each site, review and finalize the environmental needs in terms of the following:

- Power supply
- Temperature
- Ventilation
- Humidity
- Spacing needs for the equipment
- Electrical and communication wiring needs
- Physical security requirements
- Auxiliary furniture and system supplies

Prepare a detailed floor layout for each site, showing the exact location of where the hardware components will be installed and how they will be interconnected. The exact location for terminals, printers, and other system-interfacing devices of a similar nature should be in the layout diagram. Remember to include the exact location for the servers, disk drives, tape drives, device controllers, and the like. The exact location for the PC workstations and related peripheral equipment should be part of the layout, as well as any other network-related equipment.

Next, the team should define the detailed procedures that will be required to install the hardware, software, and networking components at each specific site. Develop the detailed hardware, software, and networking installation test cases that will be used to verify that the newly installed equipment functions properly. Describe in detail the roles and responsibilities of each group involved in the procurement and installation cycle of the hardware, software, and networking commodities.

7.4 Develop Installation Rollout Plan

As a first step in the development of the product deliverable's Installation Rollout Plan, ensure that the Core Team conducts a review of the interdependencies that might exist among the hardware, software, and networking facilities intended to be used by the system. Finalize the sequence in which these hardware, software, and networking facilities will be installed at each specific site. Provide a detailed estimate of the time it should take to install each of them, along with the expected delivery and installation dates. Special care should be given to subtle dependencies that might exist, such as the following:

- Hardware-to-hardware dependencies
- Software-to-software dependencies
- Network-to-network dependencies
- Hardware-to-software dependencies

7.5 Rollout Plan (ROP)

This plan is used by the various project teams to successfully roll out the application to all users. This plan should include timelines, special hardware and software installation requirements, any known issues to overcome or anticipate, contingency plans, and so on. Timelines should be generated for all hardware and software requirements, any known issues to overcome or anticipate, all contingency plans, and any anticipated defect removal activities that will occur. Having multiple timelines allows various teams to concentrate on the timelines that are relevant to their specific activities and not get bogged down in unrelated activities and timelines.

7.6 Rollout Schedule (RS)

The Rollout Schedule is a top-level timeline document indicating the schedule to be used for rolling out the application to all user groups. This is especially important for phased rollouts. Major activities are usually planned around the Rollout Schedule because implementation teams commonly tend to work backward from the Rollout Schedule to determine how to accomplish their tasks. It is common practice for teams to squeeze lag or lead time into a project from the top-level schedule. This is done because it is well-known in project management circles that things only go as planned on the surface. Although the duck looks like it is calm and serene on the surface, beneath the surface, imagine the duck's feet paddling as quickly as possible to keep the duck afloat and moving forward! That analogy is not unlike the project management team's shared experience.

7.7 Training and Implementation

It is time to put all of the planning and talk about what will be done into action. At this point in the process, it is time to actually have things done. Equipment should be delivered, installed, removed, and so on. Software installations, training, and so on should take place. It all comes together here. Frequent communications to the organization to build up interest and understanding of the new system should be made by the Project Sponsor and Executive Stakeholder at this point. It is time to announce this effort and its success to the rest of the organization. Also, it is a good time to single out top performers for rewards and recognition and laud the team for coming to this point. This is a high-water mark and a great milestone for your organization, so do not make the mistake of underselling its importance.

7.8 Rollout Signoff (RSO)

This is *the* document. It is obtained from the user or appropriate team member indicating that the product was successfully rolled out to all users. It is the culmination of a lot of people's hard work and should be a shared reading experience across the Core Team. Each member has contributed to the success of the project and deserves to see it formally accepted by the user community; however, the work has only just begun for those folks in the SPMO.

7.9 Chapter 7 Review

1. What are a Core Team's responsibilities during the Implementation phase?
2. What is the User Training Plan used for?
3. Why should the Core Team develop a cost-benefit analysis for training?
4. Why is it important to define the scope and objectives of a training program?
5. Why is it important to define training methods to be used before providing training?
6. What is the benefit of having a Training Roster?
7. What is the Equipment Installation Plan?
8. What dependencies should you be aware of when developing the Installation Rollout Plan?
9. What is significant about the Rollout Signoff?

8

SEP Phase VII: Support Phase

The Customer Support phase represents a formal handoff from the development team to organizational MIS or IT support. The associated documents and steps in this phase provide formal procedures for ensuring proper knowledge transfer has been completed between the two parties. First, as always, let's look at the SEP Phase VII roadmap (Figure 8.1).

Figure 8.1 *SEP Phase VII Roadmap.*

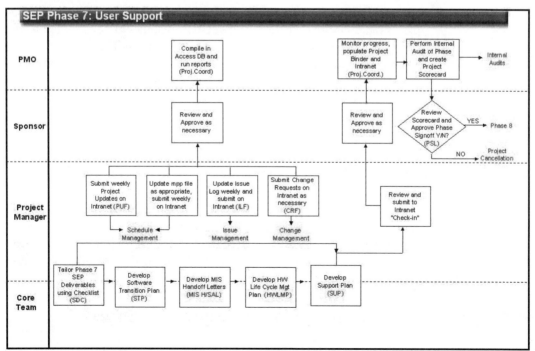

Figure 8.2
SEP Phase VII Deliverables Checklist.

			• Phase 7: User Support	Comments:
☒			Develop Software Transition Plan	
☒			Develop MIS HW/SW Handoff Letters	
☒			Develop HW Lifecycle Mgt Plan	
☒			Develop Help Desk Checklist(s)	
☒			Develop Support Plan	
☒			Phase Signoff Letter	

Six significant tasks are necessary for the Core Team to work on in this phase. Just as in every phase, the review of the deliverables checklist is first. The Phase VII Deliverables Checklist appears as Figure 8.2. We cover each of these six areas in the following paragraphs.

8.1 Software Transition Plan (SWTP)

The Software Transition Plan transitions the software from the development phase to the user support phase. It should include plans for handing off the server and user support to the appropriate departments in the organization. It is an outline of how to transfer the entire system to a state of production environment operations. The plan should verify that all of the system elements are successfully transferred into production libraries. The plan should ensure that the various system manuals are distributed to the official user and systems department representatives. The recipient of the system must turn on or stand up the production system and verify if its level of operability is adequate. Then, the system will be turned over to the users for their use. When applicable, this plan will include provisions for turning off the old system. A last step should be completion of a production systems migration report.

8.2 MIS Hardware and Software Handoff Letter

This is a letter from the MIS organization indicating it has reviewed, approved, and accepted full responsibility for both the software applications and all of the related hardware deliverables that the project team has developed and will provide ongoing support as needed to maintain it. Sometimes, this step is broken into two separate letters.

8.3 Hardware Life Cycle Management Plan

This is the plan to be used for maintaining the hardware throughout the life cycle of the application. The plan should include instructions for when and how to install recommended hardware and software upgrades, how and when to benchmark CPU utilization limits, how to determine anticipated memory usage, and so on, in order to help the MIS team make future upgrade decisions.

8.4 Develop Support Plan

A support plan outlines how problems will be handled once the software is released. The support plan should be tailored to the needs of different audiences as appropriate for the tasks they may be asked to perform. At a minimum, it is recommended that the support plan contain the following:

- Software Configuration Management Plan
- Service Level Agreements
- Help Desk Checklists

8.5 Software Configuration Management Plan (SCMP)

Once an official baseline release of the product has been made, configuration management should be implemented in all circumstances. Ideally, configuration management will have been started early on in the code development process by the developers, and transfer of the configuration management responsibility can be made from the development teams to a configuration management group. In planning for software configuration management, well-respected software engineering expert Watts Humphrey[10] recommends that your plan include several key tasks:

- Configuration control
- Change management
- Revisions
- Versions
- Deltas
- Conditional code

Configuration control begins with the establishment of a single baseline copy of the product source code. A library for the master copy of the source code should be established, and managed check-in and check-out procedures should be instituted. This single copy should be used for all subsequent builds. All changes and updates are reflected in the build. Interim checks are often established to prevent corruption of the master by requiring strict quality assurance and enforcing audit control procedures. The use of a single master for builds ensures that all changes are reflected in the latest version, and testing will account for such changes.

Change management and revision control refers in part to how modules that are checked in and out of the master source library are tracked. Generally, a release has a major version ID, a minor version ID, and a build number associated with it. It would be unwise to mix release 2.2 build 1104 with release 3.1 build 100. Although it may have no bad side effects, you cannot be sure. It is better to regenerate all modules used in major release 3 as version 3.0 baseline code and have all builds, starting with the first one, increment from that. Mixing and matching among revisions is a sure way to court disaster.

Revisions of the current working release of code will generally increment the build number. In some places, a daily build-and-test (smoke test) process is done to ensure that all code worked on to that point will still compile and execute. While these daily revisions generally increment the build number, cutovers to periodic code fixes or updates, such as quarterly maintenance releases, will usually increment the minor version ID. Changes that add significant functionality or upgrade the performance of an application will usually be done through a new release, complete with marketing collateral, advertising, and so on. These changes generally increment the major version ID.

Deltas can best be described as changed copies of the same code. The differences that exist in one of the identical code modules when compared with the original are referred to as deltas. The deltas between current and original are tracked for various reasons. Applications often need to be generated for different platforms, and one platform may require something to be done slightly differently from the other platform. Rather than creating completely different modules, sometimes it is more efficient to manage the deltas and incorporate the changes separately into the master build. Another means of solving this problem is using conditional code. Conditional code may make logic distinctions, such as comparing which version of software is running and performing one task if the version number is equal to or above a version number and another if it is below the version number.

8.6 Service Level Agreement(s) (SLA)

SLAs are most often the key to customer satisfaction in any deployment. In their book *Foundations of Service Level Management*[11], authors Sturm, Morris, and Jander provide an excellent overview of what is necessary in managing reasonable expectations between the user community and the support community. They define the SLA as a process and state that in creation of any SLA, there are four key points to keep in mind:

1. There should be equal representation from the service provider and the client.
2. The leaders of the team should be peers.
3. The members of the team should be stakeholders.
4. The team members need to be subject matter experts.

Strum et. al., point out that equality between sides is important because too many players on one side of the table can create an unfair psychological advantage. Peers are required to negotiate effectively because some people are not going to speak their minds when they feel subordinated to another person's position in the organization. Stakeholders are essential to success! Everyone must have skin in the game to succeed. Each individual representing his or her organizational unit to succeed must have a vested interest.

As this SLA creation process unfolds in an organization, the path should follow a fairly standard course. A team is assembled with representation from those who provide the service and those who expect it. The team will then assemble and a negotiation will occur among the team members. They will be required to document the negotiation and publicize it. Finally, a decision will be required in order to designate an administrator of the SLA. Now, let's take a look at how this works.

Assembling the team is the first step. Remember the key point made previously about equal representation. Generally, it is best if this representation is limited to three or four people from each side. Too few participants and the decisions made will not be respected because you will be perceived as having done the work in a vacuum. Too many participants and you will never get a decision because it will be impossible to gain a consensus on anything.

Before negotiations begin, start doing your homework. Come to the table prepared to discuss costs, metrics, performance standards, and industry-standard expectations for the type of deliverable that is to be supported. Remember that in a negotiation, both sides must leave the table feeling good about the agreement or it is doomed to fail. Do not push unreasonable expectations on the opposite side of the table. Demands are never acceptable because they are almost never met. When something is asked for, it should be substantiated with costs, metrics, data from industry standards, and so on. It is important to show that you are trying to have things established to adhere to a benchmark that all parties can agree is best for the business.

8.7 Components of an SLA

The basic elements in an SLA comprise the contract that is established between the users and the support team. These basic elements of the agreement are as follows:

I. Parties to the Agreement
II. Term of the Agreement
III. Scope of the Agreement
IV. Limitations
V. Service Level Objectives
VI. Service Level Indicators
VII. Nonperformance
VIII. Optional Services
IX. Exclusions to the Agreement
X. Reporting Procedures
XI. Administration Process
XII. Reviews
XIII. Revisions
XIV. Approvals

8.7 Components of an SLA

The Parties to the Agreement section of the SLA should simply identify who is providing the support services and who is expecting to receive the support services. The length of time the agreement is in effect is referred to as the term. The term is generally for one or two years at a time and is often set up to be renewable. Because technology changes so rapidly, renewable term conditions in an SLA are not recommended. This allows both sides an opportunity to come back to the negotiating table and reassess the SLA based on new input data.

The Scope section defines the services that are to be provided in the agreement. This is the section where you specify exactly what is supported, by whom, and when the support is expected to be rendered. For each application or piece of hardware, have a separate paragraph. This helps when technology changes or makes something obsolete and you want the SLA to remain in effect. You simply amend the relevant paragraph found in the scope section of the SLA by striking it and adding a new paragraph for the new equipment or software.

The Limitations paragraph is meant to clarify or place caveats on the level of support that is to be rendered within the scope of the SLA. These conditions or caveats are designed to protect the support team from being subjected to coverage of an SLA for any and all conditions imaginable. For example, if software performance were being measured based on response time, a part of the Limitations section may confine the terms of the SLA to performance under normal load conditions of 500 concurrent users, with a maximum of 750 users. Beyond that level of 750 users, the software named specifically in the Scope section of the SLA cannot be guaranteed to be operational by the support group.

The Objectives section is the part of an SLA that most people refer to when talking about SLAs. This is where levels of service are identified and defined. This includes measures of accuracy, number of users (as cited earlier), availability, volume, speed, response time, performance, timing, and so on. This section is where criteria are benchmarked and determined to be the standard to which the support team must adhere to as part of the agreement. Often, it is recommended that two standards, expected and minimum, are defined for each criteria in the Objectives section. The next section, Indicators, is used to define how these Objectives are measured or recorded.

The Nonperformance section of the SLA is where the stipulations of what happens when the support group fails to meet the objectives of the SLA will be found. If performance of the support team is such that objectives of the SLA fail to be met, this section will define what remedy occurs, at what point, and by whom. The consequences of failure on the part of the support team are negotiated in advance in this section. Recourse for the group receiving support is spelled out here. Both sides must agree that such consequences are fair and reasonable, or this section is meaningless. The penalty for nonperformance should be measured in terms of equal effect to the impact such nonperformance had on the group expecting support. Do not allow one side or the other to be treated too lightly or too strongly in this section. Remember that meaningful contracts mean having a goal of fair-mindedness and equity achieved on both sides of the negotiating table.

The Optional Services section would be where definitions of activities performed outside the normal scope of operations are added. This may include activities performed only occasionally, such as year-end close of the company books, where system availability may be required over weekends, holidays, and so on. This section would allow such situations to be spelled out and prevent surprises. It is often hard to think of such issues when first negotiating an SLA, but when doing so, try to look at operational issues for an extended period and determine what activities may require entries in the Optional Services section.

Reporting, administration, reviews, revisions, and approvals are all part of an overall SLA life cycle process. These activities revolve around communicating performance or nonperformance issues regarding the SLA to the organization, administering the SLA when situations arise where expectations are not met or unreasonable demands for support are made, providing periodic review of the SLA to ensure it is suitable to the current business environment, and making revisions as necessary to bring the SLA current with changing conditions. Approvals are required to effect such revisions and ensure the SLA is fair to all parties involved.

Books have been devoted to the development and administration of SLAs. Software exists that is focused entirely on SLA maintenance and administration. Volumes of data could be written about the details of SLAs, but the most important thing to remember is that it must be negotiated, fair, measurable, and have some level of accountability for nonperformance. It must be subject to periodic review and must go through an approval process. Otherwise, it is not worth the paper it is written on. You should never accept an SLA as valid or binding if the items defined in it cannot be benchmarked against some standards and subsequently measured against that benchmark to evaluate your performance. If that is the situation you are facing, it is definitely time to sit down and revise that SLA to something more reasonable. SLAs are often written without the proper level of participation or negotiation from the support groups, and unreasonable expectations are set (unintentionally, in most cases). The support group may try to uphold such expectations in good faith, but they are doomed to failure because the expectations are set higher than are reasonable. The support team, working as hard as they possibly can, will bear the brunt of much criticism, and it will be unwarranted because expectations were not reasonable.

8.7.1 Help Desk Checklist

This checklist identifies the type of customer support that the Help Desk may need to provide. It is intended to assist in preparing the organizational support team for handling questions or problems regarding the use of the product or deliverable. The checklist should be broken down into functional categories and common questions that have been gleaned from training classes. Issues that have been identified during the testing process should be documented and made available to the support staff. These items will be supplanted with other knowledge obtained by the support staff as the calls are handled. It is also a good idea to consider using a Help Desk software package that can preload such scenarios to save time for the support agent. Software that can readily access support data by functional categorization is most useful and will save the organization money. An example of this would be as follows:

```
OS - Linux | SFA Product - Acme | Contacts Screen |
Address Section | State Field | no selection |
1-patch 4.32 available
```

The support software used by the support agent would display these as filtered selections. In this case, the operating system is Linux. While running the Sales Force Automation software (whatever your company bought), the Contacts entry screen Address field will not display the state the contact lives in. As the user reported the problem, the support agent was making selections from a menu-driven application that narrowed the problem down to what was stated above. Ideally, the support software would inform the agent that a patch is available to fix the problem, and the agent could relay that information to the user.

8.8 Phase Completion Approval Signoff Completed

This is the last step in the evolution of the project. In reality, when this signoff is completed, it signals the end of the program. Technically, the

SPMO will maintain all documentation and history of the project until this deliverable has served its purpose and is shelved or replaced by another. When that happens, the SPMO will have the Project Sponsor or Executive Stakeholder place the final nail in the coffin by signing this Phase Completion Signoff. Doing so kicks off the final process in the SEP life cycle, Project Closeout, which is discussed in the next chapter.

8.9 Chapter 8 Review

1. To a development team, what is significant about the Support phase?
2. What are the six key tasks the Core Team must complete during the Support phase?
3. What is a Software Transition Plan?
4. What purpose does the MIS Hardware/Software Handoff Letter serve?
5. What are the three key sections every Support Plan should contain?
6. Define change management.
7. What is configuration control?
8. What key points should you remember when creating an SLA?
9. List the basic components of an SLA.
10. What is a Help Desk Checklist used for?

9

SEP Phase VIII: Project Closeout

Project Closeout is the final step in drawing the project to a close. Now, let's take a moment and, as always, review the SEP Phase VIII roadmap (Figure 9.1). In the Completion phase, you will perform all actions necessary to end project work and review project management performance. The post-mortem meeting and its corresponding report should provide an effective

Figure 9.1 *SEP Phase VIII Roadmap.*

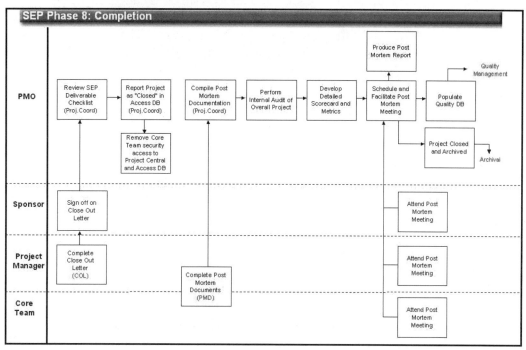

means to reflect on lessons learned and battles won (and lost). It should be used to improve on the overall process for future projects.

9.1 Disposition Phase

Disposal actions should be implemented to either eliminate a large part of a system or close down a system and end the life cycle process. The system in this phase has been declared surplus and/or obsolete and is or will be scheduled for shutdown. The chief emphasis of this phase will be to ensure that data, procedures, and documentation are packaged and archived in an orderly fashion, making it possible to reinstall and bring the system back to an operational status, if necessary, and to retain all data records in accordance with corporate policies regarding retention of electronic records.

The Disposition phase represents the end of the system's life cycle. It is usually initiated by the SPMO when a product is ready to be replaced or taken offline. A Disposition Plan should be prepared to address all facets of archiving, transferring, and disposing of the system and data (as described previously). Particular emphasis shall be given to proper preservation of the data processed by the system so that it is effectively migrated to another system or archived in accordance with applicable records management regulations and policies for potential future access. The system disposition activities preserve information not only about the current production system but also about the evolution of the system through its life cycle.

The objectives for all tasks identified in this phase are to retire the system, software, hardware, and data. The tasks and activities actually performed depend on the nature of the project. The disposition activities are performed at the end of the system's life cycle. The disposition activities ensure the orderly termination of the system and preserve vital information about the system so that some or all of it may be reactivated in the future if necessary. These activities may be expanded, combined, or deleted, depending on the size of the system.

9.2 Disposition Plan

The objectives of the Disposition Plan are to end the operation of the system in a planned, orderly manner and to ensure that system components and data are properly archived or incorporated into other systems. This will include removing the active support by the operations and maintenance organizations. The users will need to play an active role in the transition. All concerned groups will need to be kept informed of the progress and target dates. The decision to proceed with disposition will be based on recommendations and approvals from the BROC or based on a date (or time period) specified by the SPMO.

This plan will include a statement of why the application is no longer supported, a description of replacement/upgrade, a list of tasks/activities (transition plan) with estimated dates of completion, and the notification strategy. Additionally, it will include the responsibilities for future residual support issues: identification of media alternatives if technology changes; new software product transition plans; alternative support issues (once the application is removed); parallel operations of retiring and the new software product; archiving of the software product, associated documentation, movement of logs and code; and accessibility of archive, data protection identification, and audit applicability. Finally, the plan should include the five closeout actions listed in the next section.

9.3 Closeout Actions

Before closing out the project, some housecleaning activities need to be accomplished. In order to properly end the program and terminate the activities supporting the product, you should complete these actions:

1. Produce a written Software Project History containing both objective and subjective information about the project.
2. Distribute the project history to all project members.
3. Place Project History conclusions into the project binder for review when working on the next project.
4. Conduct a postmortem meeting and report all results and findings.
5. Complete all closeout paperwork.

When you write the Software Project History document, a good place to start is with the compiling all of the project status meeting notes and minutes into a chronological record of events. Remember to document concerns, decisions, and contentious items that occurred in the meeting. It is always good to reflect back on areas that caused strong feelings and try to evaluate why those feelings were expressed. You should gather all of the reports, written opinions, and so on and try to create a thorough history that reflects what you and the Core Team know to be the events that have occurred.

9.4 Postmortem Meeting Report

A postmortem meeting must be held at the end of the project. Explore all phases of SEP and ask what went well and try to learn what could have gone better. What should be changed or improved for the next project? Through answers to these questions your organization may save a lot of money by learning to prevent things from negatively affecting project outcomes. This is also a time for the SPMO to reflect on the overall administration of the program and to determine if changes are needed in administration or policy at the SPMO level.

9.5 Close-out Paperwork (COP)

This consists of all pertinent paperwork needed to verify that closure activities have been performed. These items can include receipts for returned equipment or disposal receipts, all project status reports, closeout review minutes, finalized or closed contracts, and so on. Essentially, everything associated with the project should be assembled here and prepared for archive processing. The Closeout Letter formally announces the closure of a project, so that all groups and people know that the project has been completed and the product has been phased out. This is also a good way to thank everyone involved and communicate final project statistics.

9.6 Archiving the Project

This can be done in many ways, but the most common today is to simply place everything onto a CD-ROM and store the CD in the SPMO. The CD lasts as long as any media known today and is easily copied if someone requests information on the project. One caveat, however, is to ensure that no corporate security risk is posed by creating a CD that may contain sensitive corporate data. If the CD does contain that type of data, it is a responsibility of the SPMO to protect it. Access to the CD and distribution of it to anyone in the company must be controlled as any other sensitive corporate material, even if the project is closed. A lot of valuable corporate espionage information can be gleaned from the data making up an entire project. Be safe and sensible about the risk and try to protect your organization as much as possible.

9.7 Closeout Ritual

This involves a party or some other type of ritual. During this activity, there will be ample opportunity for all persons involved in the project to be recognized and rewarded. It is good practice to seek out those "shadow people" who worked on the project and recognize them. They are the folks who work behind the scenes to make the project work. Without them, there would be no chance for success, but they do not individually stand out among the Core Team or other business leaders. They are always there, doing their part, however large or small. These folks are the backbone of the company in most cases, and your success—whether you know it or not—nearly always depends in large part on their performance. Don't always reward the stars and forget the rest. They may not work so hard for you in the future if you ignore them. A little bit of recognition can go a long way in boosting esteem and morale. It also is a reflection of your leadership to show that credit can be shared. You know the old adage, "If the project fails, you take the heat. If it succeeds, share the glory with those around you." Leadership 101.

9.8 Chapter 9 Review

1. Why is the postmortem report necessary?
2. When closing out a project, what five actions must be completed by the Core Team?
3. What purpose does a postmortem report serve to the SPMO?
4. What is the purpose of continuing to restrict access to project materials after a project has been closed?
5. Who initiates the disposition phase?
6. What is meant by the term *shadow people*?

10

Project Wizardry 101

What follows are some considerations that project leaders should be aware of when managing any effort. There are some painful lessons learned along the way during the career of Project Managers, and there is little need to repeat those painful experiences. Lessons and techniques presented in this chapter are based on many years of project management experience. This information should be taken as a subjective point of view from someone who has been there and done that.

10.1 External Factors That Dictate Success

There are many reasons for a project to fail. At every turn, throughout the project's life cycle, issues crop up that can stop the show. Good project management skills are fundamental when working in today's harried business environment. Pressures from many points in the organization—such as sales staff complaining about contact management software, revenue booking procedures, customer support procedures, and so on—all provide pressures on an in-progress project. There are expectations from each of these organizations as to how this project will solve their problems and make life better. Underlying these expectations is the assumption that you, as manager of the project, will fix everything that impedes complete success, right? The next few sections, will present some techniques to help you achieve the level of success that the business needs to obtain from your project implementations.

10.2 Business Reasons for the Project

For any project, there must be valid justification (i.e., a good business reason) to go forward and make it successful. The problem that many Project Managers face, however, is seeing eye to eye with users on the business fit for a project. Sometimes, this is a very easy task, and the business reasons are readily apparent; however, there are often situations when a business unit leader may not see eye to eye with the project leader on the business fit. For example, the EVP of sales at Company X believed their current sales booking software was too cumbersome and said it prevented his sales force from booking revenue properly. The VP of IT saw the problem as one of capacity and felt like additional hardware and bandwidth would fix the problem more than implementing new software. The CEO, who was always open to ways to get more revenue in the door, wondered if the solution could be found in taking both of these actions.

In this case, the perception of revenue booking being hindered had driven answers from the executive leadership that failed to account for the real problem, which turned out to be a lack of adequate training for the sales force in using the software. In this particular situation, the company could have spent several million dollars upgrading hardware and software, and, in the end, would have accomplished nothing. The key point here is that before you find the reason for the problem, know what the problem is—then worry about fixing the right problem. In the aforementioned situation, the leadership concluded that the problem to be fixed was something that turned out to be entirely wrong. Let's see if we can find ways to avoid that situation by understanding this process a bit better.

10.2.1 Where Is the Business Fit?

The first step in determining business fit is to understand the problem completely. It is literally impossible to solve a problem that is not understood. This means it is incumbent on you, as the project leader, to ask questions—lots of questions. Each project is different, but some things are constants. For example, it is almost always true that visiting with the end users—the folks in the trenches, so to speak—will reveal loads more than hearing the business unit leader sum the problem up for you. Don't hesitate to take time to find root causes for problems that have been reported. The solution obtained from those in the trenches is often very different from what is postulated by those standing over the trenches.

Once you have made the trek to the trenches and discovered what people working on the problem have to say about it, you are better informed in the decision-making process. This information will often drive decision making in a different direction and enable more focused effort at solving the problem. Once you have identified the root cause, you are now able to take that issue and tie it to a true business justification for the proposed solution.

10.2.2 How Business Fit Influences Project Success

In the previous scenario, the solution of training sales staff to use the software properly was certainly a more cost-effective approach than retrofitting a new package to the problem. It also solved the problem in a fraction of the time. While this example seems simplistic, the lesson it teaches is important. Know what the problem is before you go fix it. Once you are absolutely sure the right problem has been identified, then identifying a solution is much easier. It is also a significant factor in project success. If you fix the right problem, the situation is corrected and everyone is happy. In the aforementioned scenario, proper training of sales force staff eliminated the need to spend lots of money on hardware and software, consultants, and training on a new product. Wizardly advice–knowing which problem to solve is key to success.

10.3 Project Customers

In the simplest terms, a project's customers are defined as the beneficiaries of the project implementation. They are the ones that directly receive the benefits of all the effort of putting the project into an organization's infrastructure. Often, they are called users. At the same time, they also receive the negative effects of a project, and you can bet they will not be shy in telling you about those negative factors. Because they are so directly affected by the project, it is wise to include them in every aspect of the identification of the root cause, the determination of a solution that meets the needs of a good business fit, and the overall planning, design, and testing of the solution. Without their participation at each of these critical junctures, the likelihood of the project going south increases significantly.

10.4 Project Objectives

This is an important step to success. Defining the objectives is probably the single most important factor that can mitigate risk and ensure success. This definition can only come when the root cause of the problem is identified. The best approach to defining project objectives is to go back into the trenches and have the user community identify subject-matter experts (SMEs) and empower them to outline what the project objectives should achieve. Once these objectives are identified, the process of ensuring that each objective fits a business need is started. For every stated objective, there should be a direct tie to satisfaction of a legitimate business need. If that cannot be done, the objective should be brought up to the team as a questionable necessity and discussed. For all those objectives that are directly tied to business need, the process will continue into the requirements analysis phase. The key points to remember about objectives are that they need to be clearly articulated by the folks who are closest to the source of problems, and they need to be tied directly to a legitimate business need.

10.5 End-State Visions

This is sometimes referred to as the "to be" state of the project. This is where many Project Managers spike themselves by painting the rosy cheeks, blue skies, and happiness vision that is almost never the case. When defining the end state, it is important to keep the descriptions at a process level. Taking it to any other level invites trouble. Process descriptions are less colorful, but they keep the focus on what the process will be and not what expectations should come of that. This is an important distinction, because many things are often attributed to items in a project that are next to impossible to deliver. Focusing on process keeps things at a level that can be documented, observed, measured, and communicated.

It is impossible to predict whether implementing new software will increase profits or create customer satisfaction. It is possible to say that implementing new software will change Process A from this current state to that found in Process B. The effect of the change can be measured if the old process is baselined before the project starts. The new process can be compared to the baseline, and the differences can be used to make inferences about the performance of the product. Making comparisons in any other fashion is just not an apples-to-apples comparison and is meaningless.

10.6 Making Success a Team Effort

In the modern technology environments of today's businesses, there are no one-person shows. Teamwork is essential at all levels because the sophistication of business processes and technology surpasses the capabilities of a single individual. For a project to be successful, the selection of a team is an essential skill. More about teamwork and team composition will be discussed later in this chapter. The key message here is that a project should never be attempted without forming a Core Team that consists of representation from the user community and other business units across the organization. Core Teams are an essential, gating factor to success. Enlightened Project Managers intuitively know that teams can be the determining factor to their success, and they are careful to scrutinize the composition and representation of a team early on in the project process. It is the project leader's role to properly empower and motivate the team members to do their respective parts in the project effort to make it succeed.

10.7 Building Customer Confidence

When a baby begins to learn to walk, it starts out learning to stand, keep balanced, look where it wants to go, and take baby steps. The baby will often fall down. It gets up and tries again and again until it walks. Project Managers do not have the luxury of falling down and trying over and over again until they get it right. They are expected to know how to prevent themselves from falling down and are rarely afforded a second chance if they do fall. One thing they have learned over time is to control risk, take calculated steps that are measured in terms of milestones, and decompose the larger task at hand into chunks that can be observed by the user or customer. As the customer sees the project arrive at and surpass these milestones, confidence is slowly gained in the project leader's ability to deliver the goods. The more milestones are achieved, the more confidence is gained. On top of the achievement of milestones, the project leader must be able to effectively communicate the achievements to the customer in a way the customer will understand.

Generally, when the customer is involved through adequate representation in the Core Team, this becomes a process of status updates and progress meetings. As the project nears the next milestone in the plan, the customer attempts to hold the project leader to the target of completion, regardless of the state of the project. This places great pressure on a project leader to hit targets and communicate any deviations well in advance of the meeting. Ideally, the project leader will see and mitigate such factors before they become burning issues, but sometimes it is out of his or her control.

For example, I once led a project that was very tightly scheduled, and it wound up being delayed by two weeks; a computer manufacturer failed to deliver the necessary equipment on time because it was heavily back-ordered. Only by forcing them to deliver equipment of lesser capability on a loaner basis until our proper equipment arrived was I able to keep the project from falling even farther behind. The point here is that sometimes, despite the best plans and intentions, things are just out of your control and you will have to get creative to keep your project on track. Wizardly advice—be ready to adjust, adapt, and overcome.

10.8 Choosing a Development Strategy

I certainly would not advocate using a hammer to put a thumbtack in a wall. Likewise, with project deliverables, it is often not necessary to constitute a full-blown project team and incur the additional costs for implementing something simple. Of course, you want standardized processes to be followed, you want to be able to account for all resources and expenses, and you want to know that the job will get done correctly. There is a middle ground. It is unreasonable to hold the development of a simple utility to sort business records to the same level of scrutiny that you would the implementation of a new expense-processing module in your financial system. Is it possible to use the same processes, even at a generalized level, to accomplish both tasks? Yes! It is done by using project tailoring techniques, which are explained later in this chapter.

10.9 Software Development Life Cycle (SDLC) Models

There are lots of SDLC models to choose from. My belief is that the model presented in this book will satisfy almost any type of project whose scope is more than a trivial effort. While some advocate the need to choose a model for a project, I have found that the project is better off adhering to the chosen model. As I stated earlier in this book, the SEP model may not be the only game in town, but it is one of the most venerable. Why would there be reason to deviate from this model? My answer is that there is very little reason for a project leader ever to do so—leave that to the SPMO itself. Adoption of the SDLC Model, for example, over the SEP process described herein is a matter of choice for an organization's SPMO leadership to make, not a project leader. I find the two systems so closely aligned that there is really very little difference. There are, of course, other models too. My point is that as long as all of the tasks required in this book are accomplished, by whatever model, the SPMO can select and use the model that best suits its business needs.

10.9.1 How to Identify the Right Model

From an SPMO perspective, selection of the SDLC model should involve a review of the types and scope of projects undertaken. If most projects average $1 million or more in costs, then SEP is appropriate. On the other hand, if most projects cost $25,000, it may be wise to modify the SEP or select another SDLC to suit the scope of effort. This is a business-tailoring process that should not be taken lightly because the costs of choosing the wrong model, or using the SEP to overengineer a process, are very high. The SEP is designed to take small and large projects and tailor them to suit the business need. In some organizations, however, I recognize that SEP may be a drag on resources because the process piece of SEP must be enforced by the SPMO in order to be effective. In organizations where the order of the day is small, nimble projects with small scope, my recommendation is to tailor, at the SPMO level, the SEP to streamline everything that seems to be unnecessary to your specific business. Be careful about trimming indiscriminately, however. Remember, everything you find in the SEP is there for a reason.

10.10 Setting Expectations: Staged Deliveries

The decomposition of a project into tasks, milestones, and phases is a crucial factor to success. The project leader must be able to take a step back, look at a project from an "out of the weeds" perspective, and decide how to break it down. The project team will assist, of course, but the ultimate responsibility for this rests firmly on the shoulders of the project leader. The SEP breaks the project into clearly identifiable stages, or phases, as they are called. Using the SEP will help the project leader decompose the tasks in each phase into something that can be tracked by the entire organization. It minimizes risk because everything is brought down to a level that is manageable for that particular phase. When project leaders communicate to their organizations the status of projects, using the phases and milestones described in the roadmaps can be of great assistance. The organization has expectations that each milestone will be met, and that is what they will use to track your success.

10.11 Rapid Application Development (RAD)

RAD is a valuable tool when used to help users see the "to be" state of a project. I have often found mock-ups of user interfaces and process flows to be extremely beneficial. RAD tools enable developers to quickly create such mock-ups without worrying about how it all works behind the scenes. They can simulate that part using canned data or fabricated results. RAD tools facilitate expectations users will have of an end product. During the design phase, I recommend having SMEs work directly with the design team to create their interfaces—the developers easily modify and build such elements, and there is nothing more satisfying to a user group than saying they got exactly what they wanted in the project design. RAD is discussed a bit more later in this Chapter.

10.12 Alternative SDLC Work Patterns

An important objective of an SDLC methodology is to provide flexibility that allows tailoring of the methodology to suit the characteristics of a particular system development effort. One methodology does not fit all sizes and types of system development efforts. For instance, it is not reasonable to expect a very small system development project to produce 35 deliverables. However, a different approach might be needed for a high-risk system development project that has very uncertain functional and technical requirements at the beginning of development. Therefore, the SEP methodology provides for a full sequential SDLC work pattern and for alternative SDLC work patterns. It also provides a work pattern to accommodate the acquisition and implementation of a commercial off-the-shelf (COTS) product. In the standard SEP methodology, from the Initiation phase through the Closeout phase, this process is termed a full sequential work pattern, which creates the maximum number of deliverables.

During the Planning phase, the Project Manager evaluates the documentation of the system concept, as contained in supporting documentation, and determines if the standard SEP methodology should be used or if an alternative work pattern should be selected instead. The selection of work patterns is based on the selection criteria and the judgement of the involved management. In general, the full sequential work pattern is used (1) if the development type is new or a large modification, (2) if the system development size is large, (3) if the associated mission is critical, (4) if the system development risks are normal or high, and (5) if the complexity of the system development effort is normal or high.

In the full sequential work pattern, a project is divided into phases; the phases are conducted sequentially, and the initiation of each phase depends on a decision to continue that is made during a formal review near the end of the immediately preceding phase. This work pattern reflects a desire to follow a conservative approach to project management.

10.13 Other Alternative Work Patterns

Alternative work patterns provide flexibility for the SEP methodology. An alternative work pattern permits a project planner to tailor a project management plan to meet the specific needs of the project and still conform to

10.13 Other Alternative Work Patterns

SEP standards. Alternative work patterns provide the opportunity for the Core Team and related specialists to predefine the permitted tailoring and to ensure that a project planner's customization does not overlook necessary activities or include unneeded ones. The alternative work patterns suggested are as follows:

- Reduced-effort work pattern
- Rapid Application Development (RAD) work pattern
- Pilot development work pattern
- Managed Evolutionary Development (MED) work pattern
- Operations and maintenance (O&M) small-effort enhancement work pattern
- O&M project work pattern
- Commercial off-the-shelf (COTS) acquisition

The following are operational definitions for terms associated with these types of projects:

- *Proof of concept:* A project that defines what will be proven and determines both the criteria and methods for the proof of concept. Once the proof of concept is demonstrated, a prototype project may be initiated.
- *Prototype:* An ensemble that is suitable for the evaluation of design, performance, and production potential and is not required to exhibit all the properties of the final system. Prototypes are installed in a laboratory setting and are not installed in the field; nor are they available for operational use. They are maintained only long enough to establish technical feasibility.
- *Proof of technical feasibility:* The result of a successful prototype.
- *Pilot:* A system installed in the field to demonstrate that the system's concept is feasible in an operational environment. The pilot system installed has a predetermined subset of functions and is used by a bounded subset of the user population. Its features may not all function smoothly. The goal of the pilot is to provide feedback that will be used to refine the final version of the product. The pilot will be

fielded for a preset, limited period of time only to permit pilot systems to be evaluated for operational feasibility.

- *Proof of operational feasibility:* The result of a successful pilot.
- *Production:* A fully documented system, built according to the SEP, fully tested, with full functionality, accompanied by training and training materials, and with no restrictions on its distribution or duration of use.

10.14 Alternative Work Pattern Selection

During the Planning phase, the Project Manager evaluates the project statement and High-Level Solutions Document and uses the criteria for selecting either the full sequential work pattern or an alternative work pattern. This section proposes some criteria for selecting an alternative work pattern. (Note: Criteria for selection may not be mutually exclusive [e.g., complexity and size because size] may be a factor of complexity.)

Determine the type of system development:

- New development
- Modification or enhancement of existing system
- Prototype system
- Procurement of a COTS system
- O&M small-scale enhancement
- O&M project

Determine the cost of the system development project using the following guidelines:

- *Class 1:* Very large projects with estimated development or life cycle costs of more than $20 million
- *Class 2:* Large projects with estimated development or life cycle costs between $10 million and $20 million
- *Class 3:* Midsize projects with estimated development or life cycle costs between $2.5 and $10 million

- *Class 4:* Small projects with estimated development or life cycle costs between $500,000 and $2.5 million
- *Class 5:* O&M enhancements with estimated life cycle costs less than $500,000

Determine mission criticality of the proposed system development effort: Most critical (C1) to non–mission critical (C5).

Determine the risk of inability to achieve the project objectives from highest (R1) to lowest (R4), based on one or more of the following:

- Risk due to high uncertainty associated with the system's requirements, the technology that the system will employ, or the way that the system will affect the SEP's business process
- Risk due to highly compressed development time (low turnaround time) because of an emergency or legal, business, or political requirements
- Risk due to high visibility resulting from public or political attention or requirements

Determine the complexity of the system development effort from highest (E1) to lowest (E3), based on one or more of the following:

- The project affects many organizations or functional areas within an organization, thus adding a level of difficulty regarding the definition of requirements.
- The project results from business process reengineering, dramatically altering the use of information technology.
- The project requires new or rapidly advancing technology.
- The project requires a long time for development.

10.15 Alternative Work Pattern Descriptions

The subsequent sections provide descriptions for each alternative work pattern, including tasks and activities, required deliverables, and reviews for each relevant phase. Deliverables for alternative work patterns are often created, revised, and finalized across multiple life cycle phases, as with the full sequential work pattern.

Reduced-Effort (Small Application Development) Work Pattern

A reduced-effort work pattern combines some phases, eliminates some of the deliverables otherwise required, and combines some of the reviews to reduce project formality in those situations where a conservative approach is not necessary.

Rapid Application Development (RAD) Work Pattern

In the RAD work pattern, the Initiation and Planning phases are conducted according to the full sequential work pattern. The Requirements Analysis and Design phases are iteratively conducted, using prototyping tools to rough out and incrementally improve the understanding of requirements through a series of design prototypes. The Functional Requirements Document and the System Design Document are started at the beginning of this activity, but are not completed until the end of the Design phase; these documents use, as much as is possible, the outputs of the prototyping tool to create this documentation. In the process, an initial set of requirements is used to create an initial version of the application, giving users visibility into the look, feel, and navigation capabilities of the application. User evaluation and feedback provide revisions to the statements of requirements, and the process is repeated—always involving the user.

Typically, three cycle iterations will result in a completely understood set of requirements, but the iteration process can continue until successive differences in requirements are so small as not to be noticeable. Following the completion of design prototyping, a full sequential work pattern is again engaged to accomplish the Development, Integration, Test, and Implementation phases. The only deviation is the possibility of using some of the generated code from the design prototype to start the development process.

Pilot Development Work Pattern

In a pilot development work pattern, either a full sequential work pattern or a RAD work pattern is used to go from the Initiation through the Development phases. Decisions regarding full deployment of the application are held until after field trials and evaluations have proven the concept because of the risk involved in the complexity, visibility, and uncertainty of the project. The field trials and evaluations accomplish portions of user acceptance testing and implementation; after they are complete, possibly requiring one or more years, the remainder of implementation is completed. This means that migration to the Support phase is possibly deferred for more than a year.

Managed Evolutionary Development (MED) Work Pattern

The U.S. Patent and Trademark Office developed and documented the MED methodology[16]. The MED approach is particularly suited to situations where existing business processes will be altered considerably and where the full set of detailed functional requirements cannot be reliably defined early in the development life cycle. The MED discipline supports iterative definition, development, and deployment of subsystems by defining system-level functional and data requirements and a modular system architecture, which allows for subsequent refinement, development, and deployment of subsystems that can evolve to meet future business needs. A particular release level containing partial, but incomplete, functionality is often referred to as a build. During the Planning and Requirements Analysis phases, an entire series of successive builds is planned, each of which gets designed, developed, tested, and implemented.

MED Incremental and Evolutionary Strategies. The MED-based development process combines an evolutionary development strategy with incremental delivery. System development using MED proceeds by defining a bounded vision of a future system and then iteratively refining the reengineered business processes, information system requirements, and technical architecture. The incremental delivery strategy within MED is used to encapsulate part of the overall system as a subsystem to be built and deployed. Subsystems are constructed when there is sufficient confidence that they will provide a cohesive, user-validated set of business functionalities. As usage experience is obtained, lessons learned are fed back into each subsystem, improving each in subsequent versions of the system.

MED Program Management. The Planning phase is where the Project Manager, with approval of the sponsor, determines that the functional requirements will best be fulfilled by assigning them to distinct, but functionally related, subsystems. The Requirements Analysis phase will be split into a Systems Requirements Analysis phase to define overall system requirements and architecture and a Subsystem Requirements Analysis phase for detailed definition of each subsystem. At the completion of the Requirements Analysis phase, each subsystem begins its own branch of the life cycle to define a target subsystem architecture, business process, and requirements.

Risk Management within the Context of MED. The order in which a MED-based work pattern proceeds is heavily influenced by risk. MED is designed to focus explicitly on the development decisions around risk derived from uncertainty about the target system in the areas of business process, system requirements, technical architecture, cost, and schedule. This risk management strategy addresses two fundamental time-related risks of uncertainty and dependence. Uncertainty is reduced by acting on gathered information, such as from prototypes, simulations, studies, or models; dependence is eliminated by structuring parts of the system to be independently deployed as subsystems. To accomplish this goal, the Project Manager must define the target system. This consists of determining the system boundaries, specifying the target characteristics, assessing system risks and defining and executing risk mitigation activities, and developing subsystems, which is done as a project within the overall program. Projects are initiated once system-level risk is reduced to an acceptable level as documented in the risk management plan.

Reviews and Approvals. When using the MED work pattern, there is an explicit milestone for the system-level requirements and a milestone for each subsystem requirement.

Operations and Maintenance (O&M) Small-Scale Enhancement Work Pattern

This work pattern is appropriate for small-scale revisions to existing applications. Each O&M enhancement must be initiated by the Project Initiation Form and submitted to the SPMO. Typically, multiple O&M enhancements will be bundled into a planned software release identified by a version number. The intent is to limit the use of this work pattern to simple, small-scale changes that will require no more than 160 (suggested) labor hours for the total effort, including any needed updates to product documentation and any required user training.

O&M Project Work Pattern

This work pattern is appropriate for ongoing maintenance of existing applications. Each project must be specifically organized and staffed to conduct corrective, adaptive, or perfective maintenance on installed applications, including conversions needed to support upgrades and/or changes to the hardware and software operating environment. User Help Desk support and other small enhancements may also be provided and delivered by the assigned project team. System revisions and conversions will be accomplished on an as-needed basis at a fixed level of support and within a corresponding fixed annual operating budget. The intent is to limit the use of this work pattern to ongoing support activities that typically do not fit within the definition of a systems development or enhancement project.

Procurement of Commercial Off-the-Shelf Products

This effort is designed for the purchase of COTS products to be used in SEP within the framework of existing or planned systems. These COTS products may be used at a single site, or they may be installed to operate across the organization or a significant portion thereof.

Additional Work Patterns

Project teams should endeavor to follow the full sequential work pattern or one of the alternatives described; however, from time to time, new project environments or system requirements into which these work patterns will not fit will evolve. In those cases, the Project Manager, working with the Core Team, should develop and document proposed new work patterns, submit them as updates to the SPMO to be documented, and use them as the basis of the future project management plans.

10.16 Matching Resources to Business Need

Having the ability to look at the project from an overall scope-of-effort-required point of view will assist you in determining how much process is necessary to achieve the goals of standardization and delivery of business value to your organization. It makes no sense to form a Core Team and begin work on a project that can be completed by a single developer in a day. Generally, the BROC in an organization will set a dollar limit on the value of a project. This is a tradeoff—as is much in life—regarding the value of the effort versus the cost. If a programmer can solve this problem on his or her own in a day at a cost of less than $1,000, compare that to the cost of having a meeting with eight Core Team members for an hour and getting nothing but discussion and agreement accomplished. In one instance, you have agreement and no solution; in the other, you have a working solution. The point here is that each organization needs to determine the threshold at which constituting a team makes sense. In most organizations, that spending limit is set at $50,000 to $100,000. I have been in other organizations where it was only done for projects costing $500,000 or more. It is all relative to the business you support.

10.17 Developing an Effective Approach to Software Projects

When a project is undertaken, and the scope appears to be large enough to constitute formation of a Core Team, a process is undertaken by the Core Team to determine how much effort will be expended in tracking and managing the project (described in Chapter 2). Use of the Project Customization Matrix is essential to help determine how much process is required to effectively manage the project. Aside from the responsibilities of the Core Team, the BROC should also be involved at this stage to provide limits on how far the Core Team should take this before formalizing the process and adhering to the SEP process.

10.18 Having "Just Enough" Process

It is important to have the project tailored to the point that everyone involved is comfortable with the decisions made. The tailoring process is generally accomplished by a project Core Team. This team's role, based on its cross-functional representation of the various business units, is to determine just how much work is required and whether the benefits of doing the project are worth effort and money spent. In Chapter 2, we presented the Project Framework Rules Document as a tool to satisfy this purpose. The reader is encouraged to download and use the PFRD from the software package that accompanies this book.

10.19 Optimizing Time, Cost, Function, and Quality

Optimization, in general, should be a mantra of the project team. Finding ways to cut delivery times and costs and improve functionality and quality are all desirable aspects that are often attainable. The key thing project leaders need to remember is that opportunity is always presenting itself to do things better. Take advantage of every opportunity to refine processes, reduce cost, and so on. This is easy to say, but how does a project leader know when such opportunities present themselves?

The answer is often found by asking questions—lots of questions. The best advice I could give any project leader is to question everything, and I do mean everything. Do not accept that something is the way it is presented without asking why. A person will often do it that way because he or she knows of no other way or because that is how it has always been done. By asking questions, you are challenging basic assumptions; the answers that follow are often enough to force a rethink of the whole process. That someone is an SME in a given area does not mean you cannot engage that person by challenging him to explain why he is doing what he does. I have often seen people start to answer questions, only to light up and say something like, "You know, maybe we could do this instead, and it would help . . ."

When looking at costs, be sure to challenge vendors to lower their costs for everything. They certainly will not volunteer to do so, and you will quickly learn that if you do not ask, they will not volunteer. I once talked a software vendor down from $21 million to less than $7 million for an enterprise package by never being satisfied with their pricing and continually telling them I was searching for alternatives to their product. Never mind that their product was the core piece of our ERP and CRM systems, and that it would have cost me a lot more to replace their system with anything else. The fact that they believed they were not going to get any business forced them to make concessions they never dreamed possible. Wizardly advice–vendors can be quite creative and responsive when pushed a bit.

10.20 Building Realistic Project Plans

When starting to plan a project, it is important to divide up the work and plan it in a phased approach. In general, a basic five-step process should be accomplished for any project. This five-step process is intended to help you and your team think about, plan, and carry out successful projects. As you go about planning a project, review these five steps to help you organize and coordinate your efforts. You can also look back on these steps later after you've completed your project and use them as a way to evaluate what you have accomplished. The basics of the five-step process are as follows:

- *Step 1: Identify a project.* Describe your project idea in a nutshell (i.e., is it a crawl, walk, or run?).
- *Step 2: Set an objective or goal.* Ask what your goals are for this project? What do you hope to accomplish?
- *Step 3: Design the project.* When will this project be taking place? What materials will you need? Create a project timeline.
- Step 4: *Do the project.*

- *Step 5: Evaluate the project.* Did you meet your project goals? What went well? What will do you differently next time?

10.21 A Step-by-Step Process Using SEP

For SEP, the five-step process has been expanded somewhat, and a template has been drafted to help you plan out a project using the recommended phases of the SEP. You might find it helpful to refer to this template as you plan your first few projects. This template operates at a macro level for the project. Figure 10.1 on the following page shows the top level of the project template contents.

As you can see, the eight major phases of SEP are identified, along with the essential steps. When using this template, the core team should add additional tasks to each section as appropriate. For large projects, each phase can be broken into subprojects. The advantage of using SEP is that regardless of the project undertaken, each of these areas needs to be addressed. This method provides standardization and makes the job of the SPMO and the Project Manager much easier.

10.22 Identifying Tasks, Milestones, and Phases

Essentially, using the aforementioned template will break out the phases automatically for you. The next step is to look at each phase and determine the critical milestones. A good rule of thumb for determining whether something is a milestone is that it should *always* be accompanied by two things: a deliverable and a status update meeting. The next section shows how to use the Microsoft Project^{TM} tool to manage tasks in the SEP environment.

10.22.1 Using MS Project with SEP

Phase 1: Initiation Phase

After receiving the PIF from the Project Manager, the Project Coordinator e-mails the Microsoft Project Plan (.mpp) file template to the Project Manager. The Project Manager populates the .mpp file with project information and specific tasks. Next, the Project Manager saves the .mpp file as the appropriate project "codename.mpp" to both the hard drive and a backup disk. The Project Manager then submits and saves the .mpp file as a baseline and submits the project plan to the "Project Document Check-In" URL found within the appropriate Functional Group file folder on the SPMO Intranet.

Figure 10.1
Project Plan Using SEP.

ID	0	% Complet	Task Name	Duration	Start	Finish
1		0%	IT - Template	32 days?	Mon 8/26/0:	Tue 10/8/02
2		0%	**Initiation Phase**	20 days?	Mon 8/26/0:	Fri 9/20/0:
3	⊞	0%	Sponsor Formalization Letter	2 days?	Mon 8/26/C	Fri 9/13/0
4		0%	Project Manager Letter of Appointme	1 day?	Mon 9/16/C	Mon 9/16/C
5		0%	Core Team Roster	1 day?	Tue 9/17/C	Tue 9/17/C
6		0%	Project Guidelines Document	1 day?	Wed 9/18/0	Wed 9/18/0
7		0%	User Requirements Document	1 day?	Thu 9/19/C	Thu 9/19/C
8		0%	Phase Signoff	1 day?	Fri 9/20/0	Fri 9/20/0
9		0%	**Planning Phase**	3 days?	Mon 9/23/0:	Wed 9/25/0:
10		0%	High Level Solution	1 day?	Mon 9/23/C	Mon 9/23/C
11		0%	Project Definition Document	1 day?	Mon 9/23/C	Mon 9/23/C
12		0%	Cost Estimating Worksheet	1 day?	Tue 9/24/C	Tue 9/24/C
13		0%	Vendor Selection Checklist	1 day?	Tue 9/24/C	Tue 9/24/C
14		0%	Risk Analysis Matrix	1 day?	Tue 9/24/C	Tue 9/24/C
15		0%	Phase Signoff	1 day?	Wed 9/25/0	Wed 9/25/0
16		0%	**Design Phase**	5 days?	Thu 9/26/02	Wed 10/2/0:
17		0%	Marketing/Communication Plan	1 day?	Thu 9/26/C	Thu 9/26/C
18		0%	Quality Assurance Plan	1 day?	Fri 9/27/0	Fri 9/27/0
19		0%	Design	1 day?	Mon 9/30/C	Mon 9/30/C
20		0%	Design Complete	1 day?	Tue 10/1/C	Tue 10/1/C
21		0%	Phase Signoff	1 day?	Wed 10/2/0	Wed 10/2/0
22		0%	**Construction Phase**	4 days?	Thu 10/3/02	Tue 10/8/02
23		0%	Construction	1 day?	Thu 10/3/C	Thu 10/3/C
24		0%	Construction Complete	1 day?	Fri 10/4/0	Fri 10/4/0
25		0%	Product Assurance Signoff Letter	1 day?	Mon 10/7/C	Mon 10/7/C
26		0%	Phase Signoff	1 day?	Tue 10/8/C	Tue 10/8/C
27		0%	**Testing Phase**	3 days?	Mon 8/26/0:	Wed 8/28/0:
28		0%	Testing	1 day?	Mon 8/26/C	Mon 8/26/C
29		0%	Testing Plan Checklist	1 day?	Mon 8/26/C	Mon 8/26/C
30		0%	Testing Complete	1 day?	Tue 8/27/C	Tue 8/27/C
31		0%	Phase Signoff	1 day?	Wed 8/28/0	Wed 8/28/0
32		0%	Implementation Phase	4 days?	Mon 8/26/0	Thu 8/29/0

The Project Coordinator then retrieves the .mpp file from the "Project-Document Check-In" URL, reviews it, and loads the contents of the file into a master .mpp file. The master .mpp file is accessible as a read-only file through Project Central[12] on the Intranet. During the course of the project, the Project Coordinator is responsible for monitoring the progress of the project and ensuring that all reports and milestones are tracked.

Phases 2–7: Planning, Design, Construction, Testing, Implementation, and Support

During each of these phases, the Project Manager updates the .mpp file as appropriate and submits the current .mpp file weekly to the project-specific "Project Document Check-In" URL on the SPMO Intranet. The Project Coordinator reviews and retrieves the .mpp file from the "Project Document Check-In" URL and loads the file into the master .mpp file appropriately. Throughout the duration of the project, the Project Coordinator monitors the progress of the project, ensuring continuity in reporting and management. The Project Coordinator extracts .mpp file weekly from the Master .mpp file and creates reports with varying levels of detail: Enterprise Rollup, Functional Rollup, Cross-Functional Rollup, and so on.

The Enterprise Rollup reports project schedules for all projects in progress within the company. This rollup is sent to specific executives on a weekly basis. The Functional Rollup reports project schedules for all projects within a

Functional Group. Each functional director receives the appropriate Functional Rollup on a weekly basis. The Cross-Functional Rollup reports project schedules for any project that is managed by more than one functional group. These are typically large projects in which more than one functional director has a stake. This rollup is sent to the appropriate functional directors on a weekly basis. At any time, a Project Manager can view the status of the project(s) by using the centralized project repository.

Phase 8: Completion Phase

Once a project has been completed, the appropriate .mpp file is moved to the archive folder within the Functional Group file folder. All archived project information can be viewed at your designated local intranet project server location. Specific executives and directors can access archived project information on the SPMO Intranet at any time. Project Managers can access archived project information on the Intranet by placing a request with the SPMO.

10.23 Building a Project Plan Using the Template

Open the MS Project Plan (.mpp) template sent by the Project Coordinator (found with the software accompanying this book). The initial "task name" should be the assigned code name of the project.

10.23.1 Adding Start and Finish Dates

Fill in the appropriate start and finish dates for each task. To do this, double-click on the date and then use the pop-up calendar to choose the appropriate date. The duration of days will automatically reflect the number of workdays between the start and finish dates. Start and finish dates of parent tasks (in bold) cannot be manipulated—only the dates of subtasks can be modified.

10.23.2 Inserting Additional Tasks and Subtasks

Insert any additional tasks or subtasks where appropriate. To do this, click on the task that will follow the newly inserted task, then "Alt I", "Alt N" to insert "New Task." The "New Task" will be inserted above the task highlighted. You can then type in the name of the new task or subtasks, adding both the appropriate start and finish dates.

10.23.3 Inserting Predecessor Tasks into the Project Plan

Predecessors (dependencies) have already been inserted on the template, but to add additional predecessors, type the predecessor number in the appropriate predecessor cell. This creates links between tasks, showing task dependencies. It is possible to have multiple predecessors for a given task. To enter multiple predecessors, separate each predecessor number with a comma. To create subtasks, use the arrows pointing left and right on the toolbar menu. These arrows can be used to shift a task one way or another, creating the appropriate subtask at various levels. On the Gantt chart, subtasks are indented to the right, beneath the parent task.

10.23.4 Inserting Task Notes into the Project

To add a predecessor to a task that is a separate project altogether, highlight the task, and click on the note icon on the toolbar. Type in the name of the separate project and any other concerns or details you may want to add. Adding a task note to any task is a good way to communicate additional details that the project plan does not include. The Project Coordinator will insert dependencies between projects and functional groups on the appropriate .mpp rollup reports.

10.23.5 Inserting Resources into the Project Plan

Add the name of the Project Manager in the first cell under "Resource Names." You may assign resource names to any task as needed. More than one resource name can be assigned to any given task. The resource(s) that are assigned to a task should be the individual(s) who are responsible for completing that particular task. Here is an additional method for defining resources:

- Click on the "Resource Sheet" icon or select View Resource Sheet from the menu.
- Double-click on the resource name to bring up resource information.
- Enter the Internet e-mail address for the user.
- Leave the selection for Workgroup as "Default."
- Select "Work" as the resource type.
- Click on the "Windows Account" button to select the user's correct windows account.

Note: At this point, project planners should focus more on getting the tasks defined correctly and less on defining the resources correctly.

10.23.6 Tracking Task Completion

Indicating the percentage of a task that is complete helps track actual progress. By specifying a percentage of completion between 0 (the task hasn't started) and 100 (the task is finished), we can compare actual progress against planned progress. When you specify the percentage of completion for a task, Microsoft Project calculates the actual duration and remaining duration according to the formulas:

```
Actual Duration = Duration x Percent Duration Complete
Remaining Duration = Duration - Actual Duration
```

To change the task view, simply perform the following steps:

- On the View menu, click More Views.
- In the Views list, click Task Sheet, and then click Apply.
- On the View menu, point to Table, and then click Tracking.
- In the % Comp. (percentage complete) field, type the percentage complete for the task.
- The recalculated values for actual duration and remaining duration will appear in the Act. Dur. (actual duration) and Rem. Dur. (remaining duration) fields, respectively.
- To return to the Gantt chart view, click on the Gantt chart icon on the left.

An easy way to enter "% Complete" into the project plan template is to insert the "% Complete" in each appropriate cell and update this as the project moves forward. To record the percentage complete for an individual task, one option is to use the General tab of the Task Information box (double-click on a given task). It is not necessary to update the percentage complete for summary-level tasks. Microsoft Project calculates the percentage of a summary task that is complete based on the progress of its subtasks.

10.23.7 Saving the Project Plan from the Project Template

When all project updates have been made, the file should be saved as the code name assigned to it (e.g., codename.mpp). Once you have saved the .mpp file, move the file to the "Project-Document Check-In" URL under the appropriate Functional Group file on the server designated by your SPMO. From this point, your local Project Coordinator will move the .mpp file to the appropriate rollup for reporting purposes. When making continuous updates to the .mpp file, follow the same process and save the document into the "Project-Document Check-In" URL found under the appropriate Functional Group file folder designated by your SPMO.

10.23.8 Updating the New Project Plan

If your organization uses Project Central as a project management tool, you should try to make updates using the Project Central server file when possible. This will help maintain the current links and dependencies between the files in the server folder and allow others to create new dependencies to your tasks as needed. If you must take a copy of the project file home, it is recommended that you observe the following rules:

- Copy the current file from the server to your floppy. Do not perform a "Save As" feature from within MS Project. It is best to use Windows Explorer to copy the file to the A: drive.
- When opening the file outside of the current server folder, you may see a Link message dialog box indicating that files are Not Found. Simply close the dialog box. The predecessor and successor links will not be lost.
- When returning the updated file to the server, use Windows Explorer to copy the file back into the SPMO Files server folder location.
- Open the file from the server location.

10.24 Project Work Breakdown Structure

The Work Breakdown Structure (WBS) is a family-tree structure that relates to products produced and tasks performed at the various phases of the project life cycle. A WBS displays and defines the product(s) to be developed or produced and relates the elements of work (tasks) to be accomplished to each other and to the end product(s). Typically, three levels of WBS are developed during the system development process: Summary, Project, and Contract. A WBS Dictionary is also helpful for creating and recording the WBS elements.

10.24.1 Summary Work Breakdown Structure

The Summary WBS is a high-level WBS that covers the first three levels of the Project WBS. The Summary WBS is used for management presentations, but is not used for detailed day-to-day project management. The structure of the Summary WBS may vary depending on the nature of the project.

10.24.2 Project Work Breakdown Structure

The Project WBS is the detailed WBS that is used for day-to-day project management. The Project WBS includes all important products and work elements, or tasks, of the project, regardless of whether these tasks are performed by organizational personnel or by a contractor. The Project WBS may be modified, if necessary, during the life cycle. Work elements requiring more than two person-weeks of calendar time should be subdivided until the largest bottom-level work element represents work that can be accomplished in an interval of at least one person-week, but not more than two person-weeks. This subdivision may appear arbitrary, but the bottom-level work elements should focus on finite tasks performed by a single individual. When that is done, the application of standard productivity rates can generally predict the expected duration of the work element and eliminate wide variation in work element duration.

For a software system development project, the structure of the Project WBS should also reflect the project life cycle approach. The structure of the Project WBS may vary depending on the nature of the project and should be customized by the Project Manager to reflect the particular project and the particular path through the life cycle. For example, a full-scale initial information systems development project and a software conversion process would be expected to have a much different WBS.

10.24.3 Contract Work Breakdown Structure

The Contract WBS (CWBS) is a further breakdown of the contract-specific WBS that covers the products and work elements, or tasks, from the Project WBS that will be performed by a contractor. In addition to items derived from the Project WBS, the CWBS includes contractor-specific items that may not be reflected in the Project WBS. Depending on the nature of the project, the contractor may be responsible for a given part of the project development activities (such as QA), for a specific part of the development life cycle (such as the Requirements Definition phase), or for the entire development process. A preliminary CWBS may be specified in the acquisition plan. The contract line items, configuration items, contract work statement tasks, contract specification, and contractor responses will typically be expressed in terms of the preliminary CWBS.

10.24.4 Work Breakdown Structure Dictionary

A WBS Dictionary provides detailed descriptions of each WBS element. Each WBS Dictionary entry should contain a title that is the same as the WBS element it amplifies, a narrative describing the work represented by the element, the effort required (in person-hours), the most likely duration (in calendar days), and references to any special skills or resources required to accomplish the work. WBS Dictionary entries should be completed only for the lowest-level WBS elements. Create one or more WBSs and a WBS Dictionary and it is possible to generate the output in the form of graphic charts.

10.25 Pert Charts

A PERT chart is a graphic representation of a project's schedule. It is designed to show the sequence of tasks, which can be performed simultaneously, and the critical path of tasks that must be completed on time in order for the project to meet its completion deadline. The chart can be constructed with a variety of attributes, such as earliest and latest start dates for each task, earliest and latest finish dates for each task, and slack time between tasks. A PERT chart can document an entire project or a key phase of a project. The chart allows a team to avoid unrealistic time tables and schedule expectations, to help identify and shorten tasks that are bottlenecks, and to focus attention on the most critical tasks.

10.26 Gantt Charts

The Gantt chart is a matrix-formatted document that lists on the vertical axis all of the tasks to be performed. Each row contains a single task identification, which usually consists of a number and name. The horizontal axis is headed by columns indicating estimated task duration, the skill level required to perform the task, and the name of the person assigned to the task, followed by one column for each period in the project's duration. Each period may be expressed in hours, days, weeks, months, or other time units. The graphics portion of the Gantt chart consists of a horizontal bar for each task connecting the period start and period end columns. Each bar is drawn on a separate line, and the name of each person assigned to the task is also printed out on a separate line, often just beside or below the bar. In many cases when this type of project plan is used, a blank row is left between tasks. When the project is underway, this row is used to indicate progress with a second bar, which starts in the period column when the task is actually started and continues until the task is actually completed. Comparison between estimated start and end dates and actual start and end dates should indicate project status on a task-by-task basis.

Variations of this method include a lower chart, which shows personnel allocations on a by-name basis. For this section, the vertical axis contains the number of people assigned to the project, and the columns indicating task duration are left blank, as is the column indicating the resource assigned. The graphics portion consists of the same bar notation as in the upper chart, but it indicates that the designated person is working on a task. The value of this lower chart becomes clear when it shows slack time for project resources. Slack time is time when resources are not actually working on a project.

10.27 Performing Reality Checks and "Fit for Purpose"

With any major undertaking, it is always a good idea to have the proposal reviewed and scrutinized before the start of work. For project plans, this walk-through should include a full review by a knowledgeable team outside the purview of the current project. The SPMO often fulfills this role and can provide guidance on areas that may have been overlooked or are incorrectly calculated. The SPMO serves an important role in this process and ensures that the plan will perform all actions needed to succeed. The SPMO's expertise should be leveraged at every opportunity, even by experienced Project Managers. Wizardly advice–another set of eyes never hurts.

10.28 Assessing Project Risk Factors

The Risk Assessment assesses the system's use of resources and controls (either implemented or planned) to eliminate or manage vulnerabilities that are exploitable by threats to the organization. It will also identify any of the following possible vulnerabilities:

- Risks associated with the system operational configuration
- System's safeguards, threats, and vulnerabilities
- New threats and risks that might exist and, therefore, will need to be addressed after the current system is replaced
- Conformance with operational Security Policy

The risk assessment is a determination of vulnerabilities that, if exploited, could result in the following:

- Unauthorized disclosure of sensitive information
- Unauthorized modification of the system or its data
- Denial of system service or access to data to authorized users

The following is a sample layout of the recommended table of contents for a risk assessment. The Core Team–appointed Risk Officer is responsible for completing this document.

Risk Assessment Executive Summary

1.0   Background
2.0   Purpose
3.0   Scope
4.0   Assumptions
5.0   Description of System
      5.1   System Attributes
      5.2   System Sensitivity
6.0   System Security
      6.1   Administrative Security
      6.2   Physical Security
      6.3   Technical Security
      6.4   Software Security

	6.5	Telecommunication Security
	6.6	Personnel Security
7.0	System Vulnerabilities	
	7.1	Technical Vulnerability
	7.2	Personnel Vulnerability
	7.3	Telecommunication Vulnerability
	7.4	Software Vulnerability
	7.5	Environmental Vulnerability
	7.6	Physical Vulnerability
8.0	Glossary of Terms	
9.0	Acronyms	

Appendix A: Information Flow Diagram

Appendix B: Hardware Configuration

10.29 Risk Identification List

The process tracking of risks in a risk identification list is a critical facet of successful system development management. The risk identification list is used from the beginning of the project and is a major source of input for the risk assessment activity. The following are examples of categories that may be a source of risk for a system development:

- The complexity, difficulty, feasibility, novelty, verifiability, and volatility of the system requirements
- The correctness, integrity, maintainability, performance, reliability, security, testability, and usability of the project deliverables
- The developmental model, formality, manageability, measurability, quality, and traceability of the processes used to satisfy customer requirements
- The communication, cooperation, domain knowledge, experience, technical knowledge, and training of the personnel associated with technical and support work on the project
- The budget, external constraints, politics, resources, and schedule of the external system environment

10.29 Risk Identification List

- The capacity, documentation, familiarity, robustness, tool support, and usability of the methods, tools, and supporting equipment that will be used in the system development

Once the risks have been identified, document them in this section as the risk identification list. Steps for developing the risk identification list include the following:

- Number each risk using sequential numbers or other identifiers.
- Identify the SEP document in which the risk is applicable. For instance, if you are working on the CM Plan and discover a CM risk, identify the CM plan as the related document.
- Describe the risk in enough detail that a third party who is unfamiliar with the project can understand the content and nature of the risk.

It is the Project Manager's responsibility to ensure the Core Team appointed Risk Officer will use the risk identification list throughout the life cycle phases to ensure that all risks are properly documented.

10.29.1 Risk Assessment

The project management plan and the risk identification list are inputs to the risk assessment. Categorize the risks as internal or external risks. Internal risks are those you can control. External risks are events over which you have no direct control. Examples of internal risks are project assumptions that may be invalid and organizational risks. Examples of external risks are government regulations and supplier performance. Evaluate the identified risks in terms of probability and impact. For each risk item, determine the probability that this will occur and the resulting impact if it does occur. Use an evaluation tool to score each risk. For example, a simplistic model could be to assign numerical scores to risk probability (1 = low, 2 = moderate, 3 = high) and severity of impact (same rating system). A risk score would be the product of the two scores. Management attention would then be focused on those risks with a score of 9, followed by 6, and so on.

10.29.2 Risk Action Plan

Review the risk items with high rankings from the risk assessment and determine if the significant risks will be accepted, transferred, or mitigated. With the acceptance approach, no effort is made to avoid the risk item. This approach is usually employed because the risk items are the result of external factors over which you have no direct control. Two types of action are usually taken under the acceptance approach: contingency planning and no action. You can plan contingencies in case the risk does occur. Thus, the project team has a backup plan to minimize the effects of the risk event. Or, you can take no action and accept responsibility if the risk event does occur.

With the transfer approach, the objective is to reduce risk by transferring it to another entity that can better handle it. Two methods of transferring risk are the use of insurance and the alignment of responsibility and authority. With the mitigation approach, emphasis is on actually avoiding, preventing, or reducing the risk. Some risks can be avoided by reducing the number of requirements or defining them more completely. For example, careful definition of the scope of a project can avoid the possible consequence of scope creep or indecisive, protracted, and uncertain scope objectives.

Identify and describe in detail the actions that will be taken to transfer or mitigate risks that are prioritized as high in the risk assessment. These actions should ultimately result in the reduction of project risk and should directly affect the project plan and the metrics used for the project. Activities for reducing the effects of risk will require effort, resources, and time, just like other project activities. These actions need to be incorporated into the budget, schedule, and other project plan components. Update the project plan components to ensure the planning and execution of risk action activities. Also, refer to contingency plan documents for any contingency plans that have been identified with the risk acceptance approach. Risk action plans will be used to direct all risk mitigation activities. The risk management plan will need to be monitored and updated throughout the SEP life cycle phases.

10.30 Building Confidence in the Plan and Selling It Internally

Once the plan has had the reality check from the SPMO and both the SPMO and the Project Manager are comfortable with it, it should be presented to the Executive Stakeholder and other members of the Executive Team. This presentation is a critical step in gaining internal support and provides a sense of control to the executive management team as well as satisfaction on their part that you have done your job correctly. Senior executives often have a way of injecting their criticisms into the plan during these types of reviews. The best advice I can give for dealing with that situation is to take the criticism and state that you will look into the matter and see what impact it will have on the overall plan. After the meeting, review all of the input, go over it with the SPMO, and *jointly* make the decision as to whether the comment merits change or not. This way, you have the SPMO backing you up on the outcome of the matter. Once this review process has been completed, the executives should be encouraged to put a positive spin on the project and inform their respective staffs of the plan and how it will benefit the organization.

10.31 Managing for Success: Day-to-Day Project Management Insights

Anyone who has managed projects for more than a few rounds knows that something could always have been done during the course of the project to eliminate pain. Even the best Project Managers learn painful lessons. What distinguishes the best Project Managers from run-of-the-mill types is good memory and a willingness to be flexible. The following sections point out some areas of commonality shared by the best Project Managers.

10.31.1 Focus on Process

Everything moves according to plan. The plan is composed of multiple phases, each phase broken down into tasks and milestones. Everything that touches any aspect of the plan should be done according to some process, standard, or pre-agreed method. Good Project Managers never focus on individuals, but on the tasks those individuals perform. Everyone associated with work on a project is an equal cog in the big wheel. When project leaders stay focused on the processes that drive the tasks to completion and move the effort from milestone to milestone, they avoid the pitfalls of dependency on a few key individuals. They also demonstrate leadership and show an equality among participants. This mitigates pain.

10.31.2 Put Theory into Practice

Change control is a good idea. Quality is nice. Periodic reviews will help create a better understanding of what we are doing. This product should be tested using test cases developed during the development stage. Boy, all these are nice things to hear at the beginning of a project, but all too often, when time constraints put pressure (pain) on the project team, corners get cut in these areas. This is not the place to cut corners, folks. Change control is essential and should *never* be optional. Quality is demanded from sophisticated users and, personally, I would not want to deliver anything less than the best project I could put into reality. During the initial stages of planning, remember all these things that sound good—and take their implementation to heart. Putting theory into practice mitigates pain.

10.31.3 Detect Early Warning Signs

A team leader takes off for the weekend without submitting his weekly status report. Is that a problem? A developer misses a delivery date and you find out at the time it is supposed to be compiled into a larger drop. Is that a problem? Remember, in project management, everything is done according to a plan executed in an orderly and proficient manner. It is wise to question even the most minor deviations. Either of the above incidents could be the early warning signs of a larger problem—or not. The point here is that you must get down into the trenches and ask some questions to be sure. Emphasize to your team that missing deliverables is not the way to inform you they are running into problems. The team leader who took off without submitting his status report may have intended to submit it to you from home on Saturday morning or may have been so frustrated at his progress in the project that he decided to try and hide it. Either way, you won't know until you go find out for yourself. Good project leaders are like bloodhounds; they can sense when something is not quite right, and they will begin to ask questions at meetings, probing into the issue until someone comes clean and confesses or the issue is answered to their satisfaction. Even the most trivial slips can be early warning signs of a much larger issue looming in the shadows. Think of these warning signs as tips of an iceberg and leap into action. Being proactive mitigates pain.

10.31.4 Set Communications Ground Rules

At the beginning of every project, I like to set the stage for all team members to feel free to open up and speak their minds about issues. In order to prevent this from turning into a melee, I have found it a good idea to establish some communications ground rules. Here they are:

Speak up and speak for yourself.

1. Speak up when you have an idea or a problem; don't let others speak for you in a meeting.

2. Be constructive, be concise, and be to the point; be prepared to say what you would do to forward the idea or solve the problem.

3. Be accountable for your agenda. Insist that others answer the questions you bring to the table unless (or until) there is a clear reason to move on.

Be open-minded.

1. Listen actively; make sure others know that you're listening. Be prepared to re-create what they said and how they felt about it before you share your point of view. Don't interrupt—ever.

2. Be patient with others' need to develop their own thoughts; don't interpret for them.

3. Be willing to engage in constructive conflict. Hear out a new idea before you react. Separate the goal of understanding from the goal of agreeing with others.

Keep the team's satisfaction and productivity uppermost in your mind.

1. Encourage focus (i.e., finish a topic before you move on). Do not allow emotion to cloud an issue.

2. Define consensus as completion, not unanimity. Ensure that all who need to speak have had their say and feels that they've been heard. You're committed to support the decision as if it were your own.

3. Plan and think things through before acting. Beware overcommitting. Seek needed input, and be considerate of others' feelings.

4. Create and use mechanisms for offline/nontask discussions.

10.32 Daily Tracking and Management

If your project is tracked consistently, your people will expect things to go according to plan. If you are remiss in your duties to check on the progress daily, they will become remiss in their duties to perform tasks too. You can never let your guard down on showing your involvement in every aspect of the project. So you have six groups performing concurrent tasks in six different parts of the enterprise campus. That translates into at least six meetings a day to keep up on the progress. It is true that during the course of task completion, some groups will need more time and attention than others, but if you let up, the others will feel they fulfill a lesser role in the project and act accordingly. Your dedication and diligence will show through, and they will see that you lead projects by setting a strong example. Bottom line: If you don't let up, they won't either, and that mitigates pain.

10.33 Measuring Progress with Milestones

In most projects, there are hundreds of tasks to complete, dozens of milestones, and often more than a few phases. You cannot celebrate the completion of every task, of course, but completion of each milestone is an opportunity to communicate progress to the whole organization. It allows the team to share the success with the whole company and keeps everyone focused on the importance of what you are doing. It is a good idea to print a chart of milestones so that everyone knows where in the chain of events the project is at any given time. I have even posted sanitized versions of this progress indicator in the elevators around work areas to keep everyone advised of where we are in the course of project completion. It works. When people are informed and know you are tracking the status that closely, they are satisfied that the project is in good hands. That mitigates pain.

10.33.1 Defect Detection and Prevention

At the conclusion of each task, someone should check the work to ensure that it was done to standard, meets the quality levels expected, and can stand up to the scrutiny of objective evaluation. Who does that? Why did they not think to go over that stuff at the beginning of the task—at task start? How did the person performing that task know that you were going to come along and check that stuff? If you put it into the plan as a gating factor to task start and completion for every task, that's how they will know. It is a bit more work, but when people are accustomed to having someone else check their work, it is amazing how well they can do that work. It builds a mentality of quality into the organization, and that mitigates pain.

10.34 Pressures to Expect at Each Stage

During the course of your career managing projects, you are going to endure some stress. Pressures come in from all directions. At the end of the

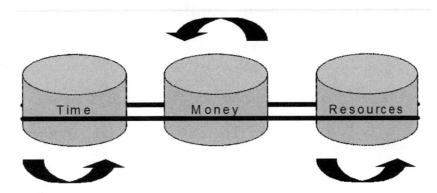

Figure 10.2
The Radio Dial Analogy.

day, there are only three things to worry about: time, money, and resources. There is an old adage about these being much like the dials on an old radio, as is illustrated in Figure 10.2:

It does not matter which dial you turn up or down, the other two dials are affected by that action. Such is the life of a Project Manager. The pressures faced during execution of a project always boil down to one of these three issues. Managing these at their most basic level, rather than getting wrapped up in the details of specific reasons why one of these three areas is a problem, will certainly cause ulcers. Bottom line: Reduce the problem to its most basic element and then solve that issue. That mitigates pain.

10.35 Managing Conflict Effectively

Fair, impartial, unbiased, process focused—even so, problems will crop up that cause conflict. Never let conflict take away from your meetings. Take it to another time and place and resolve it in a manner that shows you to be fair, impartial, unbiased, and, most importantly, focused on the process, not on the individuals. If the conflict revolves around something outside the scope of your project, and it cannot be resolved by a decision you make, it is a matter to be resolved by someone other than you. You must emphasize that it has an impact on your work and either encourage instant resolution or arrange for the leadership of the individuals involved to join you in resolving the issue. The main thing is that it should never be put off until another day and cannot be ignored. Sometimes personalities clash. That has to be resolved, and ground rules are a good place to start. Getting the individuals' management involved is another good move. What is not a good move is to make an arbitrary decision that is not really yours to make. Avoiding that scenario and keeping everyone focused on the project is your job. Doing that mitigates pain.

10.36 Estimating for Reality

Every project is part art, part science, and part wizardry. Estimates are a high form of wizardry. Good estimates come from good project planning. The ability to fully comprehend the depth and scope of the effort is not something everyone intuitively knows. How is it that some Project Managers can be so far off the mark while others are so close to the mark? It boils down to knowing how to scope things out at a level of detail that can be tracked and that accurately reflects reality. How do you learn that? Experience is a good teacher, but not for the person who never hits the mark. Well, how then?

Several techniques are used for project cost estimation, but the two basic approaches are top-down and bottom-up. In a top-down approach, cost is derived from a business analysis of the major project components. In a bottom-up approach, cost is derived by accumulating estimates from the people responsible for various components. Formal software project estimation depends on analysis of four key factors: size, complexity, capability, and process. Models that quantified these factors and compare them with industry norms can yield highly accurate estimates for software efforts. The primary techniques used most often for cost estimation of these components are explained in the following paragraphs.

10.36.1 Size

Software size is rated based on either quantification of physical characteristics of an application (e.g., source code, tables, screens) or logical characteristics about the work that an application performs (i.e., function points). Physical characteristics such as source lines of code are useful for estimating if all you want to predict is the time and cost of coding. That might sound reasonable, but keep in mind that coding is only a small part of the overall budget. If you're developing in a modern environment using C++, for example, odds are that coding will only account for 5 to 10 percent of your cost. It's not much different than for mainframe COBOL either, by the way. Function points correlate extremely well to *all* aspects of a software project. If you want to manage software development, predict cost, effort, duration, staffing, and other key factors, this is the only real choice.

10.36.2 Complexity

When gauged for the purpose of software estimation, complexity operates as an adjustment for technology (required as in algorithmic complexity or as a function of the technology, as with code or data complexity.) Three commonly used types of complexity factor are the following:

1. *Algorithmic complexity:* Correction for the level of effort required to resolve complex business problems
2. *Structural complexity:* Quantitative scale that describes recursive statements in the source code.
3. *Relational complexity:* Extent of data organization complexity

10.36.3 Capability

Software organization capability (also referred to as maturity level) is a significant factor in the estimation of software projects. Addressing the factors cited as follows throughout a software project mitigates risk:

- *Personnel:* Experience and skills of managers, developers, users
- *Technology:* Software tools and platform issues
- *Process:* Development methods, quality assurance, testing, documentation
- *Product:* Hardware and software requirements, constraints, and architectures
- *Environment:* Organization, office and physical environment

10.36.4 Process

The WBS reflects the activities undertaken during a project. This may be a formal methodology (e.g., Waterfall, Spiral, Object-Oriented) or it may be *ad hoc*. In any case, the following information from each task may be identified and/or quantified:

- Work effort and associated cost
- Capital (fixed) costs
- Duration
- Staffing (roles and number of full-time equivalents)

- Deliverables (e.g., source code, documentation, test cases, defects found)
- Predecessor and dependent tasks

The following excerpted from the DoD *Parametric Cost Estimating Handbook*[17], describes this process approach in further detail.

```
The work breakdown structure provides a framework for spec-
ifying the technical objectives of the program by first
defining the program in terms of hierarchically related
product-oriented elements and the work processes required
for their completion. Each element of the work breakdown
structure provides logical summary points for assessing
technical accomplishments, and for measuring the cost and
schedule performance accomplished in attaining the speci-
fied technical objectives.
```

For each work breakdown structure element, the detailed technical objectives are defined as well as the specific work tasks assigned to each of the resources, materials, and processes required to attain the objectives. As resources are employed and work progresses on the task, current technical, schedule, and cost data are reported. The task data may then be summarized to provide successive levels of management with the appropriate report on planned, actual, and current projected status of the elements for which they are responsible. Management will, thus, be better able to maintain visibility of status and to apply their efforts to assure desired performance.

Work is effort performed by people to transform or create products to solve identified problems in order to verifiably meet specified objectives. Just as the organization hierarchically structures the people who perform work, so the work breakdown structure hierarchically structures the products to be produced and on which the people work. Examples of these products include equipment (hardware/software), data, services and facilities for such systems as missile systems, helicopter systems, automated systems, etc.

In order to use the work breakdown structure as a framework for structuring the technical objectives of a program, in addition to its use as a management tool for cost and schedule control, it is important that the work breakdown structure be product-oriented. Its elements should represent identifiable work products whether they be equipment (hardware, software), data, or service products. Because any work breakdown structure is a product structure, not an organizational structure, complete definition of the effort encompasses the work to be performed by all participants.

The program work breakdown structure should be developed in the conceptual stages of the program. The program work breakdown structure evolves during conceptual design from an iterative analysis of the program objective, functional design criteria, program scope, technical performance requirements, proposed methods of performance, including procurement strategy, as well as drawings, process flow charts, and other technical documentation.

10.37 Creating an Initial Estimate and Revising Estimates

An estimate is an imprecise best guess. When an initial plan is put together, you can start with the required tasks for each of the eight phases of the SEP. Then, for each phase, on a task-by-task basis, your team will need to insert all of the known data points to start building an initial estimate. As with any project, the more that is known at the beginning, the better the estimate that can be derived. As the project team learns new data points, the plan should be revised to reflect the new knowledge and the schedule adjusted accordingly. Sometimes this causes the initial schedule to change and deadlines may become compressed or extended.

10.38 Handling Deadlines

Deadlines are a fact of life. Sometimes, for whatever reason, something happens that causes a crunch on the deadline. How do Project Managers deal with slips? Well, start with the facts. Avoid any other type of discussion but the facts, and only those relevant to the problem should be brought up for discussion. For example, a sandbox environment necessary for software testing was not set up because the hardware was not available. Sticking to the facts, when asked why the hardware was not available, the Project Manager told the CEO that since he (the CEO) did not approve the purchase order, the equipment was not obtained and this part of the project could not proceed as planned. The CEO, visibly upset, demanded to know why it was not made clear to him that this was a necessity. The Project Manager stated that he was at a loss to explain it because he had sent no fewer than 11 e-mails to the CEO explaining the need, had set up two meetings through the CEO's administrative assistant, both of which were blown off, and tried to call several times on the CEO's business line over the course of the last few days. Magically, the purchase order was signed on the spot, ordered to be expedited that day, and within 48 hours the equipment was available for the sandbox. True story: The Project Manager survived unscathed because facts are undeniable. That fact mitigates pain.

10.39 Knowing When and How to "Give and Take"

There are certain circumstances in which a project will slip because someone has mucked something up. Regardless of who or what it was, the Project Manager is the one who bears the brunt of the negative reaction to bad news. That is part of the job; however, it is easier to accept responsibility for the problem and be prepared to present alternatives when the Project Manager knows it is something that should have been avoided. Admitting human flaws is something most people don't like to do, but when it is done, the folks you admit such flaws to are often quick to forgive and move on. The fact that you know and admit there was or is a problem and are able to explain that it can be fixed by taking the alternative actions you are prepared to present shows that you are on the ball. This is the "give" part of give and take. When something under your watch goes wrong, bear the burden of responsibility and show that you can and are willing to fix the problem. So, where does the "take" part of this come into play?

When tasks are completed early, that is a take. When things are working like a well-oiled machine and all cogs seem to be turning exactly the way you want in the big project wheel, some free slack is gained, and that is a take. If equipment is delivered early, there is an opportunity. Take advantage of it. There are takes all around any project. Good Project Managers leverage every single one of them to their advantage. Never pass on an opportunity to gain some time or save money by jumping at such opportunities. If you can do that, it mitigates pain.

Many times in the course of a project, the opportunities to give and take are missed because Project Managers and those around them become way too focused on the delivery of the next milestone and overlook the "golden eggs" lying all around. When assessing the relevance or value of anything that pertains to a project, it is important—no, imperative!—that good Project Managers step back from the task of the moment and review the issue in light of the whole project. Take a holistic view and don't rush to judgment on the matter between sips of coffee while running from one meeting to the next.

10.39 Knowing When and How to "Give and Take"

A story comes to mind about a Project Manager who was hiring staff to help code a CRM deliverable for a company in the San Francisco Bay Area. One young man's résumé was pretty light in coding experience for this CRM product, and it was tossed off the hire pile without much thought. He only had two years of coding experience for this particular product. What was overlooked was the fact that he had spent nine years writing and executing test scripts for the same product using the test software that our project required. The review of his résumé was far too narrow-minded in scope, and the Project Manager almost missed a great talent that would be sorely needed at a later stage in the project. Fortunately, the HR manager brought the matter to my attention and the young man found a spot on the team. The team still owes him, big time, by the way. He helped mitigate a lot of pain.

11

Some Software Best Practices to Consider

Material in this section was graciously contributed by Thomas J. Beltz of Integrated Computer Engineering (ICE), is adapted with their permission from an original paper[18] that outlines their recommended 16 Critical Software Practices™ that serve as the basis for implementing effective performance-based management of software-intensive projects. ICE is recognized in the IT marketplace for its expansive knowledge and execution of risk management services in support of more than 250 federal, Department of Defense, state, and commercial software acquisition and development programs. As a cofounder and administrator of the Tri-Services Software Program Managers Network, ICE's dominance in project risk management is firmly established. The 16 Critical Software Practices™ are intended to be used to implement effective high-leverage practices to improve bottom-line measures: time to fielding, quality, cost, predictability, and customer satisfaction, to name a few, and they are for use by CIOs, Project Managers, sponsoring agencies, software Project Managers, and others involved in software engineering.

These practices (nine best practices and seven sustaining practices) are the key to avoiding significant problems for software development projects. These practices have been gathered from the crucible of real-world, large-scale software development and maintenance projects. Together they constitute a set of high-leverage disciplines that are focused on improving a project's bottom line. These practices are the starting point for structuring and deploying an effective process for managing large-scale software development and maintenance. They may be tailored to the particular culture, environment, and phases of a program. Of course, these practices cannot help death march programs that are expected to deliver under impossible schedule deadlines with inadequate funding and without the required staffing with essential skills. They are broken into three main areas, outlined as follows:

Project Integrity

1. Adopt continuous risk management.
2. Estimate cost and schedule empirically.
3. Use metrics to manage.
4. Track earned value.
5. Track defects against quality targets.
6. Treat people as the most valuable resource.

Construction Integrity

7. Adopt life cycle configuration management.
8. Manage and trace requirements.
9. Use system-based software design.
10. Ensure data and database interoperability.
11. Define and control interfaces.
12. Design twice, code once.
13. Assess reuse risks and costs

Product Stability and Integrity

14. Inspect requirements and design.
15. Manage testing as a continuous process.
16. Compile and smoke test frequently.

11.1 Project Integrity

11.1.1 Practice 1. Adopt Continuous Program Risk Management

Practice Essentials

A. Risk management is a continuous process beginning with the definition of the concept and ending with system retirement.

B. Risk management is a program responsibility impacting on and supported by all organizational elements.

11.1 Project Integrity

C. All programs need to assign a Risk Officer as a focal point for risk management and maintain a reserve to enable and fund risk mitigation.

D. Risk needs to be identified and managed across the life of the program.

E. All risks identified should be analyzed, prioritized—by impact and likelihood of occurrence—and tracked through an automated risk management tool.

F. High-priority risks need to be reported to management on a frequent and regular basis.

Implementation guidelines

A. Risk management should commence prior to contract award and shall be a factor in the award process.

B. The DEVELOPER needs to establish and implement a project Risk Management Plan that, at a minimum, defines how best practices 3 through 8 will be implemented. The plan and infrastructure (tools, organizational assignments, and management procedures) will be agreed to by the ACQUIRER and the DEVELOPER and need to be placed under Configuration Management (CM).

C. DEVELOPER and ACQUIRER senior management should establish reporting mechanisms and employee incentives in which all members of the project staff are encouraged to identify risks and potential problems and are rewarded when risks and potential problems are identified early. The ACQUIRER needs to address risk management explicitly in its contract award fee plan, and the DEVELOPER needs to provide for the direct distribution to all employees in furtherance of establishing and maintaining a risk culture.

D. Risk identification should be accomplished in facilitated meetings attended by project personnel most familiar with the area for which risks are being identified. A person familiar with problems from similar projects in this area in the past should participate in these meetings when possible. Risk identification should include risks throughout the life cycle in at least the areas of cost, schedule, technical, staffing, external dependencies, supportability, and maintainability and should include organizational and programmatic political risks. Risk identification needs to be updated at least monthly. Identified risks should be characterized in terms of their likelihood of occurrence and the impact of their occurrence. Risk mitigation activities need to be included in the project's task activity network.

E. Both the DEVELOPER and the ACQUIRER should designate and assign senior members of the technical staff as Risk Officers to report directly to their respective Program Managers and should charter this role with independent identification and management of risks across the program and grant the authority needed to carry out this responsibility.

F. Each medium-impact and high-impact risk should be described by a complete Risk Control Profile.

G. Periodically updated estimates of the cost and schedule at completion should include probable costs and schedule impact due to risk items that have not yet been resolved.

H. The DEVELOPER and ACQUIRER Risk Officers need to update the risk data and database on the schedule defined in the Risk Management Plan. All risks intended for mitigation and any others that are on the critical path and their status against the mitigation strategy should be summarized. Newly identified risks should go through the same processes as the originally identified risks.

11.1.2 Practice 2. Estimate Cost and Schedule Empirically

Practice Essentials

A. Initial software estimates and schedules should be looked on as high risk due to the lack of definitive information available at the time they are defined.

B. The estimates and schedules should be refined as more information becomes available.

C. At every major program review, costs-to-complete and rescheduling should be presented to identify deviations from the original cost and schedule baselines and to anticipate the likelihood of cost and schedule risks occurring.

D. All estimates should be validated using a cost model, a sanity check should be conducted comparing projected resource requirements, and schedule commitments should be made.

E. Every task within a work breakdown structure (WBS) level needs to have an associated cost estimate and schedule. These tasks should be tracked using earned value.

F. All costs estimates and schedules need to be approved prior to the start of any work.

Implementation Guidelines

A. Estimate the cost, effort, and schedule for a project for planning purposes and as a yardstick for measuring performance (tracking). Software size and cost need to be estimated prior to beginning work on any incremental release.

B. Software cost estimation should be a reconciliation between a top-down estimate (based on an empirical model [e.g., parametric, cost]) and a bottom-up engineering estimate.

C. Software cost estimation should also be subjected to a sanity check by comparing it with industry norms and specifically with the DEVELOPER's past performance in areas such as productivity and percentage of total cost in various functions and project phases.

D. All of the software costs need to be associated with the appropriate lower-level software tasks in the project activity network. Allocate the estimated total project labor effort among all the tasks in the activity network.

11.1.3 Practice 3. Use Metrics to Manage

Practice Essentials

A. All programs should have in place a metrics program to monitor issues and determine the likelihood of risks occurring.

B. Metrics should be defined as part of the definition of process, identification of risks or issues, or determination of project success factors.

C. All metrics definitions need to include description, quantitative bounds, and expected areas of application.

D. All programs need to assign an organizational responsibility for identification, collection, analysis, and reporting of metrics throughout the program's life.

E. Metrics information should be used as one of the primary inputs for program decisions.

F. The metrics program needs to be continuous.

Implementation Guidelines

A. Every project should have a project plan with a detail activity network that defines the process the team will follow, organizes and coordinates the work, and estimates and allocates costs and schedules among tasks. The plan should be broad enough to include each subprocess/phase. The project plan needs to include adequate measurement in each of these five categories:

1. Early indications of problems
2. Quality of the products
3. Effectiveness of the processes
4. Conformance to the processes
5. Provision of a basis for future estimation of cost, quality, and schedule

B. Metrics should be sufficiently broad based. Data should be collected for each process/phase to provide insight into the above five categories.

C. To use these metrics effectively, thresholds need to be established for these metrics. These thresholds should be estimated initially using suggested industry norms for various project classes. Local thresholds will evolve over time, based upon experience (see Practice 1.E above). Violation of a threshold value should trigger further analysis and decision making.

D. Examples of data, initial thresholds, and analysis of size, defect, schedule, and effort metrics can be found at www.qsm.com.

E. Continuous data on schedule, risks, libraries, effort expenditures, and other measures of progress should be available to all project personnel along with the latest revision of project plans.

11.1.4 Practice 4. Track Earned Value

Practice Essentials

A. Earned value project management requires a work breakdown structure, work packages, activity networks at every WBS level, accurate estimates, and implementation of a consistent and planned process.

B. Earned value requires each task to have both entry and exit criteria and a step to validate that these criteria have been met prior to the award of the credit.

C. Earned value credit is binary, with 0 percent being given before task completion and 100 percent when completion is validated.

D. Earned value metrics need to be collected on a frequent and regular basis consistent with the reporting cycle required with the WBS level. (At the lowest level of the work package, the earned value reporting should never occur less frequently than every two weeks.)

E. Earned value and the associated budgets schedules and WBS elements need to be replanned whenever material changes to the program structure are required (e.g., requirements, growth, budget changes, schedule issues, organizational change).

F. Earned value is an essential indicator and should be used as an essential metric by the risk management process.

Implementation Guidelines

A. Progress toward producing the products should be measured within the designated cost and schedule allocations.

B. THE DEVELOPER should develop and maintain a hierarchical task activity network based on allocated requirements that includes the tasks for all effort that will be charged to the program. All level of effort (LOE) tasks need to have measurable milestones. All tasks that are not LOE should explicitly identify the products produced by the task and have explicit and measurable exit criteria based on these products.

C. No task should have a budget or planned calendar time duration that is greater than the cost and schedule uncertainty that is acceptable for the program. The goal for task duration is no longer than two calendar weeks of effort.

D. Each task that consumes resources needs to have a cost budget allocated to it and the corresponding staff and other resources that will consume this budget. Staff resources should be defined by person-hours or -days for each labor category working on the task.

E. For each identified significant risk item, a specific risk mitigation/resolution task should be defined and inserted into the activity network.

F. The cost reporting system for the total project needs to segregate the software effort into software tasks so that the software effort can be tracked separately from the nonsoftware tasks.

G. Milestones for all external dependencies should be included in the activity network.

H. Earned value metrics need to be collected for each schedule level and be made available to all members of the DEVELOPER and government project teams monthly. These metrics are: a comparison of Budgeted Cost of Work Scheduled (BCWS), Budgeted Cost of Work Performed (BCWP), Actual Cost of Work Performed (ACWP), a comparison of BCWP and ACWP, a Cost Performance Index, a Schedule Performance Index, and a To-Complete Cost Performance Index.

I. The lowest-level schedules should be statused weekly.

J. The high-level schedules should be statused at least monthly.

K. Earned value reports should be based on data that is no more than two weeks old.

11.1.5 Practice 5. Track Defects against Quality Targets

Practice Essentials

A. All programs need to have prenegotiated quality targets, which is an absolute requirement to be met prior to acceptance by the customer.

B. Programs should implement practices to find defects early in the process and as close in time to the creation of the defect as possible and should manage this defect rate against the quality target.

C. Metrics need to be collected as a result of the practices used to monitor defects, which will indicate the number of defects, defect leakage, and defect removal efficiency.

D. Quality targets need to be redefined and renegotiated as essential program conditions change or customer requirements are modified.

E. Compliance with quality targets should be reported to customers on a frequent and regular basis, along with an identification of the risk associated with meeting these targets at delivery.

F. Meeting quality targets should be a topic at every major program review.

Implementation Guidelines

A. The ACQUIRER and the DEVELOPER need to establish quality targets for subsystem software depending on its requirements for high integrity. A mission-critical/safety-critical system may have different quality targets for each subsystem component. System Quality Assurance needs to monitor quality targets and report defects as per the Quality Plan.

B. Quality targets can be under change control and established at the design, coding, integration, test, and operational levels.

C. Quality targets should address the number of defects by priority and by their fix rate.

D. Actual quality or defects detected and removed should be tracked against the quality targets.

E. Periodic estimates of the cost and schedule at completion should be based on the actual versus targeted quality.

11.1.6 Practice 6. Treat People As the Most Important Resource

Practice Essentials

A. A primary program focus should be staffing positions with qualified personnel and retaining this staff throughout the life of the project.

B. The program should not implement practices (e.g., excessive unpaid overtime) that will force voluntary staff turnover.

C. The staff should be rewarded for performance against expectations and program requirements.

D. Professional growth opportunities such as training should be made available to the staff.

E. All staff members need to be provided facilities, tools, and work areas adequate to allow efficient and productive performance of their responsibilities.

F. The effectiveness and morale of the staff should be a factor in rewarding management.

Implementation Guidelines

A. DEVELOPER senior management needs to work to ensure that all projects maintain a high degree of personnel satisfaction and team cohesion and should identify and implement practices designed to achieve high levels of staff retention as measured by industry standards. The DEVELOPER should employ focus groups and surveys to assess employee perceptions and suggestions for change.

B. DEVELOPER senior management should provide the project with adequate staff, supported by facilities and tools to develop the software system efficiently. Employee focus groups and surveys should be used to assess this adequacy.

C. The training of DEVELOPER and ACQUIRER personnel should include training according to a project training plan in all the processes, development and management tools, and methods specified in the software development plan.

D. The DEVELOPER and the ACQUIRER should determine the existing skills of all systems, software, and management personnel and provide training, according to the needs of each role, in the processes, development and management tools, and methods specified in the Software Development Plan (SDP).

11.2 Construction Integrity

11.2.1 Practice 7. Adopt Life Cycle Configuration Management

Practice Essentials

A. All programs, irrespective of size, need to manage information through a preplanned Configuration Management (CM) process.

B. CM has two aspects: (1) formal CM, which manages customer-approved baseline information, and (2) development CM, which manages shared information not yet approved by the customer.

C. Both formal and development CM should uniquely identify managed information, control changes to this information through a structure of boards, provide the status of all information either under control or released from CM, and conduct ongoing reviews and audits to ensure that the information under control is the same as that submitted.

D. The approval for a change to controlled information must be made by the highest-level organization which last approved the information prior to placing it under CM.

E. CM should be implemented in a centralized library supported by an automated tool.

F. CM needs to be a continuous process implemented at the beginning of a program and continuing until product retirement.

Implementation Guidelines

A. CM plans need to be developed by the ACQUIRER and the DEVELOPER to facilitate management control of information they own. The CM procedures of the ACQUIRER serve as the requirements for the CM plan, which describes and documents how the DEVELOPER will implement a single CM process. This plan should control formal baselines and will include engineering information, reports, analysis information, test information, user information, and any other information approved for use or shared within the program. The CM process should include DEVELOPER-controlled and -developed baselines as well as ACQUIRER-controlled baselines. It should also include release procedures for all classes of products under control, means for identification, change control procedures, status of products, and reviews and audits of information under CM control. The CM plan needs to be consistent with other plans and procedures used by the project.

B. The two types of baselines managed by CM are developmental and formal. Developmental baselines include all software, artifacts, documentation, tools, and other products not yet approved for delivery to the ACQUIRER but essential for successful production. Formal baselines are information/products (software, artifacts, or documentation) delivered and accepted by the ACQUIRER. Developmental baselines are owned by the DEVELOPER, while formal baselines are owned by the ACQUIRER.

C. All information placed under CM as a result of meeting task exit criteria needs to be uniquely identified by CM and placed under CM control. This includes software, artifacts, documents, commercial off-the-shelf (COTS), government off-the-shelf (GOTS), operating systems, middleware, database management systems, database information, and any other information necessary to build, release, verify, and/or validate the product.

D. The CM process should be organizationally centered in a project library. This library will be the repository (current and historical) of all controlled products. The ACQUIRER and the DEVELOPER will implement an organizationally specific library. The library(s) will be partitioned according to the level of control of the information.

E. All information managed by CM is subject to change control. Change control consists of the following:

  1. Identification
  2. Reporting
  3. Analysis
  4. Implementation

F. The change control process needs to be implemented through an appropriate change mechanism tied to who owns the information:

  1. Change control boards, which manage formal baseline products
  2. Interface boards, which manage jointly owned information
  3. Engineering review boards, which manage DEVELOPER-controlled information

G. Any information released from the CM library should be described by a Version Description Document (Software Version Description under 498). The version description should consist of any inventory of all components by version identifier, an identification of open problems, closed problems, differences between versions, notes and assumptions, and build instructions. Additionally, each library partition should be described by a current version description that contains the same information.

11.2.2 Practice 8. Manage and Trace Requirements

Practice Essentials

A. Before any design is initiated, requirements for that segment of the software need to be agreed to by all parties.

B. Requirements tracing should be a continuous process providing the means to trace from the user requirement to the lowest-level software component.

C. Tracing shall exist not only to user requirements, but also between products and the test cases used to verify their successful implementation.

D. All products that are used as part of the trace need to be under configuration control.

E. Requirements tracing should use a tool and be kept current as products are approved and placed under CM.

F. Requirements tracing should address system, hardware, and software and the process should be defined in the system engineering management plan and the software development plan.

Implementation Guidelines

A. The program needs to define and implement a requirements management plan that addresses system, hardware, and software requirements. This plan should be linked to the SDP.

B. All requirements need to be documented, reviewed, and entered into a requirements management tool and put under CM. This requirements information should be kept current.

C. The CM plan should describe the process for keeping requirements data internally consistent and consistent with other project data.

D. Requirements traceability needs to be maintained through specification, design, code, and testing.

E. Requirements should be visible to all project participants.

11.2.3 Practice 9. Use System-based Software Design

Practice Essentials

A. All methods used to define system architecture and software design should be documented in the system engineering management plan and software development plan and frequently and regularly evaluated through audits conducted by an independent program organization.

B. Software engineering needs to participate in the definition of system architectures and should provide an acceptance gate before software requirements are defined.

C. The allocation of system architecture to hardware, software, or operational procedures needs to be the result of a predefined engineering process and tracked through traceability and frequent quality evaluations.

D. All agreed-to system architectures, software requirements, and software design decisions should be placed under CM control when they are approved for program implementation.

E. All architecture and design components need to be approved through an inspection prior to release to CM. This inspection should evaluate the process used to develop the product, the form and structure of the product, the technical integrity, and its adequacy to support future applications of the product to program needs.

F. All system architecture decisions should be based on a predefined engineering process and trade studies conducted to evaluate alternatives.

Implementation Guidelines

A. The DEVELOPER should ensure that the system and software architectures are developed and maintained in keeping with standards, methodologies, and external interfaces specified in the system and software development plans.

B. Software engineers need to be an integral part of the team performing systems engineering tasks that influence software.

C. Systems engineering requirements trade studies should include efforts to mitigate software risks.

D. System architecture specifications need to be maintained under CM.

E. The system and software architecture and architecture methods need to be consistent with each other.

F. System requirements, including derived requirements, need to be documented and allocated to hardware components and software components.

G. The requirements for each software component in the system architecture and derived requirements need to be allocated among all components and interfaces of the software component in the system architecture.

11.2.4 Practice 10. Ensure Data and Database Interoperability

Practice Essentials

A. All data and database implementation decisions should consider interoperability issues, and, as interoperability factors change, these decisions should be revisited.

B. Program standards should exist for database implementation and for the data elements that are included. These standards should include process standards for defining the database and entering information into it and product standards that define the structure, elements, and other essential database factors.

C. All data and databases should be structured in accordance with program requirements to provide interoperability with other systems.

D. All databases shared with the program need to be under CM control and managed through the program change process.

E. Databases and data should be integrated across the program with data redundancy kept to a minimum.

F. When using multiple COTS packages, compatibility of the data/referential integrity mechanisms needs to be considered to ensure consistency between databases.

Implementation Guidelines

A. The DEVELOPER needs to ensure that data files and databases are developed with standards and methodologies.

B. The DEVELOPER needs to ensure that data entities and data elements are consistent with the DoD data model.

C. All data and databases should be structured in compliance with DII COE to provide interoperability with other systems.

D. Data integrity and referential integrity should be maintained automatically by COTS DBMSs or other COTS software packages. The DEVELOPER should avoid developing its package, if at all possible. Before selecting multiple COTS software packages, the DEVELOPER should study the compatibility of the data/referential integrity mechanisms of these COTS packages and obtain assurance from the COTS vendors first.

E. Unnecessary data redundancy should be reduced to minimum.

F. Data and databases should be integrated as much as possible. Except data for temporary use or for analysis/report purposes, each data item should be updated only once, and the changes should propagate automatically everywhere.

11.2.5 Practice 11. Define and Control Interfaces

Practice Essentials

A. Before completion of system-level requirements, a complete inventory of all external interfaces needs to be completed.

B. All external interfaces need to be described as to source, format, structure, content, and method of support, and this definition, or interface profile, needs to be placed under CM control.

C. Any changes to this interface profile should require concurrence by the interface owners prior to being made.

D. Internal software interfaces should be defined as part of the design process and managed through CM.

E. Interfaces should be inspected as part of the software inspection process.

F. Each software or system interface needs to be tested individually and a test of interface support should be conducted in a stressed and anomalous test environment.

Implementation Guidelines

A. All internal and external interfaces need to be documented and maintained under CM control.

B. Changes to interfaces require concurrence by the interface owners prior to being made.

C. Milestones related to external interfaces should be tracked in the project activity network. (Keep these milestones off your critical path.)

D. Subsystem interfaces should be controlled at the program level.

11.2.6 Practice 12. Design Twice, Code Once

Practice Essentials

A. All design processes should follow methods documented in the software development plan.

B. All designs need to be subject to verification of characteristics, which are included as part of the design standards for the product produced.

C. All designs should be evaluated through a structured inspection prior to release to CM. This inspection should consider reuse, performance, interoperability, security, safety, reliability, and limitations.

D. Traceability needs to be maintained through the design and verified as part of the inspection process.

E. Critical components should be evaluated through a specific white-box test level step.

F. Design can be incrementally specified when an incremental release or evolution life cycle model is used, provided the CM process is adequate to support control of incremental designs and the inspection process is adapted to this requirement.

Implementation Guidelines

A. When reuse of existing software is planned, the system and software architectures should be designed to facilitate this reuse.

B. When an incremental release life cycle model is planned, the system and software architectures need to be completed in the first release or, at most, extended in releases after the first without changes to the architecture of previous releases.

C. The system and software architectures will be verified using methods specified in the SDP. This verification will be conducted during a structured inspection of the software architecture and will include corroboration that the architecture will support all reuse, performance, interoperability, security, safety, and reliability requirements. The architecture will be under CM.

11.2.7 Practice 13. Assess Reuse Risks and Costs

Practice Essentials

A. The use of reuse components, COTS, GOTS, or any other non-developmental items (NDI) should be treated as a risk and managed through risk management.

B. Application of reuse components, COTS, GOTS, or any other NDI will be made only after successful completion of an NDI acceptance inspection. This inspection needs to consider the process used to develop it, how it was documented, number of users, user experience, and compliance with essential program considerations, such as safety or security.

C. Before a decision is made to reuse a product or to acquire COTS, GOTS, or NDI, a complete cost tradeoff should be made considering the full life cycle costs, update requirements, maintenance costs, warranty and licensing costs, and any other considerations that impact use of the product throughout its life cycle.

D. All reuse products, COTS, GOTS, or NDI decisions should be based on architectural and design definitions and be traceable back to an approved user requirement.

E. All reuse components, COTS, and GOTS need to be tested individually first against program requirements and in an integrated software and system configuration prior to release for testing according to the program test plan.

F. Reuse, COTS, GOTS, and NDI decisions will be continuously revisited as program conditions change.

Implementation Guidelines

A. The DEVELOPER will establish a reuse plan for the integration of COTS, GOTS, and in-house software. This plan needs to include discussion and allocation of by whom and by what process reused software code is tested, verified, modified, and maintained.

B. The reuse plan should be in the SDP and document an approach for evaluating and enforcing reused functionality against system requirements.

C. The reuse plan should suggest a system engineering process that identifies software requirements by taking existing, reusable software components into account.

D. The test plan should identify the testing of the integrated reused code.

E. When integrating COTS, GOTS, and in-house software, ensure accurate cost estimation of integrating the reused code into the system. The cost of integrating unmodified reused code is approximately one-third the cost of developing code without reuse.

F. The DEVELOPER and the ACQUIRER need to be able to plan for the estimated costs of obtaining the necessary development and runtime licenses over the system's life cycle and the maintenance/support critical to the product, including source code availability.

11.3 Product Stability and Integrity

11.3.1 Practice 14. Inspect Requirements and Design

Practice Essentials

A. All products that are placed under CM and are used as a basis for subsequent development need to be subjected to successful completion of a formal inspection prior to their release to CM.

B. The inspection needs to follow a rigorous process defined in the software development plan and should be based on agreed-to entry and exit criteria for that specific product.

C. At the inspection, specific metrics should be collected and tracked that will describe defects, defect removal efficiency, and efficiency of the inspection process.

D. All products to be placed under CM should be inspected as close to their production as feasible.

E. Inspections should be conducted beginning with concept definition and ending with completion of the engineering process.

F. The program needs to fund inspections and track rework savings.

Implementation Guidelines

A. The DEVELOPER will implement a formal, structured inspection/peer review process that begins with the first system requirements products and continue through architecture, design, code, integration, testing, and documentation products and plans. The plan needs to be documented and controlled as per the SDP.

B. The project should set a goal of finding at least 80 percent of the defects in every product undergoing a structured peer review or other formal inspection.

C. Products should not be accepted into a CM baseline until they have satisfactorily completed a structured peer review.

D. The DEVELOPER needs to collect and report metrics concerning the number of defects found in each structured peer review, the time between creating and finding each defect, where and when the defect was identified, and the efficiency of defect removal.

E. Successful completion of inspections should act as the task exit criteria for non-Level-of-Effort earned value metrics (and other metrics used to capture the effectiveness of the formal inspection process) and as gates to place items under increasing levels of CM control.

F. The DEVELOPER should use a structured architecture inspection technique to verify correctness and related system performance characteristics.

11.3.2 Practice 15. Manage Testing As a Continuous Process

Practice Essentials

A. All testing should follow a preplanned process, that is agreed to and funded.

B. Every product that is placed under CM should be tested by a corresponding testing activity.

C. All tests should consider not only a nominal system condition, but also address anomalous and recovery aspects of the system.

D. Prior to delivery, the system needs to be tested in a stressed environment, nominally in excess of 150 percent of its rated capacities.

E. All test products (test cases, data, tools, configuration, and criteria) should be released through CM and be documented in a software version description document.

F. Every test should be described in traceable procedures and have pass-fail criteria included.

Implementation Guidelines

A. The testing process must be consistent with the RFP and the contract. The award fee should incentivize implementation of the testing practices described below.

B. The ACQUIRER and DEVELOPER need to plan their portion of the test process and document this plan with test cases and detailed test descriptions. These test cases should use cases based on projected operational mission scenarios.

C. The testing process should also include stress/load testing for stability purpose (i.e., at 95 percent CPU use, system stability is still guaranteed . . .)

D. The test plan should include a "justifiable testing stoppage criteria." This gives testers a goal. If your testing satisfies these criteria, then the product is ready for release.

E. The test process should thoroughly test the interfaces between any in-house and COTS functionality. These tests should include timing between COTS functionality and the bespoken functionality. The test plans need to pay serious attention to demonstrating how, if the COTS software fails, to test that the rest of the software can recover adequately. This involves some very serious stress testing using fault injection testing.

F. Software testing should include a traceable white-box and other test process verifying implemented software against CM-controlled design documentation and the requirements traceability matrix.

G. A level of the white-box test coverage should be specified that is appropriate for the software being tested.

H. The white-box and other testing should use automated tools to instrument the software to measure test coverage.

I. All builds for white-box testing need to be done with source code obtained from the CM library.

J. Frequent builds require test automation, because more frequent compiles will force quick turnaround on all tests, especially during regression testing. However, this requires a high degree of test automation.

K. A black-box test of integration builds needs to include functional, interface, error recovery, stress, and out-of-bounds input testing.

L. Reused components and objects require high-level testing consistent with the operational/target environment.

M. Software testing includes a separate black-box test level to validate implemented software. All black-box software tests should trace to controlled requirements and be executed using software built from controlled CM libraries.

N. In addition to static requirements, a black-box test of the fully integrated system will be against scenarios/sequences of events designed to model field operation.

O. Performance testing for systems (e.g., performing 10,000 tests per second still yields response times under 2 seconds) should be tested as an integral part of the black-box test process.

P. An independent QA team should periodically audit selected test cases, test traceability, test execution, and test reports, providing the results of this audit to the ACQUIRER. (The results of this or similar audits may be used as a factor in the calculation of Award Fee.)

Q. Each test developed needs to include pass-fail criteria.

11.3.3 Practice 16. Compile and Smoke Test Frequently

Practice Essentials

A. All tests should use systems that are built on a frequent and regular basis (nominally no less than twice a week).

B. All new releases should be regression tested by CM prior to release to the test organization.

C. Smoke testing should qualify new capabilities or components only after successful regression test completion.

D. All smoke tests should be based on a preapproved and traceable procedure and run by an independent organization (not the engineers who produced it).

E. All defects identified should be documented and subject to the program change control process.

F. Smoke test results should be visible and provided to all project personnel.

Implementation Guidelines

A. From the earliest opportunity to assess the progress of developed code, the DEVELOPER needs to use a process of frequent (one- to two-week intervals) software compile-builds as a means for finding software integration problems early.

B. It is required that a regression facility that incorporates a full functional test suite be applied with the build strategy.

C. The results of the testing of each software build should be made available to all project personnel.

12

Putting It All Together

At the beginning of this book, in Chapter 1, I mentioned the absolute need for an SPMO to embrace a methodology and to use it for all software projects an IT organization will undertake. The next eight chapters described each phase of the SEP methodology in terms of how a business leader would expect the project to flow. Each chapter has provided a solid, evolutionary progression of the project development effort from a management viewpoint. The overview of each phase of the methodology is important because it sets standards and expectations for you, the IT leader. When you are looking at taking on any new effort, you want to ensure that you have the best set of tools, practices, procedures, and so on available to help you succeed. Understanding the SEP process is a key gating factor to your success. Granted, you may personally believe in another methodology and be more comfortable with it, but it really does not matter which methodology is used as long as it achieves the desired level of results and has been defined and documented with an equivalent level of detail as what has been provided in this book.

SEP was chosen because it is the most widely recognized software development project model used in the business world today. There are newer models out there, but the truth of the matter is that most IT leaders choose to go with an industry-proven model that will not limit their ability to succeed. When your reputation and your job are on the line for a project deliverable, it is not worth taking chances by using a model that is not widely known or proven across the software industry and over the course of years of use. Remember, you are reaping the benefits of the evolution of this methodology over those many years of trial by fire in the trenches of businesses worldwide.

12.1 Beyond SEP Methodology: Making It All Work

It is my strong belief that one of the greatest strengths an SPMO adds to an organization is process standardization. Part of this process standardization includes having the organization align its activities to a standard method of getting work done (e.g., SEP) and by using the same activities defined in a process for each phase of each project the SPMO has under management. Additionally, enterprise project document standardization is achieved as a side effect of the combination of process and methodology standardization.

When every project is using the same approach to get work done, people begin to align their thoughts, expectations, vocabularies, and efforts toward the goal; they begin to function as a team. This team effect strengthens the overall expectation of project success, and I believe it allows people the opportunity to fully commit themselves to their work. It is my experience that once expectations are known and work assignments are understood, people generally tend to step up and get the job done far beyond my expectations.

The net effect of this process standardization is a common understanding of what is expected when a project request is submitted. The project initiation request sets expectations for a series of known activities and events to take place. In effect, it raises the bar of expectations in an organization because the new minimum standard is to do better than the last project. With the SPMO processes in place, all of the resources, documents, histories, work products, and so on of the previous project (including the things that went wrong) are available to the new core team as it begins to take on a new project. It is part of the SPMO team's responsibility to ensure this ideal is upheld and adhered to for each new project that is started.

12.2 SPMO Implementation Thoughts

We described the SPMO organizational structure and project team composition in Chapter 1. In addition to these defined roles for the project and SPMO, the SEP roadmaps defined which activities are to be performed by the Core Team, the SPMO, and the other project team members during the project's phased effort. Figure 12.1 illustrates the SPMO domain.

The single most significant activity of the SPMO is that of tracking the progression of each project and managing the completion of the deliverables during the course of the project development. Doing this will focus

12.2 SPMO Implementation Thoughts

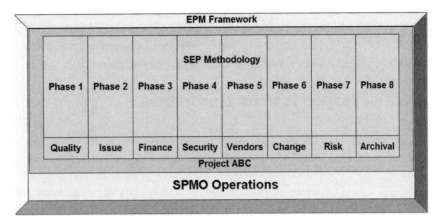

Figure 12.1
SPMO Scope and Methodology Domain.

the Core Team on what work will need to be accomplished next in the work effort and keep them aligned with a steady progression of task completion activities. Review of the deliverables is an absolute must. Quality should never be sacrificed for the sake of completion.

As an IT leader, you benefit from having all information for every project at your disposal. Cyclical status reports and data taken from the project database will allow you to communicate better across the organization. You will be able to better track project costs and manage budgets collectively. You will find that the wealth of information at your disposal becomes useful to other business leaders, and they will ask for access to your project data (because you have raised the bar and set higher expectations). Executive meetings will be much easier to prepare for, and communication of project data will become less and less a focus of executive staff meetings. Business objectives will take more of the spotlight in these meetings.

My experience has been that the better the SPMO and you do your job, the less visible you become in these staff meetings. Businesspeople tend to spend their time focusing on problems, and if you take away the problems, they are free to focus their energies elsewhere. You may be thinking that less visibility is a double-edged sword. True, but it should be viewed as an opportunity to allow you to communicate your vision, strategy, and ideals to other business leaders in more of a one-on-one setting instead of using the staff meeting to try and achieve these goals. Taking such a vis-à-vis approach tends to strengthen bonds and build trust in a relationship. It also allows other executives a forum in which to ask you so-called dumb questions without being embarrassed in a staff meeting. You will most likely be surprised by the number of times executives from other business units begin to value these sessions as a mini-learning event and request recurring meetings on your calendar. You should always take the time to cross-pollinate your views with your peers. It builds strong trust and alliances in an organization, and there is nothing more powerful than an executive team that trusts each other and works well together.

12.3 People Issues Revisited

During the initial stages of setting up the SPMO, you will likely spend most of your time communicating your vision of how projects will work to your team, to other business leaders, and to other members of the organization. First and foremost, make sure you have a solid grasp of what you want the SPMO to become. Always describe the SPMO in terms of the end state and not what you have in place at the moment. Make sure the people you choose to staff the SPMO understand your vision. Spend as much time as needed to ensure this, or you will be doomed from the start. Your SPMO staff should possess enough understanding of this undertaking to believe in it. It is not uncommon for the establishment of a working SPMO to take two or three months from start to go-live. Most of this time will be in transitioning staff, creating the BROC, training, communicating the new vision of how project work will be done, and training the development teams on how you want them to work on projects. It is not an easy undertaking by any means, but with the tools and templates provided in this book, you will be off to a good start.

I have found one key success factor in transferring the knowledge of an SPMO end state is to spend as much one-on-one time with your team as possible to reinforce the vision and keep the SPMO staff focused on the end state of what you want. As they see your commitment and gain confidence in their understanding of the vision you are espousing, they will begin to offer suggestions for improvement of the process. Listen to every suggestion made. Do not reject anything without bringing up the matter with your SPMO staff. Empower them to be the ones to decide if the suggestion is on track with the end-state vision or not. Remember, you can always overrule them when the decision is wrong or you disagree with it, but the point here is to empower your team to take control of the process. You should truly want them to own it. Anytime you overrule them, you take away from that empowerment and create an artificial dependency on your approval. My advice is to avoid that situation as much as possible. Empowerment gives people the chance to take responsibility for their actions. People tend to want to do a good job, and having the freedom to decide how that job gets done strengthens their bond with the organization. You will find out very soon that they dedicate themselves to creating a work product that usually goes far beyond your expectations. In more than 20 years of IT management, I have seldom been disappointed by taking this approach.

12.4 Project Management Tools

Most carpenters find a good hammer and use it for many years. They generally do not evaluate their hammer every six months and compare it with newer hammers or different brands of hammers. They seldom have any need to pilot the use of a different brand of hammer. They generally use the hammer they have for as long as it reliably does the job they bought it to do. My point is that the use of a particular project management tool is not a significant factor to success. The use of any software tool should be based on criteria related to business objectives. For me, selection of a given software tool is based on the following key criteria:

- Is the tool considered a de facto standard that other tool vendors compare themselves to?
- Is the tool already in widespread use in the organization?
- If it is not currently used, is the expense of introducing the tool justified?
- Will the tool significantly enhance productivity? How?
- Will use of this tool allow the interchange of data between teams, units, and vendors?

Many other criteria can be applied to the tool selection process, but the answers to these questions are gating factors in my book. If these questions can all be answered with a yes, then I am most likely to be receptive to using the tool. A no answer for any one of these questions usually becomes a showstopper. In cases where no tool is present, the answers to these questions, for each product evaluated, will help you decide what is best for your business. It is quite common to create a decision matrix and evaluate several vendor products against these criteria before making a decision.

To put things into proper perspective, a press release from the NIST is reprinted below[19]. The NIST is a nonregulatory agency of the U.S. Department of Commerce's Technology Administration that develops and promotes measurement, standards, and technology to enhance productivity, facilitate trade, and improve the quality of life. What follows is a truly staggering report of the loss of money resulting from software errors. This only emphasizes the absolute need for an organization to use the SPMO to establish order and structure in its development processes. The full text of the press release follows:

Software Errors Cost U.S. Economy $59.5 Billion Annually

NIST Assesses Technical Needs of Industry to Improve Software-Testing

FOR IMMEDIATE RELEASE:

June 28, 2002

Contacts: Michael Newman

(301) 975-3025

NIST 2002-10

Software bugs, or errors, are so prevalent and so detrimental that they cost the U.S. economy an estimated $59.5 billion annually, or about 0.6 percent of the gross domestic product, according to a newly released study commissioned by the Department of Commerce's National Institute of Standards and Technology (NIST). At the national level, over half of the costs are borne by software users and the remainder by software developers/vendors.

The study also found that, although all errors cannot be removed, more than a third of these costs, or an estimated $22.2 billion, could be eliminated by an improved testing infrastructure that enables earlier and more effective identification and removal of software defects. These are the savings associated with finding an increased percentage (but not 100 percent) of errors closer to the development stages in which they are introduced. Currently, over half of all errors are not found until "downstream" in the development process or during post-sale software use.

NIST funded the study, which was conducted by the Research Triangle Institute (RTI) in North Carolina, as part of a joint planning process with industry to help identify and assess technical needs that would improve software-testing capabilities. Findings of the 309-page report are intended to identify the infrastructure needs that NIST can meet through its research programs.

> "The impact of software errors is enormous because virtually every business in the United States now depends on software for the development, production, distribution, and after-sales support of products and services," said NIST Director Arden Bement. "Innovations in fields ranging from robotic manufacturing to nanotechnology and human genetics research have been enabled by low-cost computational and control capabilities supplied by computers and software."
>
> In 2000, total sales of software reached approximately $180 billion, supported by a large workforce encompassing 697,000 software engineers and 585,000 computer programmers.

Software is error-ridden in part because of its growing complexity. The size of software products is no longer measured in thousands of lines of code, but in millions. Software developers already spend approximately 80 percent of development costs on identifying and correcting defects, and yet few products of any type other than software are shipped with such high levels of errors. Other factors contributing to quality problems include marketing strategies, limited liability by software vendors, and decreasing returns on testing and debugging, according to the study. At the core of these issues is difficulty in defining and measuring software quality.

The increasing complexity of software, along with a decreasing average product life expectancy, has increased the economic costs of errors. The catastrophic impacts of some failures are well-known. For example, a software failure interrupted the New York Mercantile Exchange and telephone service to several East Coast cities in February 1998. But high-profile incidents are only the tip of a pervasive pattern that software developers and users agree is causing substantial economic losses.

12.5 Study Design and Background Facts

In the study, RTI identified a set of quality attributes and used them to construct metrics for estimating the cost of an inadequate testing infrastructure. Two in-depth case studies were conducted, one in the manufacturing sector (transportation equipment) and one in the service sector (financial services).

For the analysis of transportation equipment industries, data were collected from 10 vendors of computer-aided design/manufacturing/engineering

(CAD/CAM/CAE) and product data management (PDM) software, and from 179 users, primarily automotive and aerospace companies. Approximately 60 percent of the automotive and aerospace manufacturers surveyed reported significant software errors in the previous year. Respondents who experienced errors reported an average of 40 major and 70 minor software bugs per year in their CAD/CAM/CAE or PDM software systems.

The total cost impact on these manufacturing sectors from an inadequate software-testing infrastructure is estimated to be $1.8 billion, and the potential cost reduction from feasible infrastructure improvements is $0.6 billion. Users of CAD/CAM/CAE and PDM software absorb approximately three-fourths of the total impact, with the automotive industry representing about 65 percent and the aerospace industry representing 10 percent. Software developers experience the remaining one-fourth of the costs.

For the analysis of financial services, data was collected from four developers of financial electronic data interchange (FEDI) and clearinghouse software as well as the software embedded in routers and switches that support electronic data exchange, and from 98 software users, primarily banks and credit unions. Approximately two-thirds of the software users surveyed reported experiencing major software errors in the previous year. Respondents that did have major errors reported an average of 40 major and 49 minor software bugs per year in their FEDI or clearinghouse software systems. Approximately 16 percent of those bugs were attributed to router and switch problems, and 48 percent were attributed to transaction software problems. The source of the remaining 36 percent of errors was unknown. Typical problems encountered due to bugs were increased person-hours used to correct posting errors, temporary shut down leading to lost transactions, and delay of transaction processing.

The total cost impact on the financial services sector from an inadequate software-testing infrastructure is estimated to be $3.3 billion. Potential cost reduction from feasible infrastructure improvements is $1.5 billion. Software developers absorb about 75 percent of the economic impacts. Users experience the remaining 25 percent of costs, with banks accounting for the majority of user costs.

The annual cost to these two major industry groups from inadequate software infrastructure is estimated to be $5.18 billion. Based on similarities across industries with respect to software development and use and, in particular, software-testing labor costs, RTI projected the cost to the entire U.S. economy. Using the per-employee impacts for the two case studies, an extrapolation to other manufacturing and service industries yields an approximate estimate of $59.5 billion as the annual cost to the nation of inadequate software testing infrastructure.

Thus, if all software bugs could be identified and removed instantly (in real time), the combined economic benefits to the two industry groups and to the economy would be $5.85 billion and $59.5 billion, respectively. Realizing that such a "perfect infrastructure" is not attainable, industry experts were asked for estimates of a plausible reduction in delayed identification and removal of software errors. Based on this information, a "feasible improved infrastructure" scenario was constructed. For this scenario, software developers were asked to estimate the potential cost savings associated with enhanced testing tools, and users were asked to estimate cost savings if the software they purchase had 50 percent fewer bugs and errors. This improved infrastructure scenario is estimated to result in a combined annual benefit of $2.10 billion to the two industry groups studied, and $22.2 billion to the U.S. economy.

12.6 Next Steps

The path to higher software quality is significantly improved software testing. Standardized testing tools, suites, scripts, reference data, reference implementations and metrics that have undergone a rigorous certification process would have a large impact on the inadequacies currently plaguing software markets. For example, the availability of standardized test data, metrics and automated test suites for performance testing would make benchmarking tests less costly to perform. Standardized automated testing scripts, along with standard metrics, also would provide a more consistent method for determining when to stop testing.

12.7 Additional Resources for Managing Software Projects

One of the best sources for project-related information is the Web site for the Project Management Institute, www.pmi.org, where a wealth of data can be found. The Software Program Management Group Web site, www.pm-group.co.uk, is also very useful. Another very good resource for software program management information is www.spmn.com, which is home for the Software Program Manager's Network Web site. Many other Web resources are available. I recommend you check the links section at the www.pmi.org Web site for more resources.

Glossary

NOTE: This glossary was originally printed in the *Systems Development Life Cycle Manual*, dated July 2002, a product of the State of Maryland's Department of Budget & Management (DBM) Office of Information Technology. It is freely available at URL: http://www.dbm.state.md.us.

–A–

Acceptance Test: Formal testing conducted to determine whether a system satisfies its acceptance criteria and to enable the customer to determine whether to accept the system. See *User Acceptance Test*.

Accreditation: Formal declaration by an accrediting authority that a computer system is approved to operate in a particular security mode using a prescribed set of safeguards.

Acquisition Plan: A formal document showing how all hardware, software, and telecommunications capabilities, along with resources, are to be obtained during the life of the project.

Activity: A unit of work to be completed in order to achieve the objectives of a work breakdown structure. See *Work Breakdown Structure*. In process modeling, an activity requires inputs and produces outputs. See *input/output*.

Adaptability: The ease with which software satisfies differing system constraints and user needs.

Adaptive maintenance: Maintenance performed to change a system in order to keep it usable in a changed environment.

Alias: A name of a data entity or data attribute that is different from its official name.

Allocated baseline: The approved documentation that describes the design of the functional and interface characteristics that are allocated from a higher-level configuration item. See *baseline*.

Alternative work patterns: Work pattern that permits tailoring a project plan to meet the specific needs of the project and still conform to SDLC standards.

Application: A system providing a set of services to solve some specific user problem.

Application model: A model used to graphically and textually represent the required data and processes within the scope of the application development project.

Application software: Software specifically developed to perform a specific type of work (e.g., a word processor). Compare with *system software*.

Architecture: The structure of a computer system, either a part or the entire system; can be hardware, software, or both.

Audit: A formal review of a project (or project activity) to assess compliance with contractual obligations.

Availability: The degree to which a system (or system component) is operational and accessible when required for use.

–B–

Backup: *v.* To copy software files onto a different media that can be sorted separately from the original files and used to restore the original files, if needed. The act of creating these files. *n.* The set of copied files.

Baseline: A work product (such as software or documentation) that has been formally reviewed, approved, and delivered and can only be changed through formal change control procedures. See *allocated baseline, functional baseline, operational baseline, product baseline*.

Benchmark: A standard against which measurements or comparisons can be made.

Bottom-up: The process of designing a system by designing the low-level components first, then integrating them into large subsystems until the complete system is designed; bottom-up testing tests these low-level components first, using software drivers to simulate the higher-level components. See *top-down*.

Build: An operational version of a software product incorporating a specified subset of the complete system functionality. See *version*.

Business Process Reengineering: The redesign of an organization, culture, and business processes to achieve significant improvements in costs, time, service, and quality.

–C–

Capability: A measure of the expected use of a system.

Capacity: A measure of the amount of input a system could process and/or amount of work a system can perform (e.g., number of users, number of reports to be generated).

Certification: Comprehensive analysis of the technical and nontechnical security features and other safeguards of a system to establish the extent to which a particular system meets a set of specified security requirements.

Change: In configuration management, a formally recognized revision to a specified and documented requirement. See *change control, change directive, change impact assessment, change implementation notice.*

Change control: In configuration management, the process by which a change is proposed, evaluated, approved (or disapproved), scheduled, and tracked. See *change, change directive, change impact assessment, change implementation notice.*

Change Control Documents: Formal documents used in the configuration management process to track, control, and manage the change of configuration items over the systems development or maintenance life cycle. See *system change request, change impact assessment, change directive, and change implementation notice.*

Change directive: The formal change control document used to implement an approved change. See *Change Control Documents.*

Change Impact Assessment: The formal Change Control Document used to determine the effect of a proposed change before a decision is made to implement it. See *Change Control Documents.*

Change Implementation Notice: The formal Change Control Document used to report the actual implementation of a change in a system. See *Change Control Documents.*

Client/server: A network application in which the end-user interaction with the system (server) is through a workstation (client) that executes some portion of the application.

Code: *v.* To transform the system logic and data from design specifications into a programming language. *n.* The computer program itself; pseudocode is code written in an English-like logical representation; source code is code written in a programming language; object code is code written in machine language.

Compatibility: A measure of the ability of two or more systems (or system components) to exchange information and use the information that has been exchanged. Same as *interoperability*.

Component: General term for a part of a software system (hardware or software). See *product*.

Computer-aided software engineering: An electronic tool that is used to assist in the design, development, and coding of software. See *tools*.

Computer System Security Officer: The person who ensures that all activities are undertaken at the user site. Includes security activities for planning, awareness training, risk management, configuration management, certification and accreditation, compliance assurance, incident reporting, and guidance and procedures.

Concept of Operations: A formal document that describes the user's environment and process relative to a new or modified system; defines the users, if not already known. Called a CONOPS.

Configuration: The functional and/or physical collection of hardware and software components as set forth in formal documentation. Also, the requirements, design, and implementation that define a particular version of a system (or system component). See *configuration control, configuration item, configuration management, configuration management plan, configuration status accounting*.

Configuration Audit: Formal review of a project for the purpose of assessing compliance with the Configuration Management Plan.

Configuration control: The process of evaluating, approving or (disapproving), and coordinating changes to hardware/software configuration items.

Configuration Control Board: The formal entity charged with the responsibility for evaluating, approving (or disapproving), and coordinating changes to hardware/software configuration items.

Configuration item: An aggregation of hardware and/or software that satisfies an end-use function and is designated by the customer for configuration management; treated as a single entity in the configuration management process. A component of a system requiring control over its development throughout the life cycle of the system.

Configuration management: The discipline of identifying the configuration of a hardware/software system at each life cycle phase to control changes to the configuration and maintain the integrity and traceability of the configuration through the entire life cycle.

Configuration Management Plan: A formal document that establishes formal configuration management practices in a systems development/maintenance project. See *configuration management*.

Configuration status accounting: The recording and reporting of the information that is needed to effectively manage a configuration, including a listing of the approved configuration identification, status of proposed changes to the configuration, and the implementation status of approved changes. See *configuration*.

Contingency Plan: A formal document that establishes continuity of operations processes in case of a disaster. Includes names of responsible parties to be contacted, data to be restored, and location of such data.

Conversion: The process of converting (or exchanging) data from an existing system to another hardware or software environment.

Conversion Plan: A formal document that describes the strategies involved in converting data from an existing system to another hardware or software environment.

Corrective maintenance: Maintenance performed to correct faults in hardware or software.

Correctness: The degree to which a system or component is free from faults in its specification, design, and implementation.

Cost analysis: The costs for design, development, installation, operation and maintenance, and consumables for the system to be developed.

Cost-benefit analysis: The comparison of alternative courses of action or alternative technical solutions to determine which alternative would realize the greatest cost benefit; cost-benefit analysis is also used to determine if the system development or maintenance costs still yield a benefit or if the effort should stop.

Cost estimate: The process of determining the total cost associated with a software development or maintenance project, to include the effort, time, and labor required.

Criteria: A standard on which a decision or judgement may be based (e.g., acceptance criteria to determine whether to accept a system).

Critical path: Used in project planning; the sequence of activities (or tasks) that must be completed on time to keep the entire project on schedule; therefore, the time to complete a project is the sum of the time to complete the activities on the critical path.

Critical Review Board: A formal board that guides and monitors the development of requirements that affect current and future state systems.

Customer: An individual or organization that specifies the requirements for and formally accepts delivery of a new or modified system; one who pays for the system. The customer may or may not be the user. See *user*.

–D–

Data dictionary: A repository of information about data, such as its meaning, relationships to other data, origin, usage, and format. A data dictionary manages data categories such as aliases, data elements, data records, data structure, data store, data models, data flows, data relationships, processes, functions, dynamics, size, frequency, resource consumption, and other user-defined attributes.

Database Administrator: The person responsible for managing data at a logical level, namely data definitions, data policies, and data security.

Database: A collection of logically related data stored together in one or more computerized files; an electronic repository of information accessible via a query language interface.

Database Management System: A software system that controls storing, combining, updating, retrieving, and displaying data records.

Data store: A repository of data; a file.

Demonstration: A procedure to verify system requirements that cannot be tested otherwise.

Deliverable: A formal product that must be delivered to (and approved by) the customer.

Delivered system documentation: Includes the Software Development Document, User Manual, Maintenance Manual, and Operations Manual.

Design phase: The period of time in the Systems Development Life Cycle during which the designs for architecture, software components, interfaces, and data are created, documented, and verified to satisfy system requirements.

Development phase: The period of time in the Systems Development Life Cycle to convert the deliverables of the Design phase into a complete system.

Disposition phase: The period time when a system has been declared surplus and/or obsolete, and the task performed is either eliminated or transferred to other systems.

Disposition Plan: A formal plan providing the full set of procedures necessary to end the operation or the system in a planned, orderly manner and to ensure that system components and data are properly archived or incorporated into other systems.

Document: Written and/or graphical information describing, defining, specifying, reporting, or certifying activities, requirements, procedures, reviews, or results. See *product*.

–E–

Effectiveness: The degree to which a system's features and capabilities meet the user's needs.

Efficiency: The degree to which a system or component performs its designated functions with minimum consumption of resources.

Element: A subsystem, component, or unit; either software or hardware, as defined by the project.

Enhancement: Maintenance performed to provide additional functional or performance requirements.

Entity: Represents persons, places, events, things, or abstractions that are relevant to the state and about which data is collected and maintained.

–F–

Fault tolerance: The ability of a system (or system component) to continue normal operation despite the presence of hardware or software faults.

Feasibility: The extent to which the benefits of a new or enhanced system will exceed the total costs and also satisfy the business requirements.

Feasibility Study: A formal study to determine the feasibility of a proposed system (new or enhanced) in order to make a recommendation to proceed or to propose alternative solutions.

Field Test: Testing that is performed at the user site.

Fielded system: An operational system installed at the user site.

Full sequential: The systems development work pattern defined by life cycle phases described in SEP documentation (Chapter 10).

Functionality: The relative usefulness of a functional requirement as it satisfies a business need.

Functional baseline: The approved documentation that describes the functional characteristics of the system, subsystem, or component. See *baseline*.

Functional Configuration Audit: An audit to ensure that the functional requirements have been met by the delivered configuration item. See *audit*.

Functional requirement: A requirement that specifies a function (activity or behavior, based on a business requirement) that the system (or system component) must be capable of performing.

Functional Requirements Document: A formal document of the business (functional) requirements of a system; the baseline for system validation.

Functional Test: Testing that ignores the internal mechanism of a system (or system component) and focuses solely on the outputs generated in response to selected inputs and execution conditions. Same as black-box testing.

–G–

Gantt chart: A list of activities plotted against time, showing start time, duration, and end time; also known as a bar chart.

–H–

Hardware: The physical portion of a system (or subsystem), including the electrical components. Compare with *software*.

Host: The computer that controls communications in a network that administers a database; the computer on which a program or file is installed; a computer used to develop software intended for another computer. See *target*.

–I–

Implementation: Installing and testing the final system, usually at the user (field) site; the process of installing the system.

Implementation phase: The period of time in the Systems Development Life Cycle when the system is installed, made operational, and turned over to the user (for the beginning of the Operations and Maintenance phase).

Implementation Plan: A formal document that describes how the system will be installed and made operational.

Information Technology: The application of engineering solutions in order to develop computer systems that process data.

In-Process Review: Formal review conducted (usually annually) during the Operations and Maintenance phase to evaluate system performance, user satisfaction with the system, adaptability to changing business needs, and new technologies that might improve the system.

In-Process Review Report: A formal document detailing the findings of the in-process review. See *In-Process Review*.

Input/output: The process of entering information into a system (input) and its subsequent results (output). A hardware device that enables input (for example, a keyboard or card reader) and output (for example, a monitor or printer). Collectively known as I/O.

Inspection: A semiformal to formal technique in which software requirements, design, or code are examined in detail by a person or group other than the originator to detect errors. See *peer review, walk-through*.

Integrated Product Team: A multidisciplinary group of people who support the Project Manager in the planning, execution, delivery, and implementation of life cycle decisions for the project.

Integration Document: A formal document that describes how the software components, hardware components, or both are combined and the interaction between them.

Integration and Test phase: Life cycle phase during which subsystem integration, system, security, and user acceptance testing are conducted; done before the Implementation phase.

Integration Test: Testing in which software components, hardware components, or both are combined and tested to evaluate the interaction between them.

Integrity: The degree to which a system (or system component) prevents unauthorized access to, or modification of, computer programs or data.

Iterative: A procedure in which repetition of a sequence of activities yields results successively close to the desired state (e.g., an iterative life cycle in which two or more phases are repeated until the desired product is developed).

Glossary

Interface: To interact or communicate with another system (or system component). An interface can be software and/or hardware. See *user interface*.

Interface Control Document: Specifies the interface between a system and an external system(s).

Interoperability: A measure of the ability of two or more systems (or system components) to exchange information and use the information that has been exchanged. Same as *compatibility*.

Information Technology Systems Security Certification and Accreditation: A formal set of documents showing that the installed security safeguards for a system are adequate and work effectively.

–L–

Lessons Learned: A formal or informal set of examples collected from experience (e.g., experience in system development) to be used as input for future projects to know what went well and what did not; collected to assist other projects.

Library: A configuration controlled repository for system components (e.g., documents and software).

Life cycle: All of the steps or phases a project passes through during its system life; from concept development to disposition.

–M–

Maintainability: The ease with which a software system (or system component) can be modified to correct faults, improve performance or other attributes, or adapt to a changed environment.

Maintenance: In software engineering, the activities required to keep a software system operational after implementation. See *adaptive maintenance, corrective maintenance, enhancement, perfective maintenance*.

Maintenance Manual: A formal document that provides systems maintenance personnel with the information necessary to maintain the system effectively.

Maintenance Review: A formal review of both the completed and pending changes to a system with respect to the benefits achieved by completing the recommended changes; also provides information about the amount of maintenance required based on activity to date.

Measurement: In project management, the process of collecting, analyzing, and reporting metrics data.

Methodology: A set of methods, procedures, and standards that define the approach for completing a system development or maintenance project.

Metrics: A quantitative measure of the degree to which a system, component, or process possesses a given attribute.

Migration: Porting a system, subsystem, or system component to a different hardware platform.

Milestone: In project management, a scheduled event that is used to measure progress against a project schedule and budget.

Mission: The goals or objectives of an organization or activity.

Model: A simplified representation or abstraction (e.g., of a process, activity, or system) intended to explain its behavior.

Module: In system design, a software unit that is a logically separate part of the entire program. See *unit*.

–N–

Nontechnical: Relating to agreements, conditions, and/or requirements affecting the management activities of a project. Compare with *technical*.

–O–

Operational baseline: Identifies the system accepted by the users in the operational environment after a period of on-site testing using production data. See *baseline*.

Operations Manual: A formal document that provides a detailed operational description of the system and its interfaces.

Operations and Maintenance (O&M) phase: The period of time in the SEP Systems Development Life Cycle during which a software product is employed in its operational environment, monitored for satisfactory performance, and modified as necessary to correct problems or to respond to changing requirements.

–P–

Peer review: A formal review where a product is examined in detail by a person or group other than the originator. See *inspection, walk-through*.

Perfective maintenance: Software maintenance performed to improve the performance, maintainability, or other attributes of a computer program.

Performance measures: A category of quality measures that address how well a system functions.

Performance measurement and capacity planning: A set of procedures to measure and manage the capacity and performance of information systems equipment and software.

Performance review: A formal review conducted to evaluate the compliance of a system or component with specified performance requirements.

Phase: A defined stage in the SEP Systems Development Life Cycle.

Phase review: A formal review conducted during a life cycle phase; usually at the end of the phase or at the completion of a significant activity.

Physical Configuration Audit: An audit to ensure that all physical attributes listed in the design requirements have been met by the configuration item being delivered.

Pilot: An alternative work pattern to develop a system to demonstrate that the concept is feasible in an operational environment. Pilots are used to provide feedback to refine the final version of the product and are fielded for a preset, limited period of time. Compare with *prototype*.

Planning phase: The period in the SEP Systems Development Life Cycle in which a comprehensive plan for the recommended approach to the systems development or maintenance project is created.

Post-Implementation Review: A formal review to evaluate the effectiveness of the systems development effort after the system is operational (usually for at least six months).

Post-Implementation Review Report: A formal document detailing the findings of the Post-implementation Review. See *Post-Implementation Review*.

Post-Termination Review: A formal review to evaluate the effectiveness of a system disposition.

Post-Termination Review Report: A formal document detailing the findings of the Post-termination Review. See *Post-Termination Review*.

Procedure: A series of steps (or instructions) required to perform an activity. Defines how to perform an activity. Compare with *process*.

Process: A finite series of activities as defined by its inputs, outputs, controls (e.g., policy and standards), and resources needed to complete the activity. Defines what needs to be done. Compare with *procedure*.

Process model: A graphical representation of a process.

Process review: A formal review of the effectiveness of a process.

Product: General term for an item produced as the result of a process; can be a system, subsystem, software component, or a document.

Product baseline: The set of completed and accepted system components and the corresponding documentation that identifies these products. See *baseline*.

Production: A fully documented system, built according to the SDLC, fully tested, with full functionality, accompanied by training and training materials, and with no restrictions on its distribution or duration of use.

Product review: A formal review of a product software (or document) to determine if it meets its requirements. Can be conducted as a peer review.

Program specification: A description of the design logic in a software component, generally using pseudocode. See *code*.

Project: The complete set of activities associated with all life cycle phases needed to complete a systems development or maintenance effort from start to finish (may include hardware, software, and other components); the collective name for this set of activities. Typically a project has its own funding, cost accounting, and delivery schedule.

Project management: The process of planning, organizing, staffing, directing, and controlling the development and/or maintenance of a system.

Project Management Plan: A formal document detailing the project scope, activities, schedule, resources, and security issues. The Project Management Plan is created during the planning phase and updated throughout the project.

Project Manager: The person with the overall responsibility and authority for the day-to-day activities associated with a project.

Prototype: A system development methodology to evaluate the design, performance, and production potential of a system concept (it is not required to exhibit all the properties of the final system). Prototypes are installed in a laboratory setting and not in the field; nor are they available for operational use. Prototypes are maintained only long enough to establish feasibility. Compare with *pilot*.

Quality: The degree to which a system, component, product, or process meets specified requirements.

Quality assurance: A discipline used by project management to objectively monitor, control, and gain visibility into the development or maintenance process.

Quality Assurance Plan: A formal plan to ensure that delivered products satisfy contractual agreements, meet or exceed quality standards, and comply with approved systems development or maintenance processes.

Quality Assurance Review: A formal review to ensure that the appropriate quality assurance activities have been successfully completed, held when a system is ready for implementation.

–R–

Rapid Application Development: In a RAD work pattern, the Requirements Definition and Design phases are iteratively conducted; in this process, a rough set of requirements is used to create an initial version of the system, giving users visibility into the look, feel, and system capabilities. User evaluation and feedback provide revisions to the requirements, and the process is repeated until the requirements are considered to be complete.

Records management: The formal set of system records (e.g., files, data) that must be retained during the Disposition phase; the plan for collecting and storing these records.

Recoverability: The ability of a software system to continue operating despite the presence of errors.

Reengineering: Rebuilding a process to suit some new purpose (e.g., a new business process).

Regression Test: In software maintenance, the rerunning of test cases that previously executed correctly in order to detect errors introduced by the maintenance activity.

Release: A configuration management activity wherein a specific version of software is made available for use.

Reliability: The ability of a system (or system component) to perform its required functions under stated conditions for a specified period of time.

Requirement: A capability needed by a user; a condition or capability that must be met or possessed by a system (or system component) to satisfy a contract, standard, specification, or other formally imposed document.

Requirements Analysis phase: The period of time in the SEP during which the requirements for a software product are formally defined, documented, and analyzed.

Requirements management: Establishes and controls the scope of system development efforts and facilitates a common understanding of system capabilities between the system proponent, developers, and future users.

Requirements Traceability Matrix: Provides a method for tracking the functional requirements and their implementation through the development process.

Resource: In management, the time, staff, capital, or money available to perform a service or build a product; also, an asset needed for a process step to be performed.

Reverse engineering: A software engineering approach that derives the design and requirements of a system from its code; often used during the Maintenance phase of a system with no formal documentation.

Review: A formal process at which an activity or product (e.g., code, document) is presented for comment and approval; reviews are conducted for different purposes, such as peer reviews, user reviews, management reviews (usually for approval), or done at a specific milestone, such as phase reviews (usually to report progress).

Review Report: A formal document that records the results of a review.

Risk: A potential occurrence that would be detrimental to the project; risk is both the likelihood of the occurrence and the consequence of the occurrence.

Risk assessment: The process of identifying areas of risk; the probability of the risk occurring, and the seriousness of its occurrence; also called *risk analysis*.

Risk management: The integration of risk assessment and risk reduction in order to optimize the probability of success (i.e., minimize the risk).

Risk Management Plan: A formal document that identifies project risks and specifies the plans to reduce these risks.

Role: A defined responsibility (usually task) to be carried out by one or more individuals.

–S–

Scope: The established boundary (or extent) of what must be accomplished; during planning, this defines what the project will consist of (and just as importantly, what the project will not consist of).

Security: The establishment and application of safeguards to protect data, software, and hardware from accidental or malicious modification, destruction, or disclosure.

Security Risk Assessment: Tool that permits developers to make informed decisions relating to the acceptance of identified risk exposure levels or implementation of cost-effective measures to reduce those risks. See *Requirements Analysis phase*.

Security Test: A formal test performed on an operational system, based on the results of the Security Risk Assessment in order to evaluate compliance with security and data integrity guidelines, and address security backup, recovery, and audit trails. Also called *Security Testing and Evaluation (ST&E)*.

Segment: A major part of a larger system or subsystem; in software, a self-contained portion of a computer program.

Sensitive system: A system or subsystem that requires an IT Systems Security Certification and Accreditation; contains data requiring security safeguards.

Sensitivity analysis: Assesses the potential effect on inputs (costs) and outcomes (benefits) depending on the relative magnitude of change in certain factors or assumptions.

Software: Computer programs (code), procedures, documentation, and data pertaining to the operation of a computer system. Compare with *hardware*.

Software Development Document: Contains all of the information pertaining to the development of each unit or module, including the test cases, software, test results, approvals, and any other items that will help explain the functionality of the software.

Standard: Mandatory requirements to prescribe a disciplined uniform approach to software development and maintenance activities.

Subsystem: A collection of components that meets the definition of a system, but is considered part of a larger system. See *system*.

Survivability: A measure of the ability of a system to continue to function, especially in the presence of errors.

System: A collection of components (hardware, software, interfaces) organized to accomplish a specific function or set of functions; generally considered to be a self-sufficient item in its intended operational use.

System Administrator: The person responsible for planning a system installation and use of the system by other users.

System component: Any of the discrete items that comprise a system or subsystem. See *subsystem, system*.

System Change Request: The formal Change Control Document procedure used to request a change to a system baseline, provide information concerning the requested change, and act as the documented approval mechanism for the change. See *Change Control Documents*.

System Concept Development phase: Phase that begins after the need or opportunity has been identified in the Initiation phase. The approaches for meeting this need are reviewed for feasibility and appropriateness (e.g., cost-benefit analysis) and documented in the budget documents.

System Design Document: A formal document that describes the system architecture, file and database design, interfaces, and detailed hardware/software design; used as the baseline for system development.

System proponent: The organization benefiting from or requesting the project; frequently thought of as the "customer" for that project.

System Security Plan: A formal document that establishes the processes and procedures for identifying all areas where security could be compromised within the system (or subsystem).

System software: Software designed to facilitate the operation of a computer system and associated computer programs (e.g., operating systems, code compilers, utilities). Compare to *application software*.

System Test: The process of testing an integrated hardware/software system to verify that the system meets its documented requirements.

Systems Administration Manual: A manual that serves the purpose of an Operations Manual in a distributed (client/server) application. See *Operations Manual, Client/Server*.

Systems analysis: In systems development, the process of studying and understanding the requirements (customer needs) for a system in order to develop a feasible design.

Systems Development Life Cycle: A formal model of a hardware/software project that depicts the relationship among activities, products, reviews, approvals, and resources. Also, the period of time that begins when a need is identified (initiation) and ends when the system is no longer available for use (disposition).

Systems Manager: The individual, or group, responsible for post-implementation system maintenance, configuration management, change control, and release control. This may or may not include members of the development team.

–T–

Tailor: To modify a process, standard, procedure, or work pattern formally to fit a specific use or business need.

Target: The computer that is the destination for a host communication; see *host*. In programming, a language into which another language is to be translated.

Task: In project management, the smallest unit of work subject to management accountability; a work assignment for one or more project members fulfilling a role, as defined in a Work Breakdown Structure.

Technical: Relating to agreements, conditions, and/or requirements affecting the functionality and operation of a system. Compare with *nontechnical*.

Test: The process of exercising the product to identify differences between expected and actual results and performance. Typically testing is bottom-up: unit test, integration test, system test, and acceptance test.

Test case: A specific set of test data and associated procedures developed for a particular test.

Test files/data: Files/data developed for the purpose of executing a test; becomes part of a test case. See *test case*.

Testability: A metric used to measure the characteristics of a requirement that enable it to be verified during a test.

Test Analysis Approval Determination: The form attached to the Test Analysis Report as a final result of the test reviews for all testing levels above the Integration test. See *Test Analysis Report*.

Test Analysis Report: Formal documentation of the software testing as defined in the Test Plan.

Test and Evaluation (T&E): T&E occurs during all major phases of the Systems Development Life Cycle, beginning with system planning and continuing through the operations and maintenance phase; ensures standardized identification, refinement, and trace ability of the requirements as such requirements are allocated to the system components.

Test and Evaluation Master Plan: The formal document that identifies the tasks and activities so the entire system can be adequately tested to assure a successful implementation.

Test Problem Report: Formal documentation of problems encountered during testing; the form is attached to the Test Analysis Report. See *Test Analysis Report*.

Test Readiness Review: A formal phase review to determine that the test procedures are complete and to ensure that the system is ready for formal testing.

Tools: Software application products that assist in the design, development, and coding of software. Also called CASE tools; see *Computer-aided software engineering*.

Top-down: An approach that takes the highest level of a hierarchy and proceeds through progressively lower levels; compare with *bottom-up*.

Traceability: In requirements management, the identification and documentation of the derivation path (upward) and allocation path (downward) of requirements in the hierarchy.

Training: The formal process of depicting, simulating, or portraying the operational characteristics of a system or system component in order to make someone proficient in its use.

Training Plan: A formal document that outlines the objectives, needs, strategy, and curriculum to be addressed for training users of the new or enhanced system.

–U–

Unit: The smallest logical entity specified in the design of a software system; must be of sufficient detail to allow the code to be developed and tested independently of other units. See *module*.

Unit Test: In testing, the process of ensuring that the software unit executes as intended; usually performed by the developer.

Upgrade: A new release of a software system to include a new version of one or more system components.

Usability: The capability of the software product to be understood, learned, used; is of value to the user, when used under specified conditions.

User: An individual or organization who operates or interacts directly with the system; one who uses the services of a system. The user may or may not be the customer. See *customer*.

User Acceptance Test: Formal testing conducted to determine whether or not a system satisfies its acceptance criteria and to enable the user to determine whether or not to accept the system. See *Acceptance Test*.

User interface: The software, input/output (I/O) devices, screens, procedures, and dialogue between the users of the system (people) and the system (or system component) itself. See *interface*.

User Manual: A formal document that contains all essential information for the user to make full use of the new or upgraded system.

User Satisfaction Review: A formal survey used to gather the data needed to analyze current user satisfaction with the performance capabilities of an existing system or application; administered annually, or as needed.

–V–

Validation: The process of determining the correctness of the final product, system, or system component with respect to the user's requirements. Answers the question, Am I building the right product? Compare with *verification*.

Verifiability: A measure of the relative effort to verify a requirement; a requirement is verifiable only if there is a finite cost-effective process to determine that the software product or system meets the requirement.

Verification: The process of determining whether the products of a life cycle phase fulfill the requirements established during the previous phase; answers the question, "Am I building the product right?" Compare to *validation*.

Verification and Validation Plan: A formal document that describes the process to verify and validate the requirements. Created during the Planning phase and updated throughout the project.

Version: An initial release or rerelease of a computer software configuration item, associated with a complete compilation or recompilation of the computer software configuration item; sometimes called a build. See *build*.

Version Description Document: A formal document that describes the exact version of a configuration item and its interim changes. It is used to identify the current version; provides a packing list of what is included in the release.

Volatility: In requirements management, the degree to which requirements are expected to change throughout the Systems Development Life Cycle; opposite of *stability*.

–W–

Walk-through: A software inspection process, conducted by peers of the software developer, to evaluate a software component. See *inspection, peer review*.

Work Breakdown Structure: In project management, a hierarchical representation of the activities associated with developing a product or executing a process; a list of tasks; often used to develop a Gantt chart.

Work Pattern: The complete set of life cycle phases, activities, deliverables, and reviews required to develop or maintain a software product or system; a formal approach to systems development.

Common SPMO Acronyms and Abbreviations

BPR	Business Process Reengineering
BROC	Business Requirements Oversight Committee
BSA	Business Systems Analyst
CCB	Change Control Board
CER	Capital Expense Request
CEW	Cost Estimate Worksheet
CMP	Change Management Process
CMT	Change Management Team
COL	Closeout Letter
COTS	Commercial Off-the-Shelf
CPD	Content Pipeline Document
CPI	Continuous Process Improvement
CRF	Change Request Form
CSCI	Computer Software Configuration Item
CTR	Core Team Roster
DAD	Data Analysis Document
DBA	Database Administrator
DCP	Database Conversion Plan
DDD	Data Development Document
DDP	Data Development Plan
DDisP	Data Distribution Plan
DRA	Data Risk Analysis

EIP	Equipment Installation Plan
EVA	Economic Value Added
FRD	Framework Rules Document
FSD	Functional Specification Document
GPRA	Government Performance and Results Act of 1993
GUI	Graphical User Interface
HFP	Human Factors Plan
HFR	Human Factors Report
HLMP	Hardware Life Cycle Management Plan
HLSD	High-Level Solutions Document
HSAL	Hardware Signoff Acceptance Letter
HSTL	Hardware Software Transition Letter
IQA	Internal Quality Audit
IRF	Incident Report Form
IRS	Interface Requirements Specification
IT	Information Technology
ITMRA	Information Technology Management Reform Act of 1996
ITP	Integration Test Plan
LPA	Lease-Purchase Analysis
MAL	Master Archive List
MIS	Management Information Systems
MRS	Marketing Rollout Schedule
NTD	Near-Term Deliverable
OMG	Operations and Maintenance Guide
OTP	Optimization Tradeoff Plan
PASL	Project Assurance Signoff Letter
PAT	Product Assurance Test
PCA	Project Continuation Approval
PCL	Project Cancellation Letter
PDD	Project Definition Document

PFRD	Project Framework Rules Document
PIF	Project Initiation Form
PMD	Postmortem Documentation
POS	Project Objective Statement
PPDG	Project Planning and Documentation Guide
PRS	Performance Requirements Specification
PSUF	Project Status Update Form
PTL	Project Transition Letter
QAP	Quality Assurance Plan
QAT	Quality Action Team
RAM	Risk Assessment Matrix
RFI	Request for Information
RFP	Request for Proposal
ROI	Return on Investment
RMM	Risk Management Matrix
RTM	Requirements Traceability Matrix
SAS	Security Access Sheet
SDLC	Software Development Life Cycle
SDP	Software Development Plan
SEI	Software Engineering Institute, Carnegie-Mellon University
SEP	Systems Engineering Process
SFL	Sponsor Formalization Letter
SIM	Software Installation Manual
SIR	System Infrastructure Requirements
SIS	System Interface Specification
SLA	Service Level Agreement
SME	Subject-Matter Expert
SPMO	Software Program Management Office
SRS	Software Requirements Specification
STP	Software Test Plan

SUM	Software User Manual
TA	Technology Analysis
TAD	Technical Analysis Document
TCN	Target Completion Notice
TM	Training Manual
TPC	Test Plan Checklist
TRA	Technical Risk Analysis
UAT	User Acceptance Test
UI	User Interface
URD	User Requirements Document
WBSD	Work Breakdown Structure Dictionary

Roadmaps

SEP Phase I Roadmap

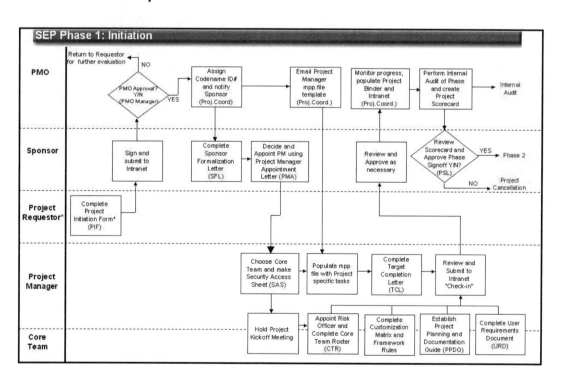

SEP Phase II Roadmap

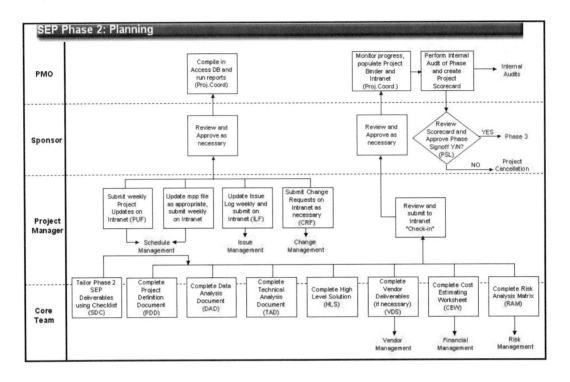

SEP Phase III Roadmap

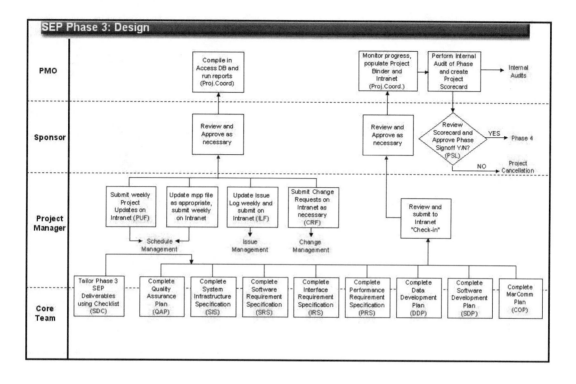

Appendix A

SEP Phase IV Roadmap

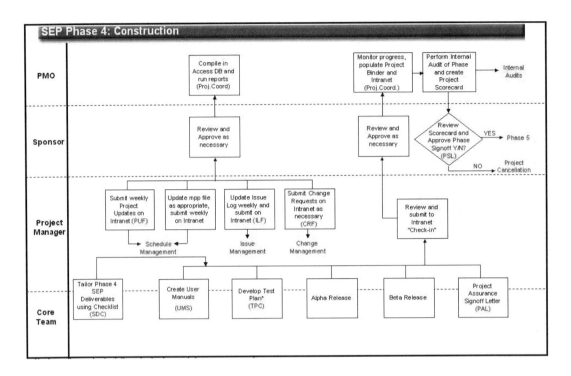

SEP Phase V Roadmap

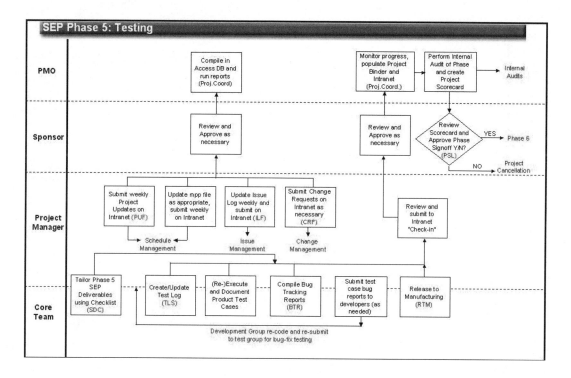

Appendix A

SEP Phase VI Roadmap

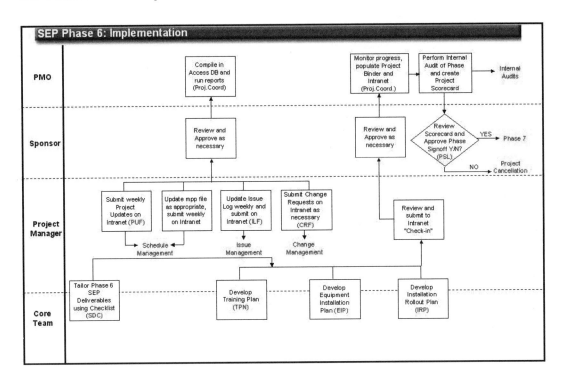

SEP Phase VII Roadmap

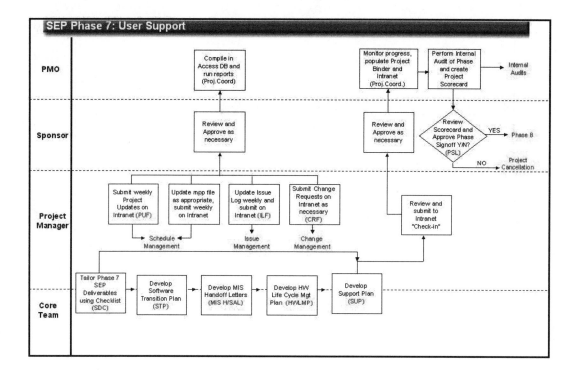

Appendix A

SEP Phase VIII Roadmap

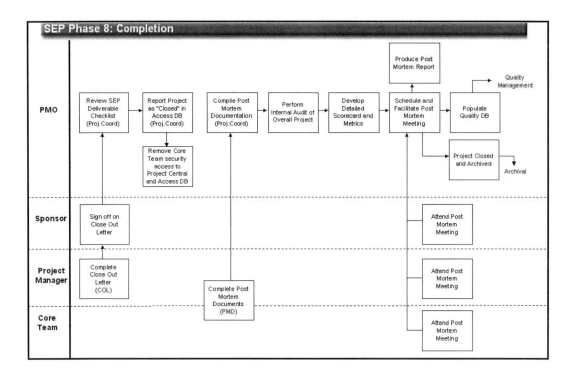

Security Access Roadmap

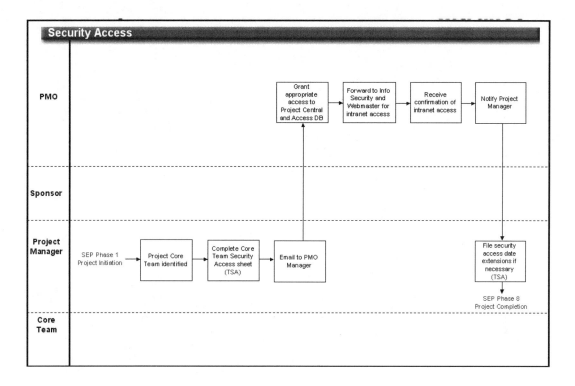

Appendix A

Project Cancellation Roadmap

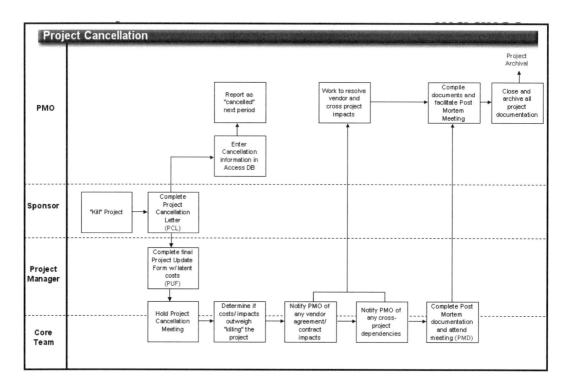

Project Archival Roadmap

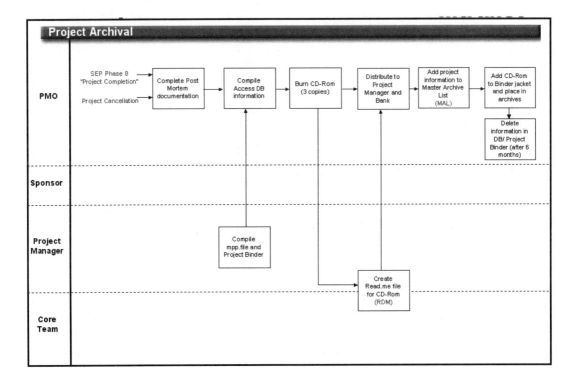

Appendix A

SPMO Documentation Updates Roadmap

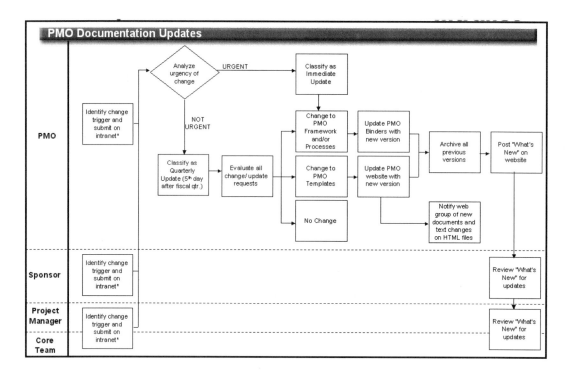

Schedule Management Roadmap

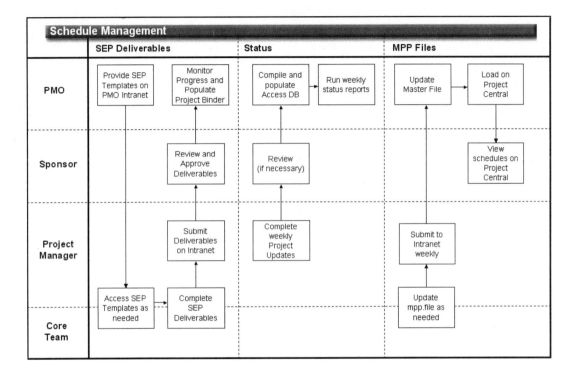

Appendix A

Risk Management Roadmap

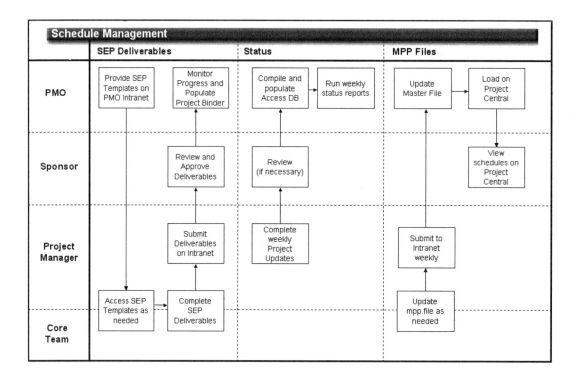

Issue Management Roadmap

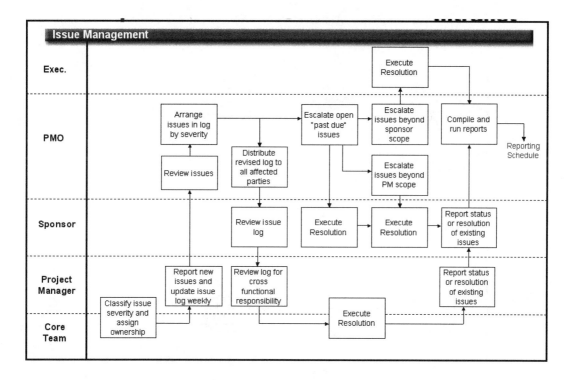

Appendix A

Financial Management Roadmap

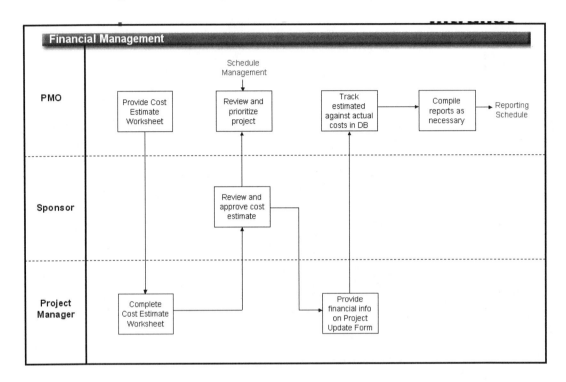

Change Management Roadmap

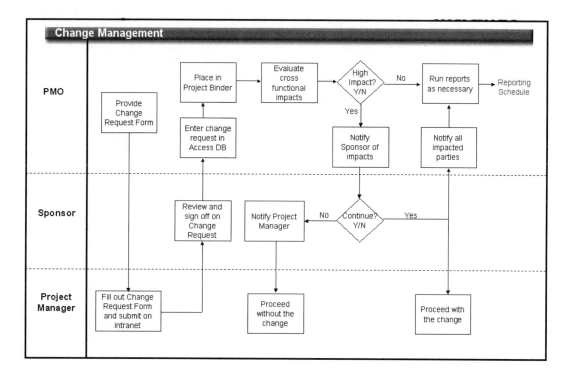

Appendix A

Vendor Management Roadmap

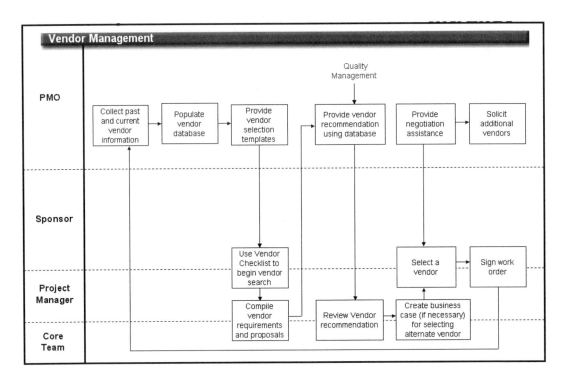

Quality Management Roadmap

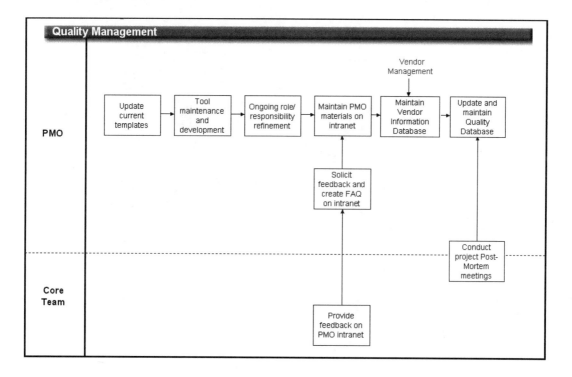

Appendix A

B

Answers

B.1 Chapter 1 Review

1. What are the key roles in an Enterprise SPMO?

    These roles are defined as the Executive Stakeholder, Project Sponsor, Program Manager, Project Manager, Project Coordinator, Project Resources, and Business Systems Analysts.

2. Describe the major service areas of an SPMO.

    They are Performance Reporting, Financial, Vendor, Issue, Quality, Change, and Risk Management.

3. What are several benefits of project performance reporting?

    Benefits of performance reporting include providing a means to ensure the project makes orderly progress toward key milestones by charting progress metrics. They tie performance reports and project financials together for a consolidated picture of the overall status of a project.

4. List the five key components of project performance reporting.

    1. Establishing program standards

    2. Requesting and collect data

    3. Consolidating information

    4. Reporting development and continuous improvement

    5. Reporting communications

5. Cite five to seven elements a project performance report should include.

Some examples of possible elements contained in a project performance report include:

1. *Scope of deliverables:* Planned, actual, and projected
2. *Cost:* Planned, actual, earned, and estimated at completion
3. *Schedule:* Planned, actual, and estimated
4. *Quality:* Planned, actual, and projected achievement
5. *Risk:* Planned, actual, and projected reduction
6. *Benefits:* Planned and achieved
7. *Issues:* Defined, corrective actions, status, management actions required

6. Why is financial management important in an enterprise SPMO environment?

Benefits of financial management include being able to explicitly define the financial controls and processes for the project and forecast project costs. It allows the team to improve estimates with consistent financial factors and to identify potential overruns and shortfalls in spending. It enables an integration with the performance reporting function and provides a process to consistently request financial approval from key stakeholders.

7. What are several benefits of effective vendor management?

Benefits of effective vendor management are cost savings obtained by working closely with vendor management to better obtain quality products and services, to develop relationships and partnering alliances with vendors, and to develop standards for vendor quality, metrics, reporting, pricing, and billing.

8. List the key components of vendor management.

1. Vendor planning
2. Vendor selection assistance
3. Establishment of contract terms and conditions
4. Monitoring
5. Contract closure

9. What is the purpose of a CCB?

Organizations set up a Change Control Board (CCB) to process and prioritize issues as they arise.

10. What are the main components of quality management?
    - Managing expectations
    - Verifying quality
    - Process management
    - Defining metrics
    - Reporting quality metrics
    - Continuous improvement
    - Establishing rewards and recognition
    - Quality training and orientation

11. Define change management as it pertains to an SPMO.

    Change management is the process of managing proposed changes to the project scope defined during the Requirements phase. This process will ensure consistent handling and escalation of all change requests. The objective of change management is to provide a defined process for managing changes to requirements and to set guidelines for approving and escalating changes. This process will provide corporate executives and project members with timely information regarding changes to requirements.

B.2 Chapter 2 Review

1. What happens when a Project Initiation Form (PIF) is submitted to the SPMO?

    Once the PIF has been submitted, the SPMO will enter the data into a project database and make some preliminary reviews against business needs, objectives, and so on. If the request is determined to meet the needs of the business, the SPMO will assign a project code name and an SPMO ID number. Generally, the task of completing the PIF is done by a Project Coordinator working within the SPMO. The Project Coordinator will also generate a Sponsor Formalization Letter (SFL) and arrange a meeting with the Project Sponsor. During this meeting, the sponsor will be required to sign the initiation document in order to approve any future work on the project.

2. What are the key points in a Sponsor Formalization Letter (SFL)?

    Key points in the SFL are statements of commitment from the sponsor such as the following:

- I will be the representative for the project to peer/upper management.
- I will appoint a Project Manager to manage the project.
- I will be the focal point for decisions beyond the Project Manager's scope of authority.
- I will approve/disapprove the scope and objectives, including schedule and budget.
- I will provide strategic direction as well as approve any project changes.
- I will apply resources to the project as deemed necessary by the Project Manager.

3. Who is responsible for establishing a project Core Team?

    It is the PM's responsibility, once he or she has been assigned to a project, to coordinate with the SPMO and choose from among many people in the organization those who will be representatives on the Core Team.

4. Describe the role of a Risk Officer.

    The Risk Officer does not have the job of stopping progress, but rather of recording and informing the team of concerns that arise during the scope of the project.

5. Who completes the Project Customization Matrix?

    The Project Customization Matrix is created and reviewed by the Core Team to make inclusion/exclusion decisions about areas that are often overlooked at the beginning of an initiative. It is up to the Core Team members to make such decisions based on their knowledge of the company and what is significant and relevant to business needs.

6. What is the purpose of a User Requirements Document (URD)?

    The URD is intended to document the intent of the system from the user perspective.

7. What is the Project Planning and Documentation Guide (PPDG)? What is it used for?

    The PPDG contains a high-level overview of the contents of each of the documents that make up a company's Systems Engineering Process (SEP). The information contained in this document can be used as a reference point for the information that can be found in each of the SEP documents.

B.3 Chapter 3 Review

1. Why is the Project Objective Statement (POS) necessary?

   The POS states what work you are going to do (the scope), by when (the schedule), with how many or how much (the resources or cost). It provides clarity and focus for the project team.

2. What is the Project Definition Document (PDD)?

   The PDD is a high-level summary of the project. It should document information in the following order: description, purpose, strategic alignment, completion criteria, project start, customers, dependencies, and hardware/software requirements.

3. What is the purpose of a Flexibility Matrix?

   This matrix is used to help the team decide and prioritize the tradeoff between scope, schedule, and resources.

4. Why should a Data Risk Analysis (DRA) be completed?

   The DRA will bring important data issues to light *before* they arise, and it can save the Core Team much time and effort in defending decisions after the fact.

5. List five key components of a Technical Analysis Document (TAD).

   These components are Software Reengineering Assessment, Technology Analysis, Technical Risk Assessment, In-House Contractor Analysis, and Lease-Purchase Analysis.

6. Who is responsible for the completion of the Technical Risk Analysis (TRA)?

   It is part of the Risk Officer's responsibilities to ensure this TRA is completed.

7. What is the High-Level Solution Document (HLSD)?

   The HLSD is an initial response from the Project Manager to the user's problems and needs as presented in the User Requirements Document (URD). This document is not intended to describe the end solution or final product in great detail. It is meant only to provide a 40,000-foot view (hence the name high-level solution).

8. When is a Request for Proposal (RFP) used?

This document, used when asking third parties to provide possible assistance, is the official request from your organization to a vendor to submit a proposal stating how the vendor would satisfy the requirements of the URD and accomplish the objectives stated in the HLS.

9. What basic elements should a funding package contain?

The funding documentation should contain all of the documents needed in your organization to request capital and/or expense dollars for the project, such as an explanation of the costs to sustain current operations, any savings to be realized, a calculation of the Return on Investment (ROI) or Economic Value Added (EVA). It should include any project development costs for hardware, software, data formatting and/or conversion, and programming. Project implementation costs such as training, publications, rollout costs, costs of sustaining the product after delivery, maintenance fees, and support costs are included in the funding documents. Finally, the funding documents should disclose funds that have already been budgeted for this project. An appendix should contain any copies of outstanding and/or approved Capital Equipment Requests (CERs), Purchase Orders (POs), and vendor invoices (paid and unpaid) that have been received to date.

10. Who manages the project budget and schedule?

The Project Manager is responsible for managing the budget and schedule.

11. What are dependency diagrams used for?

They are used to display a visual representation of project dependencies.

12. When are variance reports necessary?

The reports should be compiled upon request of the Core Team or Project Sponsor, or at minimum, at the end of each of the eight SEP project phases.

B.4 Chapter 4 Review

1. What is a Quality Assurance Plan (QAP)?

B.4 Chapter 4 Review

The QAP defines, tracks, and measures both product and process quality goals throughout the project development process. QAPs ensure the completion of defect removal activities.

2. What are some factors to consider in building a Human Factors Plan (HFP)?

   - O/S tests
   - Code testing
   - User input testing
   - General performance testing
   - User feedback
   - Graphics
   - Performance
   - Functionality

3. List the four key specifications documents required during the design phase.

   1. System Infrastructure Requirements
   2. Software Requirements Specifications
   3. Interface Requirements Specifications
   4. Performance Requirements Specifications

4. What is a Software Requirements Specification (SRS)?

   The SRS document specifies the exact functional specification for each and every item mentioned in the URD. Sometimes, these requirements are referred to as Computer Software Configuration Items (CSCI).

5. User-Interface (UI) requirements are detailed in which specification document?

   UI requirements are detailed in the Interface Requirements Specification Document.

6. Which two components are found in the Data Development Plan (DDP)?

   The first of these two components is the Content Pipeline Document. The second component is the Data Distribution Plan.

7. List the basic elements of a DCP.

   - Identifying content authors

- Defining content flow process and content correction process.
- Defining data format
- Defining data publication tool assignments
- Generating reports
- Collecting data
- formatting data

8. What is a Software Development Plan (SDP)?

   The SDP is a generalized description of a group of specifications and plans for conducting a software development effort.

9. What is the purpose of a Database Conversion Plan (DCP)?

   The DCP is used to define existing application files that need to be converted, specify the new files that need to be created, identify the volume of data that is to be converted, and stipulate which organizational entities are to be involved in defining the conversion process, target dates, data integrity, and so on.

10. What is the Marketing Communications Plan used for?

    This document communicates to the appropriate Marketing Communications organization all of the information required to develop a Marketing Communications Plan.

B.5 Chapter 5 Review

1. Why is the Software User Manual (SUM) written?

   It is written as a fundamental learning tool for the project deliverable.

2. Who uses the Software Installation Manual (SIM)?

   The SIM is used by systems administrators and gives step-by-step instructions for installing the application.

3. Why should training manuals be standardized?

   In a large organization with many large systems, it is a huge cost consideration to train people. Consistency across training programs helps reduce costs and leverage efficiencies across applications.

4. What is an Operations and Maintenance Guide (OMG)?

   The OMG describes the technical operation and maintenance specifications for the finished product.

5. Test cases should be constructed in accordance with which standard?

   ANSI/IEEE Standard 829-1983 for Software Test Documentation

6. What is the purpose of a test plan?

   The purpose of the test plan is to provide an overview of the testing effort needed for the product delivery to be successful.

7. What is a master test plan?

   It is a centralized repository to be used for all documentation relating to the testing effort.

8. What is the Test Summary Report used for?

   This is an explanation of the testing process, environment, results, and so on.

9. Name four to six major areas that a test plan should contain.

   1. Stress Test Plans

   2. Integration Test Plans

   3. Software Test Plan's

   4. Product Assurance Tests

   5. User Acceptance Tests

   6. MIS/Outside Certification Plans

10. What is a Software Test Plan (STP)?

    The STP describes the software test approach, identifies the tests to be performed for each module, and provides detailed schedules for test activities. It ensures correctness and accuracy of the program's internal logic and validates interfaces among the various modules of the program.

11. What is the purpose of the Product Assurance Test (PAT)?

    The PAT verifies that the total system solution performs as expected. This test is performed by executing a series of test cases that have been specifically constructed to demonstrate to the users that the system works properly in a production environment.

12. What is the purpose of the User Acceptance Test (UAT)?

    The UAT verifies the total system solution and ensures that it satisfies the original business requirements.

13. Who completes the Functional Certification Letter (FCL)?

    The FCL is a letter from the customer or the functional business representative that documents satisfaction or areas of concern with the functional performance of the system.

B.6 Chapter 6 Review

1. Describe the cyclical process of testing.

    The test group executes test cases and documents bugs found in the testing process. The bug reports are reviewed by the developers. The development group then attempts to correct the bugs and then will resubmit the recoded modules for retest. This iterative process generally continues until all modules have passed all appropriate test cases.

2. What is the purpose of the Test Plan Checklist?

    The Test Plan Checklist not only requires the test team to conduct reviews on the four recommended test plans (i.e., Stress Test Plan, STP, ITP, and UAT) that were created in the previous phase of work, but it also asks for an introspective look at the Test Team and the quality of the Test Plan. This review helps the team focus on more than just going through the motions of completing a test case: It asks the members of the Test Team to take responsibility for validation of the product.

3. Test log entries should contain what minimal information?
    - Execution descriptions
    - Procedure results
    - Environmental information
    - Unexpected events
    - Incident report ID number

4. List several types of test domains.
    - User-interface errors
    - Error handling
    - Boundary-related errors
    - Calculation errors
    - Initial and later states
    - Control flow errors

- Errors in handling or interpreting data
- Race conditions
- Load conditions
- Hardware
- Source, version, and ID control
- Testing errors

5. What is the most important preventive measure a Core Team can take to avoid test errors?

   Spending enough time during the design process to avoid these types of errors.

6. Name three key factors to addressing error-handling issues.

   In this domain of testing, there are three key factors to consider: prevention, detection, and recovery.

7. What is a control flow error?

   When a program executes, the program cursor moves from one part of the program to the next, executing the coded instructions sequentially. Some execution instructions force the program to jump from one routine to another. This movement in execution is referred to as program or control flow.

8. What is a load condition?

   Load conditions are the result of putting more work on the computer than it can handle.

9. Who should be included in a Test Plan Review?

   It is best for all concerned if the formal test review includes the most experienced users and developers present in an organization.

B.7 Chapter 7 Review

1. What are the Core Team's chief responsibilities during the Implementation phase?

   In this phase, the Core Team is responsible for developing training and rollout plans.

2. What is the User Training Plan (UTP) used for?

   The UTP details the activities required for getting all system users trained on the new application and understanding the new work flow procedures.

3. Why is it necessary for the Core Team to develop a cost-benefit analysis for training?

   The Core Team should develop a cost-benefit analysis for the training to determine the benefits that will result from effective training and to quantify them so they can be presented during the business leader walk-through of the training program. The business leaders will certainly want to know what the estimated costs of training are and how the numbers were derived.

4. Why is it important to define the scope and objectives of a training program?

   This is really a question of cost. Training is a costly proposition, and you should be aware of that fact. To train some or all staff internally or externally is a calculated tradeoff between the quality of training the users will receive and the time and cost of having specific training for each user.

5. Why is it important to define the training methods to be used before providing training?

   Defining the training methods to be used helps the training team clarify what is to be done and helps focus the team's efforts on delivering the right materials to the right audience in the right facilities with the right equipment.

6. What is the benefit of having a Training Roster?

   It is important for an organization to know who has had training because training equates to dollars. You want to help ensure that the organization does not waste money training those who will not benefit or do not need training. Likewise, it is imperative to train all of those in the organization who need and will use the training.

7. What is the Equipment Installation Plan?

   This document describes plans for installing hardware, software, and networking equipment at user sites and training sites, and it should also include the plans for converting equipment from old systems to the new system.

8. What kind of dependencies should you be aware of when developing the Installation Rollout Plan?

   Special care should be given to subtle dependencies that might exist, like the following:

   - Hardware-to-hardware dependencies

- Software-to-software dependencies
- Network-to-network dependencies
- Hardware-to-software dependencies

9. What is significant about the Rollout Signoff?

   This is *the* document. It is obtained from the user or appropriate team member indicating that the product was successfully rolled out to all users. It is the culmination of a lot of people's hard work and should be a shared reading experience across the Core Team.

B.8 Chapter 8 Review

1. To a development team, what is significant about the Support phase?

   The Customer Support phase represents a formal handoff from the development team to organizational MIS or IT support.

2. What are the six key tasks the Core Team must complete during the Support phase?

   1. Develop the Software Transition Plan
   2. Develop the MIS Hardware/Software Handoff Letters
   3. Develop the Hardware Life Cycle Management Plan
   4. Develop the Help Desk Checklists
   5. Develop the Support Plan
   6. Develop the Signoff Letter

3. What is a Software Transition Plan?

   The Software Transition Plan transitions the software from the Development phase to the User Support phase.

4. What purpose does the MIS Hardware/Software Handoff Letter serve?

   This letter from the MIS organization indicates it has reviewed, approved, and accepted full responsibility for both the software applications and all of the related hardware deliverables that the project team has developed; it formally declares it (MIS) will provide ongoing support as needed to maintain it.

5. What are the three key sections every support plan should contain?

At a minimum, it is recommended that the support plan contain a Software Configuration Management Plan, Service Level Agreement(s), and Help Desk Checklists.

6. Define change management.

   Change management refers in part to how software modules are managed as they are checked in and out of the master source library.

7. What is configuration control?

   Configuration control is a process that begins with the establishment of a single, baseline copy of the product source code. A library for the master copy of the source code is established and managed using check-in and check-out procedures. This single copy should be used for all subsequent builds by all groups. All changes and updates are reflected in the build. Interim checks are often established to prevent corruption of the master by requiring that strict quality assurance and audit control procedures are enforced. The use of a single master for builds ensures that all changes are reflected in the latest version, and testing will account for such changes.

8. What key points should you remember when creating a Service Level Agreement (SLA)?

   1. There should be equal representation of the service provider and the client.
   2. The leaders of the team should be peers.
   3. The members of the team should be stakeholders.
   4. The team members need to be subject-matter experts.

9. List the basic components of an SLA.

   I. Parties to the Agreement
   II. Term of the Agreement
   I. Scope of the Agreement
   II. Limitations
   III. Service Level Objectives
   IV. Service Level Indicators
   V. Nonperformance

       VI. Optional Services

      VII. Exclusions to the Agreement

    VIII. Reporting Procedures

      IX. Administration Process

       X. Reviews

      XI. Revisions

     XII. Approvals

10. What is a Help Desk Checklist used for?

This checklist identifies the type of customer support that the Help Desk may need to provide. It is intended to be used to assist in preparing the organizational support team for handling questions or problems regarding the use of the product or deliverable.

B.9 Chapter 9 Review

1. Why is the Postmortem Report necessary?

   The postmortem meeting and its corresponding report should provide an effective means to reflect on lessons learned and battles won. It should be used to improve on the process for future projects.

2. When closing out a project, what five actions must be completed by the Core Team?

   In order to properly end the program and terminate the activities supporting the product, you should complete the following five actions:

   1. Produce a written Software Project History containing both objective and subjective information about the project.

   2. Distribute the Project History to all project members.

   3. Place Project History conclusions into the project binder for review when working on the next project.

   4. Conduct a postmortem meeting and report the results and findings.

   5. Complete all closeout paperwork.

3. What good does a Postmortem Report serve to the SPMO?

   Through the answers to these questions, your organization may save a lot of money by learning to prevent things from negatively affecting project outcomes. This is also a time for the SPMO to reflect on the overall administration of the program and determine if changes are needed in administration or policy at the SPMO level.

4. What is the purpose continuing to restrict access to project materials after a project has been closed?

   Access to the archive CD and distribution of it to anyone in the company must be controlled to protect other sensitive corporate material, even if the project is closed. A lot of valuable corporate espionage information can be gleaned from the data comprising an entire project.

5. What is meant by the term *shadow people*?

   These are the folks who work behind the scenes to make the project work. Without them, there would be no chance for success, but they do not individually stand out within the Core Team or among other business leaders. They are always there and doing their part, however large or small. These folks are the backbone of the company in most cases, and your success—whether you know it or not—nearly always depends in large part on their performance.

C

Software Notes

C.1 Installing the Intranet-Based Software

The software provided with this book can be downloaded from the following URL: http://books.elsevier.com/digitalpress. Search for the title and the software can be retrieved. It is provided as is, and no support for using it is provided by the author. A single directory named /enterprise is found in the zip file. This directory contains a Web created using Microsoft FrontPage 2002. All of the files needed to use the Web are broken down in the standard FP2002 subdirectory structure. Template documents and files are stored in the directory labeled /_private. The directory labeled /images contains all graphics used for the Web page development. These graphics may be modified to suit user needs.

Copy the /enterprise directory to your hard drive and open the Web using FrontPage 2000. The software may ask if you wish to convert this directory to a FrontPage Web. If so, say yes. Once converted, you may use FrontPage to publish the Web to any location you desire. The contents of the Web may be used or modified only in accordance with the end-user license agreement that accompanies the archive file and is reprinted below for your convenience.

WARRANTY LIMITS

READ THIS AGREEMENT AND LABEL BEFORE OPENING THE ARCHIVE SOFTWARE FILE. BY OPENING THIS SOFTWARE PACKAGE, YOU ACCEPT AND AGREE TO THE TERMS AND CONDITIONS PRINTED BELOW. IF YOU DO NOT AGREE, DO NOT OPEN THE ARCHIVE PACKAGE. SIMPLY DELETE THE ARCHIVE PACKAGE FROM YOUR SYSTEM.

The software is distributed on an as-is basis, without warranty. The author makes no representation or warranty, either express or implied, with respect to the software media, it contents, accuracy, or fitness for a specific purpose. The author shall have no liability to you or any other person or entity with respect to any liability, loss, or damage, caused or alleged to have been caused, directly or indirectly, by the software media herein. This includes, but is not limited to, interruption of service, loss of data, loss of classroom time, loss of consulting or anticipatory profits, or consequential damages resulting from the use of these software products. If media is defective, you may return to download a replacement file.

References

1. Yourdon, Edward. *Decline and Fall of the American Programmer.* Englewood Cliffs, N.J.: Prentice Hall, 1992.

2. Paulk, Curtis, Chrissis, and Weber. *Capability Maturity Model for Software*, Version 1.1, Technical Report CMU/SEI-93-TR-024, ESC-TR-177. Pittsburgh, Pa.: Software Engineering Institute, Carnegie-Mellon University, February 1993.

3. Copies of document CMU/SEI-93-TR-025 are available from the National Technical Information Service and the Defense Technical Information Center. For nongovernment entities, contact Research Access, Inc., 3400 Forbes Ave., Suite 302, Pittsburgh, PA 15213.

4. Peach, Robert W., and Diane S. Ritter. *The Memory Jogger 9000: A Pocket Guide to Implementing the ISO 9000 Quality Systems Standard and QS-9000 Third Edition Requirements*, 2nd ed. Salem, N.H.: Goal/QPC, 1996.

5. Details of the GPRA can be found at

    http://www.thomas.loc.gov

6. Jeletic, Kellyann, Rose Pajerski, and Cindy Brown (eds.). *Software Process Improvement Guidebook*, NASA SEL 95-102, 1995. at http://sel.gsfc.nasa.gov/website/documents/docs/95-102.pdf.

7. For more info on the Cohen Bill, GPRA, and OMB A-130 (discussed later in this section) the reader is encouraged to visit URL

    http://www.thomas.loc.gov

8. Lewis, Bob. *IS Survival Guide*, Indianapolis, In.: Sams Publishing, 1999.

9. IEEE Standard 829-1998 for Software Test Documentation, Computer Society of the IEEE, P.O. Box 80452, Worldway Postal Center, Los Angeles, CA 90080.

10. Humphrey, Watts S. *Managing the Software Process*. Reading, Mass: Addison Wesley, 1990.

11. Kaner, Cem. *Testing Computer Software*, 1st ed. Blue Ridge Summit, Pa.: TAB Books, 1988.

12. Strum, Morris, and Jander. *Foundations of Service Level Management*. Indianapolis, Ind.: Sams Publishing, 2000.

13. Microsoft Windows 2000 Professional ©1999 Microsoft Corporation, all rights reserved. Windows is a registered trademark of Microsoft Corporation.

14. Microsoft Project Central information can be found by visiting http://support.microsoft.com.

15. Freedman, Daniel P., and Gerald M. Weinberg. *Handbook of Walkthroughs, Inspections, and Technical Reviews*. New York: Dorset House Publishing, 1990.

16. *Managed Evolutionary Development Guidebook*, 2nd ed. Washington, DC: U.S. Patent and Trademark Office, June 1993.

17. *Parametric Cost Estimating Handbook,* Washington, D.C.: U.S. Department of Defense, 1995.

18. Whitepaper, "16 *Critical Software Practices For Performance-based Management,*" Integrated Computer Engineering, retrieved September 2003 from http://www.iceincusa.com.

19. Electronic copies of NIST Planning Report 02-3, *The Economic Impacts of Inadequate Infrastructure for Software Testing*, can be obtained from www.nist.gov/director/prog-ofc/report02-3.pdf. Paper copies can be requested by e-mail from dherbert@nist.gov.

Index

Adaptive Action Plan (AAP), 72
Alternative work patterns, 170–73
  defined, 170
  deliverables, 173–74
  descriptions, 173–77
  MED, 175–76
  O&M project, 176–77
  O&M small-scale enhancement, 176
  pilot development, 174–75
  RAD, 174
  reduced-effort, 174
  SDLC, 170
  selection, 172–73
  suggested, 171
  system development, 172–73
Analysis
  cost, 59
  data risk, 58
  in-house, 57
  in-house/contractor, 61
  lease/purchase, 62
  risk, 70–71
  technical risk, 61
  technology, 60–61
Analysis and Detailed Planning phase, 53–75
  BP, 164
  checklist, 54–55
  COTS sources, 57
  CP, 68–75
  DAD, 56
  DRA, 58
  FD, 65–66
  FM, 56
  HLS, 62–63
  in-house analysis, 57
  NTD, 57
  PB, 66–67
  PDD, 55–56
  PDDN, 56
  POS, 55
  project deliverables, 164
  PS, 68
  RFP, 64–65
  roadmap, 53
  TAD, 58–62
Approval letters (AL), 74–75

Best practices, 205–27
  construction integrity, 214–23
  continuous program risk management, 206–8
  cost and schedule estimation, 208–9
  data/database interoperability, 219–20
  defects tracking, 212–13
  defined, 205
  design twice, code once, 221–22
  earned value tracking, 210–12
  interface definition/control, 220–21
  life cycle CM, 214–16

metrics for management, 209–10
people treatment, 213–14
product stability/integrity, 223–27
project integrity, 206–14
requirements and design inspection, 223–24
requirements management/tracing, 217
reuse risks and costs, 222–23
system-based software design, 218–19
testing management, 224–26
Best practices decisions, 40–41
change management, 40–41
continuous improvement/project assessment, 41
project file, 40
Bid/proposals (BP), 64
Boundary-related errors, 128
Business fit, 164–65
Business need, 177
Business Requirements Oversight Committee (BROC), 25–28
defined, 25
functions, 26
members, 27–28
project criteria, 25–26
project proposal guidelines, 26
roles and responsibilities, 27–28
SPMO role in, 28
Sponsor, 27
Business Systems Analyst (BSA), 3–4
defined, 3
responsibilities, 3–4

CAD/CAM/CAE, 235–36
Calculation errors, 128–29
Certification letters, 106–7
DCL, 107–8
FCL, 107
MISCL, 107
Change management, 23–25

as best practices decision, 40–41
communications, 24
defined, 23
evaluation, 25
plans, 24–25
programs, establishing, 24
training, 24
workforce planning, 24–25
Change Management Team (CMT), 24
Close-out paperwork (COP), 160
Closeout ritual, 161
COHEN Bill of 1996, 29–30
Commercial Off-The-Shelf (COTS) information, 57
Communications
change management, 24
ground rules, 194–95
relationship decisions, 42
reporting, 8
user-interface errors, 119–22
Configuration Management (CM), 214–16
Conflict management, 197
Construction integrity best practices, 214–23
Construction phase, 95–108
DCL, 107–8
defined, 95
deliverables checklist, 96
development process for test plans, 98–102
FCL, 107
MISCL, 107
OMB, 97–98
PASL, 107
product deliverables, 106
product signoff and certification letters, 106–8
roadmap, 95
SIM, 96–97
SUM, 96
TM, 97
Content Pipeline Document (CPD), 86

Continuous Process Improvement (CPI), 7, 20
 Core Team requirement, 7
 implementing, 20
Contracts, 87
 closure, 13
 terms and conditions, 12
 See also Vendors
Contract WBS, 186–87
Control flow errors, 129
Core Team
 as essential success factor, 166
 forming, 34–36
 initial meeting, 35
 Project Manager work with, 9
 Roster (CTR), 34
 roster revision, 36
 security access, 34–35
Cost analysis, 59
Cost Estimate Worksheet (CEW), 66, 67
Critical path (CP), 68–75
 AAP, 72
 approval letters (AL), 74–75
 defined, 68
 dependency diagrams (DD), 69
 documents from review meeting (DRM), 73
 meeting agenda (MA), 73
 optimization tradeoff plan (OTP), 69
 project team review minutes (PTRM), 74
 resource histogram (RH), 69
 review package (RP), 72
 status reports (SR), 71–72
 task duration estimate (TDE), 69
 variance reports (VR), 72
 waiver/exception to required standards (WERS), 73–74
 WBSD, 69–70
Customers
 confidence, building, 167
 project, 165
 SLAs and, 151
Customization matrix, 37

Data Analysis Document (DAD), 56
Data Analysis Team, 88–90
Database Conversion Plan (DCP), 88–91
 conversion process, 90–91
 conversion type, 90
 Data Analysis Team, 88–90
 defined, 88
Data certification letter (DCL), 107–8
Data Development Plan (DDP), 86
Data interpretation errors, 129–30
Data Risk Analysis (DRA), 58
Deadlines, 201–2
Defects
 detection, 196
 prevention, 196
 tracking, against quality targets, 212–13
Deliverables
 alternative work pattern, 173–74
 checklist, 78
 near-term, 57
 product, 106
 project, 64
Dependency diagrams (DD), 69
Design
 inspection, 223–24
 phase, 77–93
 study, 235–37
 system-based software, 218–19
 twice, 221–22
Detailed Design phase, 77–93
 CA, 87
 DCP, 88–91
 DDP, 86
 deliverables checklist, 78
 HFP, 79
 HFR, 80
 IRS, 85

MCP, 91
MRS, 91–92
PRS, 86
PRSpec, 80–82
PTL, 92–93
QAP, 78–79
roadmap, 77
SDP, 87–88
SIR, 82–84
SRS, 84–85
steps, 77
Disposition phase, 158
Disposition Plan, 158–59
   elements, 159
   objectives, 158
Documents from review meeting (DRM), 73

Earned value tracking, 210–12
   implementation guidelines, 211–12
   practice essentials, 210–11
Economic value added (EVA), 66
End-state visions, 166
Enterprise Rollout, 181
Equipment Installation Plan (EIP), 142–43
Errors
   boundary-related, 128
   calculation, 128–29
   control flow, 129
   handling, 127
   in handling/interpreting data, 129–30
   hardware, 131
   ID control, 131–32
   initial, 128
   later-state, 128–29
   source, 131–32
   testing, 132
   user-interface, 118–27
   version, 131–32
Estimates, 198–201
   capability, 199

complexity, 198–99
cost, 208–9
initial, 201
process, 199–201
revising, 201
schedule, 208–9
size, 198
Executive Stakeholder, 2
Expectations
   management, 16
   setting, 169

Financial management, 8–9
   defined, 8
   financial reports, 9
   guidelines, 8
Flexibility Matrix (FM), 56
Functional certification letter (FCL), 107
Functional Rollup, 181–82
Functional Specification Document (FSD), 84
Funding documentation (FD), 65–66

Gantt charts, 187–88

Hardware
   errors, 131
   life cycle management plan, 148–49
   training requirements, 140–41
Help desk checklist, 155
High-Level Solution (HLS), 62–63
   defined, 62
   items, 62–63
Human Factors Plan (HFP), 79
Human Factors Report (HFR), 80

ID control errors, 131–32

Implementation, 135–45
  defined, 135–36
  deliverables checklist, 136
  deliverables checklist review, 136
  Equipment Installation Plan (EIP), 142–43
  Installation Rollout Plan, 143
  roadmap, 135
  Rollout Plan (ROP), 143–44
  Rollout Schedule (RS), 144
  Rollout Signoff (RSO), 145
  training and implementation, 144
  User Training Plan, 136–42
  User Training Plan development, 136–37
Incident reports, 115–16
  guidelines, 115–16
  illustrated, 116
  See also Testing
Information Technology Management Reform Act (ITMRA), 29–30
In-house analysis, 57
In-House/Contractor Analysis (IHCA), 61
Installation Rollout Plan, 143
Integration Test Plan (ITP), 103–4
  defined, 103
  testing areas, 103–4
  in TPC, 113–14
Interface Requirements Specification (IRS), 85
Internal quality audits (IQAs), 17
Issues
  escalation, 14
  management, 13–14
  reporting, 14
  resolution, 13
  status, 14

Kickoff meeting, 35

Lease/Purchase Analysis (LPA), 62
Load condition, 130, 131

Marketing Communications Plan (MCP), 91
Marketing Rollout Schedule (MRS), 91–92
Marketing Rollout Signoff (MRS), 92
MED work pattern, 175–76
  incremental and evolutionary strategists, 175
  program management, 175
  reviews and approvals, 176
  risk management in context of, 175–76
  See also Alternative work patterns
Meeting agenda (MA), 73
Microsoft Project, 180–82
Milestones, 196
MIS Certification Letter (MISCL), 107
MIS Certification Plan (MISCP), 106
MIS hardware/software handoff letter, 148
MS Project Plan template, 182–85
  predecessor tasks, 183
  resources, 183–84
  saving plan and, 185
  start/finish dates, 182
  task completion, 184
  task notes, 183
  tasks/subtasks, 182
  updating plan and, 185

Near-term deliverables (NTDs), 57

O&M project work pattern, 176–77
O&M small-scale enhancement work pattern, 176
Operations and Maintenance Guide (OMG), 97–98
Optimization, 178–79
  questions, 178–79

tradeoff plan (OTP), 69

People issues, 232–33
Performance measurements
   determining, 18–19
   development, 18
   information management, 19
   lessons, 19
   process steps, 18
Performance reporting, 5–8
   benefits, 5–6
   components, 6
   defined, 5
   example format, 7
   report criteria, 7
   report development, 7
   use of, 6
Performance Requirements Specification (PRS), 86
PERT charts, 187
Pilot development work pattern, 174–75
Planning decisions, 37–38
   development, 37–40
   output, 38
   project tools, 38
Postmortem meeting report, 160
Pressures, 196–97
Process management, 17
Product assurance signoff letter (PASL), 107
Product Assurance Test (PAT), 104–5
   defined, 104
   minimum components, 104–5
Product deliverables, 106
Product Requirements and Specifications (PRSpec), 80–82
   analysis areas, 81–82
   defined, 80
   key specifications, 80
Product signoff, 106

Product stability/integrity best practices, 223–27
Program Manager, 2
Progress review meetings, 39
Project Budget (PB), 66–67
   defined, 66
   template, 67
Project Closeout, 157–61
   actions, 159–60
   close-out paperwork (COP), 160
   defined, 157
   Disposition phase, 158
   Disposition Plan, 158–59
   postmortem meeting report, 160
   project archiving, 160
   ritual, 161
   roadmap, 157
Project Continuation Approval (PCA), 74
Project Coordinator, 181
   defined, 3
   responsibilities, 3
Project Definition Document Notebook (PDDN), 56
Project Definition Document (PDD), 55–56
   defined, 55
   items, 55–56
Project Framework Rules Document (PFRD), 37–43
   best practices decisions, 40–41
   defined, 37
   planning decisions, 37–38
   relationship decisions, 41–42
   tracking decisions, 39–40
Project Initiation phase, 31–51
   Core Team and, 34–36
   form, 33
   PFRD, 37–43
   PPDG, 47–51
   requirements gathering, 43–45
   roadmap, 31
   SEP guidelines, 31–51

URD, 45–47
Project management, 193–95
   communications ground rules, 194–95
   early warning detection, 194
   "give and take," 202–3
   process focus, 193
   resources, 237
   theory into practice, 193–94
   tools, 233–35
Project Manager (PM)
   appointment letter, 33–34
   Core Team work, 9
   defined, 3
   in issue status, 14
   negative reaction and, 202
   responsibilities, 3
Project Objective Statement (POS), 55
Project Planning and Documentation Guide (PPDG), 47–51
   defined, 47
   outline, 47–50
   as project Bible, 51
   structure, 47
Project plans
   confidence building, 192–93
   realistic, building, 179–80
   saving, 185
   with templates, 182–85
   updating, 185
Project Resources, 4
Projects
   archiving, 160
   business reasons for, 163–65
   customers, 165
   deliverables, 64
   effective approach to, 178
   integrity best practices, 206–14
   kickoff meeting, 35
   objectives, 165–66
   risk factors, 188–90
   success factors, 163
   tools, 38
   WBS, 185–87
Project Schedule (PS), 68
Project Sponsor, 2
Project team review minutes (PTRM), 74
Project Transition Letter (PTL), 92–93
Project WBS, 186

Quality Action Teams (QATs), 20
Quality Assurance Plan (QAP), 78–79
Quality management, 14–23
   benefits, 15
   components, 14, 15–20
   CPI, 20
   defined, 14
   expectation management, 16
   IQAs, 17
   metric definition, 18
   metric reports, 20
   objectives, 15
   process management, 17
   quality goals, 16
   quality verification, 16–17
   rewards and recognition, 23

Race condition, 130, 131
Rapid application development (RAD), 169–70
   tools, 169
   work pattern, 174
Reality checks, 188
Reduced-effort work pattern, 174
Relationship decisions, 41–42
   communication, 42
   escalation, 42
   ownership, 41
Reporting, 39–40
Reports
   financial, 9

incident, 115–16
metric, 20
status (SR), 71–72
variance (VR), 72
Request for Proposals (RFPs), 64
developing, 64–65
items, 64–65
Requirements
inspection, 223–24
tracing, 217
training hardware/software, 140–41
Requirements Analysis Team, 81
Requirements gathering, 43–45
problem definition, 43
requirements definition, 44–45
work process evaluation, 44
Requirements Traceability Matrix (RTM), 85, 108
Resource histogram (RH), 69
Return on investment (ROI), 66
Reuse risks, 222–23
Review package (RP), 72
Risk
action plan, 192
assessment, 188–90, 191–92
factors, 188–90
identification list, 190–92
reuse, 222–23
Risk Analysis Matrix (RAM), 70
Risk management, 206–8
implementation guidelines, 207–8
practice essentials, 206–7
Risk Management Matrix (RMM), 70
Risk Officer, 70
appointment, 35–36
responsibilities, 35
Rollout Plan (ROP), 143–44
Rollout Schedule (RS), 144
Rollout Signoff (RSO), 145
Roster revision, 36

Security Access Sheet (SAS), 34–35
Service Level Agreements (SLAs), 151–55
acceptance, 154
components, 152–55
creation process, 151
as customer satisfaction key, 151
defined, 151
Limitations section, 153
Nonperformance section, 153–54
Objectives section, 153
Optional Services section, 154
Parties to the Agreement section, 153
Scope section, 153
Smoke testing, 227
Software configuration management plan (SCMP), 149–51
configuration control, 150
defined, 149
deltas, 150
tasks, 149
Software Development Life Cycle (SDLC), 168–69
alternative work patterns, 170
model identification, 168–69
models, 168
Software Development Plan (SD), 87–88
defined, 87
items, 87–88
Software Installation Manual (SIM), 96–97
Software process improvement organizations, 21–23
component focus, 22
elements, 21
goals, 23
Software Program Management Office. *See* SPMO
Software Reengineering Assessment (SRA), 59–60
defined, 59
intangible benefits, 60

tangible benefits, 60
Software Requirements Specification (SRS), 84–85
Software Test Plan (STP)
   defined, 104
   test variants, 104
   in TPC, 114
Software Transition Plan (SWTP), 148
Software User Manual (SUM), 96
Source errors, 131–32
SPMO
   BROC role, 28
   Business Systems Analyst (BSA), 3–4
   change management, 23–25
   Executive Stakeholder, 2
   financial management, 8–9
   implementation thoughts, 230–32
   issue management, 13–14
   mission statement, 1
   most significant activity, 230
   organization structure, 4–5
   performance reporting, 5–8
   Program Manager, 2
   Project Coordinator, 3, 181
   Project Manager (PM), 3, 9, 14, 33–34, 202
   Project Sponsor, 2
   quality management, 14–23
   roles and responsibilities, 1–4
   scope and methodology domain, 231
   service areas, 5
   staff, 232
   test/certification plans, 102–6
   understanding, 1–30
   vendor management, 9–13
Sponsor Formalization Letter (SFL), 32
Staged deliveries, 169
Status reports (SR), 71–72
Stress Test Plan (SsTP), 103, 113
Subject matter experts (SMEs), 165
Success
   factors, 163
   as team effort, 166–67
Summary WBS, 186
Support phase, 147–56
   completion, 155–56
   defined, 147
   deliverables checklist, 148
   hardware life cycle management plan, 148–49
   help desk checklist, 155
   MIS hardware/software handoff letter, 148
   plan development, 149
   roadmap, 147
   SLAs, 151–55
   software configuration management plan (SCMP), 149–51
   Software Transition Plan (SWTP), 148
System-based software design, 218–19
System Infrastructure Requirements (SIR), 82–84
   defined, 82
   requirements document TOC, 82–84
Systems Engineering Process (SEP), 2
   choice of, 229
   Microsoft Project with, 180–82
   Phase I, 31–51
   Phase II, 53–75
   Phase III, 77–93
   Phase IV, 95–108
   Phase V, 111–33
   Phase VI, 135–45
   Phase VII, 147–56
   Phase VIII, 157–61
   project plan using, 181
   step-by-step process, 180

Target Completion Notice (TCN), 43
Tasks
   completion, early, 202
   completion, tracking, 184

duration estimate (TDE), 69
identifying, 180–82
inserting, 182
notes, 183
predecessor, 183
Technical Analysis Document (TAD), 58–62
   components, 58
   In-House/Contractor Analysis (IHCA), 61
   Lease/Purchase Analysis (LPA), 62
   Software Reengineering Assessment (SRA), 59–60
   Technology Analysis (TA), 60–61
   See also Analysis and Detailed Planning phase
Technology Analysis (TA), 60–61
Test cases, 98, 101
Test domains, 116–17
Testing, 111–33
   deliverables checklist, 112
   error handling, 127–32
   errors, 132
   poor, 127
   race and load conditions, 130–32
   roadmap, 111
   smoke, 227
   test domains, 116–17
   test logs/incident reports, 115–16
   TPC, 113–15
   TP reviews, 132–33
   user-interface errors, 118–27
Testing management, 224–26
   implementation guidelines, 225–26
   practice essentials, 224–25
   See also Best practices
Test Plan Checklist (TPC), 113–15
   defined, 113
   Integration Test Plan, 113–14
   reviewing, 113
   Software Test Plan, 114
   Stress Test Plan, 113
   testing team, 113

TP quality, 114
User Acceptance Test, 114
Test plans (TPs)
   deliverable documents, 100
   development process for, 98–102
   feature inclusion/exclusion, 100
   introductory section, 99
   ITP, 103–4
   outline format, 98–99
   quality, 114
   reviews, 132–33
   SPMO recommended, 102–6
   SsTP, 103
   STP, 104
   testing process, 101
   test items section, 99–100
Tracking, 39
   daily, 195–96
   decisions, 39–40
   defects against quality targets, 212–13
   earned value, 210–11
Training
   cost, 137
   delivery, 138
   estimates, 140
   facilities, 139
   hardware/software requirements, 140–41
   implementation and, 144
   materials development, 139
   methods, 138
   timing, duration, sequencing, 139–40
   See also User Training Plan
Training Manual (TM), 97
Training Roster (TR), 141
Training Schedule (TS), 141
Training Signoff (TSO), 141–42

User Acceptance Test (UAT), 105–6
   consideration areas, 105–6
   defined, 105

in TPC, 114
User-interface errors, 118–27
   command structure and entry, 122–23
   communication, 119–22
   functionality, 118–19
   missing commands, 123–24
   output, 126–27
   performance, 125–26
   program rigidity, 124–25
User Requirements Document (URD), 43, 45–47
   defined, 45
   sample outline, 45–47
   submission, 51
User Training Plan, 136–42
   areas, 137
   defined, 136
   developing, 136–42
   hardware/software requirements, 140–41
   materials development, 139
   scopes and objectives, 137
   training delivery, 138
   training estimates, 140
   training facilities, 139
   training methods, 138
   Training Roster (TR), 141
   Training Schedule (TS), 141
   Training Signoff (TSO), 141–42

Variance reports (VR), 72
Vendor management, 9–13
   benefits, 10
   business arrangement and, 10
   components, 10–11
   contract closure, 13
   contract terms/conditions, 12
   defined, 9–10
   monitoring, 12–13
   planning, 11
   selection, 11–12

Vendors
   monitoring, 12–13
   planning, 11
   selection, 11–12
Version errors, 131–32

Waiver/exception to required standards (WERS), 73–74
Work Breakdown Structure (WBS), 185–87
   Contract, 186–87
   defined, 185–86
   Dictionary, 187
   Project, 186
   Summary, 186
Work patterns. *See* Alternative work patterns